Positive Discipline for Preschoolers

Revised 2nd Edition

Also in the POSITIVE DISCIPLINE Series

Positive Discipline: The First Three Years
Jane Nelsen, Cheryl Erwin, and Roslyn Duffy

Positive Discipline for Teenagers
Jane Nelsen and Lynn Lott

Positive Discipline A–Z,
Revised and Expanded 2nd Edition
Jane Nelsen, Lynn Lott, and H. Stephen Glenn

Positive Discipline in the Classroom,
Revised and Expanded 2nd Edition
Jane Nelsen, Lynn Lott, and H. Stephen Glenn

Positive Discipline: A Teacher's A–Z Guide
Jane Nelsen, Roslyn Duffy, Linda Escobar, Kate Ortolano,
and Debbie Owen-Sohocki

Positive Discipline for Single Parents
Jane Nelsen, Cheryl Erwin, and Carol Delzer

Positive Discipline for Blended Families
Jane Nelsen, Cheryl Erwin, and H. Stephen Glenn

Positive Discipline for Parenting in Recovery
Jane Nelsen, Riki Intner, and Lynn Lott

Jane Nelsen, Cheryl Erwin, and Roslyn Duffy

Positive Discipline

FOR PRESCHOOLERS

REVISED 2ND EDITION

For Their Early Years—

Raising Children Who Are

Responsible, Respectful, and Resourceful

PRIMA PUBLISHING

PRIMA PUBLISHING and colophon are registered trademarks of Prima Communications, Inc.

Illustrations by Lisa Cooper.

All products mentioned in this book are trademarks of their respective companies.

Library of Congress Cataloging-in-Publication Data
Nelsen, Jane.
    Positive discipline for preschoolers : for their early years—raising children who are responsible, respectful, and resourceful / Jane Nelsen, Cheryl Erwin, Roslyn Duffy.
        p.   cm.
    Includes bibliographical references and index.
    ISBN 0-7615-1515-1
    1. Preschool children. 2. Toddlers. 3. Child rearing. 4. Discipline of children.
5. Parent and child. I. Erwin, Cheryl. II. Duffy, Roslyn.
HQ774.5.N45 1998
649'.123—dc21   98-36006
                                                                                        CIP

99 00 01 02 HH 10 9 8 7 6 5 4
Printed in the United States of America

HOW TO ORDER

Single copies may be ordered from Prima Publishing, P.O. Box 1260BK, Rocklin, CA 95677; telephone (916) 632-4400. Quantity discounts are also available. On your letterhead, include information concerning the intended use of the books and the number of books you wish to purchase.

Visit us online at *www.primalife.com*

To my fifteen grandchildren, Joshua, Amber, Jimmy, Kenny, Drew,
Woody, Kristina, Mac, Scotty, Kelsie, Katie, Riley, and the preschoolers,
Melissa, Gibson, Andrew, and those to come.
—Jane

. . .

To all the children—our world's best hope; to those who have dedicated time and
energy to understanding them and helping others understand them, too; and to
Philip, who continues, at 14, to teach me day-by-day the joys of being a mom.
—Cheryl

. . .

To Vinnie; our children Blue, Manus, Rose, and Bridget;
and to all the Learning Tree parents, children, and staff for sharing their
lives with our family and from whom we learn more all the time.
—Roslyn

CONTENTS

ACKNOWLEDGMENTS

We are often asked, "Where do you get your stories?" We get them from so many people without whom this book could not be written. We owe our biggest thanks to our children. They have provided us with personal family "laboratories." As you will read throughout this book, we believe that "mistakes are wonderful opportunities to learn." Our children have put up with many of our mistakes—and have helped us learn from them. We love them, and appreciate them.

We have had many opportunities to learn from parents in our parenting classes and in our counseling offices. It is easy to be "the expert" with other people. We often tell parents in our classes, "You help me when I get emotionally hooked, and I'll help you when you are emotionally hooked." They often tell us how much we help them. We want them to know how much we have learned from them—and how grateful we are.

We have also had the opportunity to answer questions on *MomsOnline* (*www.momsonline.com*). The questions, and our answers, provided substantial material for this book. We appreciate these moms who are so eager to give their children the love and guidance they need.

We have had excellent editorial help. We gratefully acknowledge Susan Silva, who has worked with us on several books. We can always count on Susan for efficiency and encouragement. When she says she'll do something—she does. And she often takes care of tasks that are beyond the call of duty.

Jennifer Fox has been an excellent editor. She has made several suggestions for better organization and has tirelessly prodded us to take care of important details that could have been missed by less diligent editors.

How can we ever thank Susan Madden enough? Susan is the general manager for Positive Discipline Associates and often put other important tasks on hold while she helped prepare the manuscript for Prima. Her attention to detail in the editing process is awesome. And—she gives such good hugs. We can't imagine what we would do without Susan.

A special thanks to the Learning Tree Montessori Child Care for much of the background material for the chapter on finding quality child care and many of the examples in the chapter on class meetings. Such insights helped bring deeper meaning to this work.

We will always be grateful to Alfred Adler and Rudolf Dreikurs, the originators of the philosophy upon which Positive Discipline is based. These psychiatrists left a legacy that has changed the lives of thousands—including us. We feel honored to share these ideas with others.

And oh how we love our families. Instead of complaining about the time it takes for us to write books, they support and encourage us. They constantly demonstrate how capable they are to be self-sufficient instead of demanding. They are proud of us for sharing concepts that have helped us all enjoy each other so much. We love spending every moment we can with them.

PROLOGUE: BY THE CHILDREN

"MY NAME IS SUSAN and I am three and a half years old. I am discovering the power of words. I am upset when people won't read me the same book over and over again, or when they try to leave out a part. My favorite question is 'why?' I like to dress up and try on all kinds of different characters. I like to have stories told to me all the time. I like to have someone to play with me all the time, too. And I don't like to have my playtime interrupted."

. . .

"I AM JEFFREY F. FRASER. The *F* stands for Frank, like my grandpa. I am very sociable. I like talking to people. Yesterday I turned five years old. We can be friends and I will invite you to my birthday party. When I pick what I want to do, I pay attention really good. I have a little brother. He will do for a playmate if there's nobody better. I think this tooth is getting loose. Do you want to hear me count? I can sing a song for you. Do you want to play with me? Okay, you be the bad guy and I'll be the good guy . . ."

. . .

"EVERYONE CALLS ME MACKEY. I am two fingers and a half old. I like to do things—suddenly! I might scream or run or take something from somebody 'just because.' I'm not listening because I am thinking my own thoughts. I like to take blocks or anything and scoot them around like they're cars and make noises or crash them together. When I get older I want to build big block towers. Sometimes I play with Joe. We play cars together. I don't sing very much but I like to make funny noises and movements. I like to go to school now but I don't like to go early in the morning."

. . .

"I'M FOUR YEARS OLD. I'M CYNDY. I have *sparkly* shoes. Do you know what kind of underwear I have on? They have the days on them. See how sparkly my shoes are when I twirl? I'm too big to be taking naps. If you read me a story, I'll be happier. I am really not tired. Do you want to see my shoes? I am going to marry Chad. Do you know Chad? He has a Batman cape. Can you read me a story now?"

. . .

"I'M MARIA. My hair is long. I always wear dresses. I am four and three quarters years old. Callie is my bestest friend. Sometimes Callie won't play with me. She is four and a half. I can play with Gina. I like to eat lunch with Callie and Gina. I want to sit next to them—not across the table from them. I like it when the teachers teach me things."

. . .

This is a book about us—the children. Each one of us is different. Not all three-year-olds or five-year-olds will be like us, but you will probably find a little bit of us in the children you know. This book will help you get to know us and find out what the world is like for us. It will give you lots of ideas about how to help us grow and how to encourage and teach us. Jeffrey calls this "possible discipline." We are alike and we are different. We want to be loved; this book is for the people who love us.

PART ONE

The Joys and Woes of Adjusting to Your Growing Child

Parenting classes are full of parents with preschoolers. Internet parenting forums echo with questions like "Why does my three-year-old bite?" or "How do I get my five-year-old to stay in his bed at night?" Child development experts, preschool directors, and therapists all boast offices overflowing with parents whose offspring have reached the age of three or four or five and who are wondering what on earth has happened. Listen for a moment to these parents:

Our little boy was such a delight. We expected trouble when he turned two—after all, everyone had warned us about the "terrible twos"—but nothing happened. Until he turned three, that is. Now we don't know what to do with him. If we say "black," he says "white." If we say it's bedtime, he's not tired. We must be doing something wrong!

Our four-year-old reminds us of the car advertisement on television: she always wants to "go farther." And we spend all of our time yelling "too far!" What has happened to her? Is she always going to act like this?

As you will discover in the pages that follow, the years from ages three to six are busy, sometimes hectic ones for young children—and for their parents and caregivers. Children are physically active and energetic; researchers tell us that human beings have more physical energy at the age of three than at any other time in their life span—certainly more than their weary parents. Their emotional, cognitive, and physical development is urging them to explore the world around them; they're acquiring and practicing social skills and entering the world outside the protected haven of the family. And preschoolers have ideas—lots of them—about how that world should operate. Their ideas, along with their urges to experiment and explore, often do not mesh with their parents' and caregivers' ideas and plans. The power struggles and frustration this clash creates will be a primary focus of this book.

So settle down for a while; get comfortable and gather up all of your questions. Join us as we venture into the world of preschoolers.

1

The Wild and Wonderful
World of Preschoolers

PRESCHOOLERS ARE ENGAGING, charming little people. They can share ideas, show curiosity, exercise a budding sense of humor, build relationships of their own, and offer open arms of affection and playfulness to those around them. They can also be stubborn, defiant, confusing, and downright defeating. Most parents worry about the world their children will inherit; they wonder how best to raise their children so that they can live successful, happy lives. And they watch the occasionally frustrating behavior of those same children and wonder what lies ahead—and what to do about it.

Experts abound, of course. You can hardly watch television or pick up a magazine without being offered the latest advice on discipline and development. Bookstore shelves bulge with volumes covering every aspect of parenting. In fact, most parents find that the problem isn't having enough information; it's knowing where to start and whom to trust.

Why "Positive Discipline"?

POSITIVE DISCIPLINE (BOTH the philosophy and the skills that go with it) will offer you effective, loving ways to guide your youngster through these busy, often challenging years. Whether you are a parent, a teacher, or a child care provider, you will find ideas in these pages that you can really use and that will help you give the children in your care the best start in life.

Does Positive Discipline work? Yes! That is why we are so excited to share these concepts. They have worked for us, our children, our preschool students, our clients, and hundreds of parents and teachers who have attended our classes and workshops. We share many success stories in this book: our own as well as those of many parents, teachers, and caregivers who have expressed their wonder and gratitude for the success they and their children have experienced by using the Positive Discipline concepts. We've made many mistakes (where do you think we get the stories for our books?), but we truly believe that mistakes are opportunities to learn. We want to share what we have learned with you.

> Whether you are a parent, a teacher, or a child care provider, you will find ideas in these pages that you can really use and that will help you give the children in your care the best start in life.

This is indeed a challenging world. The newspapers are filled with frightening stories, and our children need all the confidence, wisdom, and problem-solving skills we can give them. They also need to believe in their own worth and dignity, to possess a healthy sense of self-esteem, and to know how to live, work, and play with those around them. It is the rare parent who doesn't occasionally feel overwhelmed and confused, who doesn't worry that his or her best just won't be good enough. The stakes are so high, and we love our children so much. Where do we begin?

The Importance of Long-Range Parenting

IT IS EASY in the rush of daily life with a preschooler to focus on the crisis at hand. There's the morning to get through, with lunches to be packed and jackets to grab and children who may or may not be willing to get dressed and put shoes on their feet. Parents must get about their work, and children must go off to child care or preschool or must be supervised at home. Later on, dinner and household duties demand time and attention, and then there's bedtime at the end of the day. Just getting everyone fed, bathed, and to sleep can take our last remaining ounce of energy.

There's more that parents must do, however. We must think and dream and plan. We must learn to know our little ones well and we must decide where all of us are going and how best to get there. These last, most important tasks are often the ones we never have time to do. But think for a moment: Wouldn't it be helpful, as you embark on the parenting journey, to know your final destination? How will you get there if you don't have a clear picture of where you want to go?

Perhaps one of the wisest things you can do right now is to take a moment to ask yourself a very important question. What do you want for your child? When your child has grown to be an adult, what qualities and characteristics do you want her to have?

You may decide that you want your child to be confident, compassionate, and respectful. You may want her to be responsible, hard-working, and trust-worthy. Most parents want their children to be happy, to have rewarding work and healthy relationships. Whatever you want for your child, how will you bring it to pass? How will your child learn to have a contented, successful life?

As you've probably guessed, the answer is that our children will have whatever skills and qualities we as parents and teachers have the courage and wisdom to help them develop. Every little crisis and catastrophe of daily life—and the way we respond to each one of them—should be moving our children closer to the qualities we value. For most of us, that responsibility feels overwhelming. What if we make mistakes? What if we lose our tempers? Say the wrong thing? Don't know what to do?

> The newspapers are filled with frightening stories, and our children need all the confidence, wisdom, and problem-solving skills we can give them.

Mistakes Are Opportunities to Learn

THE GOOD NEWS is that mistakes are wonderful opportunities to learn and grow. We will make lots and lots of them as parents and teachers; our little ones will make lots and lots of them, too. As long as we are willing to hug, forgive, and figure out a better way, we can grow closer. We can learn valuable skills. However, many adults are not aware of the mistakes they are making. They may not realize that shaming a child may stop the behavior (at least for the moment) but it does not help the child get to the destination they have in

WHAT DO YOU WANT FOR YOUR CHILDREN?

Here is a typical list from parents and caregivers:

Self-discipline	Self-reliance
Decision-making skills	Problem-solving skills
Self-motivation	Self-confidence
Cooperation/collaboration skills	Social skills
Creativity	"Good finders"—able to see positives
Values	Resilience
Leadership skills	Foresight
Endurance	Accountability
Responsibility	Respect for self and others
Empathy/caring	Tolerant
Sense of humor	Determined
Thinking skills/judgment skills	Public spirited/social interest
Honesty	Lifelong learners
Adaptability	Communication skills

The real question is: What kind of discipline works best to help children develop these skills—punitive or nonpunitive? We believe punitive methods do not work to achieve these positive, long-range results.

mind: a capable, confident child with valuable life skills. Mistakes are truly opportunities to learn, but first we need to recognize (without shaming ourselves) when we make them.

The New Toolbox

LIVING AND WORKING with young children is one of the most challenging tasks we will ever face. Regardless of how much we love our children, most of us will admit that there are moments when we feel angry, frustrated, even desperate. Children of any age can be charming, talented, and lovable. They also can be stubborn, defiant, and baffling.

This book is filled with new "tools" for your toolbox. We are fairly sure that you haven't yet tried everything. As you read through the chapters ahead, you will add some valuable knowledge and skills to your Positive Discipline toolbox, tools such as understanding developmental appropriateness (chapter 5), understanding temperament (chapter 7), social skill development (chapter 8), how your personality might affect a child (chapter 10), and the four mistaken goals of misbehavior (chapters 19, 20, and 21). We will also explore the many ways of providing discipline—and preventing misbehavior—for preschoolers.

The most valuable parenting tools of all are those you already possess: your love for your child and your own inner wisdom and common sense. Learning to trust those instincts you already have will help you evaluate the suggestions and ideas in this book and elsewhere, and will carry you far along the road to successful parenting.

Remember, too, that preschoolers learn by imitation, and the people they will most likely imitate are their parents and teachers. Not only will our children want to dig in the garden and push the vacuum cleaner with us, but they will also mirror the values we live by. Children will always pay more attention to our actions than to our words. Let your actions teach your child that she is loved, valued, and respected, that choices have consequences, and that her world is a safe and wonderful place to be.

A Word About Families

THESE DAYS, FAMILIES come in many different shapes, sizes, and configurations. Preschoolers may find themselves in families with two parents, a single parent, adoptive parents, grandparents, or stepparents. Their parents may be of different genders or of the same gender. Sometimes we wonder: Does it matter what shape a family has?

Children can grow up with a healthy sense of respect and dignity in any sort of family. The decisions parents make about what values will be taught and lived are what shape a child's early life. Young children can grow up healthy and happy in any family as long as that family is built on love, respect, dignity, and belonging.

All families these days face pressure and stress, whether it's about finances, time, or relationships. Still, if your family seems a bit different from the traditional Norman Rockwell sort, you may be wise to look for support and additional information; for example, check out *Positive Discipline for Single Parents* (Prima Publishing, 1994) and *Positive Discipline for Blended Families* (Prima Publishing, 1997). Support groups exist for adoptive parents, grandparents who are raising their grandchildren, and just about every other imaginable form of family. It is not weakness to ask for help—it is wisdom.

In the Name of Love

IT IS A rare parent who does not love his or her child. Love, however, is sometimes not enough. Parents (and teachers) do many ineffective and even harmful things in the name of "love." We may punish our child because we love him; we push our child because we love him enough to want the very best for him. We overprotect children, humiliate children, teach children, play with children, and scold children—all in the name of "love."

> Actually, love is the easy part. The real issue is whether we can show our love in ways that nurture accountability and self-esteem and that encourage our children to reach their full potential as happy, contributing members of society.

Actually, love is the easy part. The real issue is whether we can show our love in ways that nurture accountability and self-esteem and that encourage our children to reach their full potential as happy, contributing members of society. How much should we give our children? How much is too much? Is it harmful to let a child have her own way? Should we push our child or let her move at her own pace?

It is knowledge that gives legs to the love we feel. None of us is born knowing how to raise an active preschooler; we learn from our own parents and experiences and we do the best we can. And we make mistakes. Fortunately, parent education and training is finally gaining wide acceptance and credibility. Society has never questioned the need for training in occupational fields, be it surgery or bricklaying. But somewhere along the line the notion got planted that raising children should come "naturally" and that needing help was an admission of inadequacy.

The truth is that "good" parents take parenting classes, read books, and ask lots of questions. We encourage you to seek out and get involved with a parenting group in your community or to start one yourself. Reading books and attending classes will not make you a perfect parent—there is no such thing. But you will have more awareness of what works and what doesn't work for the long-range benefit of your children. When you make mistakes, you will know how to correct them—and you will be able to teach your children that mistakes provide wonderful opportunities to learn (we can't say it often enough!).

Trust Your Heart

PARENTING IS RARELY a simple matter; there is so much in our crowded lives that must be juggled and balanced. Sometimes it's hard to keep our priorities straight or to find time for even the things we know are important.

No one can challenge and stretch a parent or teacher like a young child (or a classroom full of them!) who is just learning to explore his world. In the chapters that follow, we will take time to explore the world of preschoolers. We will learn how they think and why they do the things they do. We will peek into their social relationships, discover how to select the best child care, and examine how to help our children learn. There will be ample opportunity for tips and techniques, for information and suggestions.

For now, remember that it is always the relationship between parent and child that matters most. It is often the quiet, everyday moments—the cuddle before bed, the tears after a quarrel, working and laughing side by side—where the best sort of parenting takes place. If your relationship is based on unconditional love and trust, if your children know that you love them *no matter what,* you will probably do just fine.

No one ever said it would be easy to be a parent. It isn't always easy to be a preschooler these days, either. All of us are learning, exploring new territory, and making occasional mistakes. Have patience; do a lot of listening. Trust your heart. Your love and wisdom, coupled with understanding and skills, will help you find your way to being the best parent you can be.

2

"Where Has My Baby Gone?"

From Toddler to Preschooler

*H*e doesn't toddle anymore." *Carlota Martinez watched three-year-old Manuel's progress across the playground. She felt a jolt of surprise as Manuel climbed to the very top of the domed bars with sure-footed skill. "Where has my baby gone?" she wondered out loud, with a bittersweet smile. "Who is this new little person?"*

Dana automatically reached down to take her daughter's hand when the light at their corner turned green. Five-year-old Marta looked at her mother and made a face. Marta was willing to walk beside her mom, but she would not *hold hands: that was for* babies. *Dana felt a bit silly. She realized Marta was careful and capable enough to cross the street without having her hand held, but at that moment Dana's own hand suddenly felt very empty.*

Somewhere, somehow, during the second three years of life the needy, helpless infants we used to cuddle and marvel at grow into separate beings, filled with plans, ideas, and opinions all their own. For most of us, this transformation happens so gradually that we feel a sense of shock when, at moments like those we've just witnessed, we see our children through new eyes. When was the wobbly toddler replaced by this sturdy youngster who can walk and even run (faster than his parents) without a stumble? When did the wiry, endlessly distracted little explorer disappear, to be succeeded by the careful, capable, and more responsible young person standing beside us? When can we stop checking to see if she visited the potty, has a coat on, or remembered her lunch box? When can we stop cutting her meat for her? Some of us get so much in the habit of doing these things that we're still calling out instructions and warnings even after our children become parents themselves!

Learning to Let Go

SOMETIMES IT SEEMS that all of parenting is about learning to let go. We let go of the special closeness nursing brings when our children are weaned from the breast or the bottle. When we can no longer measure how many ounces of juice our child drinks because he now uses a "big people" glass, we must let go again. When we leave our child in someone else's care, even for as little as half an hour, we must let go in still another way. Letting go is a process that begins the moment a baby separates from her mother's body, and it is essential to the healthy growth and development of a human being. Hanging on—which usually is done in the name of love— prevents healthy growth. The challenge of parenting lies in finding the balance between nurturing, protecting, and guiding on the one hand and allowing our children to explore, experiment, and become independent, unique people on the other.

Nature urges each of us to grow into separate beings. The late preschool years (from the ages of three to six) give parents their first taste of that outward-moving energy. These years are sometimes compared to adolescence, and there certainly are many similarities. At both of these crucial stages a developmental shift is taking place. Teens are leaving childhood to claim their places in the world of adults. Preschoolers are leaving babyhood behind to enter their childhood years. And it often seems to watching parents that each step they take carries them farther from our arms: the more they grow, the less they seem to need us.

The truth is that our children will always need our guidance, encouragement, and love, but parenting does take a different shape as they grow and change. At fourteen, a child still needs both love and limits, but he must make

> Somewhere, somehow, during the second three years of life the needy, helpless infants we used to cuddle and marvel at grow into separate beings, filled with plans, ideas, and opinions all their own.

many life decisions on his own. In the same way, children at four years of age are far from self-sufficient, but they need some independence with which to learn and practice new skills. Providing that balance of guidance and independence requires that our role in their lives changes dramatically. Babies are dependent on adults for every need: they can't even support the weight of their own heads. They must be fed, diapered, and dressed; they need help blowing their noses when they get a cold. One-year-olds still have most of the same needs. They must be carried much of the time, fed, and changed often. By age two, the picture is beginning to change. Not only can children walk unassisted, but many can ask for things with simple words, point at or pantomime what they want—and most have discovered how to say "no" with fervor, much to their parents' chagrin! Communication and mobility bring huge changes.

Let a scant twelve months pass by, then look again. Three-year-olds are as different from that tiny baby as a young chick is from the sealed egg it left behind. By three, most children walk, talk, and feed themselves and are beginning to use the toilet with little or no help (unless parents are hanging on to these tasks because they need control or need to be needed). In the space of only a single year, children have mastered the basics of most adult survival functions. They can communicate with simple sentences, cover the length of a room in the blink of an eye, and get into every nook and cranny imaginable. The transformation is as remarkable as if in twelve short months we were to progress from lying on the grass and watching an airplane soar far overhead to suiting up as an astronaut bound for outer space.

By four, children have matured even more. They can dress themselves, bathe, and communicate well. They have begun to reason and understand how ideas and things are connected, and they can help with simple food preparation and other household tasks. They're even ready for some organized sports and activities. What a change! No wonder we find ourselves asking, "Where has my baby gone?"

The World Out There

ANOTHER SIGNIFICANT CHANGE takes place in this second half of the preschool years. Children begin to be much more interested in the other people who share their world. They may no longer view their mom, dad, or immediate family members as the most important people in their world. Our familiar role as all-providing, all-knowing, God-like nurturers vanishes.

Children begin to make connections with other people; they discover the world of friends. Johnny figures out whether he is a boy or girl and that it is a permanent arrangement. He notices skin colors, body shapes, and lifestyles that differ from his own. He begins to make decisions about the world and how it works, what to expect from others, and what he must do to find love and belonging. Conflict may arise as parents make peace with the fact that this new person has different needs than he used to. Instead of caring for a helpless infant, we must now learn to see our child as capable, able to master new skills, and, occasionally, make mistakes; we must learn to watch our precious child experience the discomfort some of those mistakes bring. Letting go of "baby" takes a toll on both parents and children. Children waver between wanting to be independent and needing to race back into Mom or Dad's sheltering arms.

The changes keep coming. By the age of five, another shift begins. The people he now finds most interesting are other children, his peers. What these other children say, think, and do register as vitally important on his radar screen. He discovers that other children have needs, feelings, and abilities; he learns that he is not the center of the universe and he must find ways to interact with others and to solve problems. The seeds of empathy are planted, the tiny tendrils of cooperation must be nurtured, and adult tendencies to overprotect, blame, or assign labels must be avoided. He doesn't realize it, but learning to be a member of society who can build and maintain healthy relationships takes up most of a child's energy during these years. Teaching these skills (and helping smooth over the crises that are often part of the learning process) will occupy a great deal of his parents' and caregivers' time and attention during these busy years.

Helping Children with Transitions

AN UNDERSTANDING OF how preschoolers perceive and think about their world can help parents with the letting-go process. Providing a quality preschool experience with trained professionals may also ease and support parents and children through these important life changes.

Let's peek in as Jonah and his parents experience the changes that come with the preschool years.

Jonah is excited; he is three and gets to start preschool next week. Jonah also has a new prize possession; he and his dad went out to buy a lunch box, and Jonah found one with his favorite action heroes on the lid. Jonah knows he will get to carry his sandwich and milk in the lunch box when he goes to "school." He proudly shows his lunch box to his little brother when he returns home, then sets it prominently on the kitchen counter where he can guard it.

For the next week, Jonah carries the lunch box everywhere he goes. He even insists on sleeping with it at night. When the big morning arrives, he clutches the lunch box in his hand. His new teacher shows him his cubby and invites him to leave the lunch box there but Jonah refuses, holding it to his chest. The teacher smiles and does not insist. Later on, when Jonah has joined in the play at the water table, she retrieves his lunch box from the floor where he set it down. It takes Jonah most of his first week before he can part with his lunch box upon arrival.

For young children, an object such as a lunch box becomes a tangible symbol for any big change. At home the lunch box was a badge that said "I am a big boy now." At school it provided a talisman of home, family, and everything safe and comfortable. The lunch box represents a concrete or visible object symbolizing change. Whether the object is a lunch box, a new pair of shoes, or a coat for school, children often find that special possessions provide support as they experience the inevitable transitions of life.

> Whether the object is a lunch box, a new pair of shoes, or a coat for school, children often find that special possessions provide support as they experience the inevitable transitions of life.

Concrete objects can help preschoolers adapt to change and give touchable form to abstract concepts. Make a small celebration out of buying a special backpack for an upcoming trip. A child can then pack small toys, art supplies, or favorite books in the backpack to carry with her. When families separate, having a special pillow or blanket to carry between households offers a way to connect these two places.

A visit to the doctor or even a hospital stay becomes less frightening with a comforting object tucked into a little one's arms. A child needing special medical care might bring along a teddy bear who can have its temperature taken, too. Five-year-old Jordan's stuffed kangaroo rode the hospital gurney into the operating room with him when he had his tonsils removed (although Kanga had to wait outside during the actual surgery) and was waiting next to him when he woke up. A special quilt to snuggle under during uncertain times provides a constant reminder of the people in a child's life, reassures her that she is loved, and covers her with warmth.

Living with preschoolers means understanding that they perceive the world differently than do the adults around them. For instance, preschoolers are constantly asking, "How much longer?" but they don't understand the concept of "ten minutes" or "three hours"—which is why they need to ask again two minutes later! The Schultzes found a way to answer the time question that seemed to satisfy their three- and five-year-old children. When the children asked, "How much longer?" their parents would hold up a thumb and index finger with a little space (or a bigger space) and say, "About this much longer." Sometimes they would hold up both hands spread wide apart to indicate longer periods of time. Their children could relate more to the visual cues of the space between their parents' fingers than to a stated amount of time.

Having a preschooler in your life means learning to observe all the ways she is growing and changing, and adapting your parenting skills to match her needs. These years are all about change, which can make them unsettling for everyone. Understanding a child's need for special objects and her different perception of time are just two ways of knowing this emerging person better. We can use these discoveries to ease the transitions for everyone.

Helping Parents with Transitions

WHETHER WE LIKE it or not, work or school requires many parents to place their children in some sort of child care setting. But who cares for the mom and dad? Entrusting the care of a young child to another person requires a great deal of faith. Parents perform a daily act of trust when they walk through the doors of child care homes and centers or leave a child with a nanny or sitter. Compassionate caregivers include the needs of the parents as well as the children in their plans. When families part each day, a farewell ritual is vital. Holding a child while he waves from the doorway or creating another way to ease the leave-taking is critical to the emotional well-being of both parent and child.

Remember Jonah? His preschool teacher realized that his lunch box helped him feel safe and secure. She wisely allowed him to pace his own letting-go process by respecting the link his lunch box provided to his family and home. There are many small ways in which caregivers can support children and their parents through these transition times. Understanding the concrete thinking of young children and the pain parents feel when they must leave their children behind may help caregivers see their own role differently.

Each child in a child care setting represents an entire family unit. Sometimes teachers regard parents as interfering, pushy, or overprotective. When the perspective of caregivers widens to include parents as partners rather than adversaries, everyone benefits.

Celebrate Your Growing, Changing Child

OUR BABIES DO grow up, and they need us in different ways. We must learn to let go and support them as they master new skills, offer encouragement when they stumble, and provide thoughtful links to familiar places and faces as they move away from the safety of our arms. Yes, Baby is gone. But oh, what a terrific kid came along to replace him! Let's spend some time getting to know this new person.

3

"Don't Talk to Me in That Tone of Voice"

Feelings and the Art of Communication

FEELINGS CAN BE such bewildering things, and a preschooler's world is a riot of feelings. Take a moment sometime and watch a toddler or preschooler try to deal with frustration or anger. She may throw a toy across the room, stamp her foot, fall over backwards in a tantrum, or collapse in a flood of tears. Or she may do all of the above, often within the span of a few minutes.

It is difficult enough for adults to cope with emotions, but for young children there is an added wrinkle: they haven't yet learned what feelings are, how to identify and talk about them, or what each one feels like, let alone how to cope with them in a controlled and effective manner. Understanding and communicating with your young child means deciphering his nonverbal clues, understanding what he is feeling, and helping him to understand it as well. Learning to recognize and deal with children's feelings is a vitally important step in handling children's behavior.

What Is a Feeling?

JUST AS THEY learn so many other things in life, children learn to cope with their feelings by watching their parents. And all too often, parents deal with difficult feelings either through emotional displays (dumping their stronger emotions on the people around them) or by squelching them entirely. The feelings we refuse to express don't go away, however; they simply go underground. And when they're finally released, the results are often far more damaging than if the feelings had been expressed early on.

Emotional displays and emotional squelching give feelings a bad reputation, but the truth is that feelings themselves don't cause problems. Certain actions (or a failure to act at all) may cause problems. Some people put feelings in the same category as emotional displays. A temper tantrum is an emotional display; acting depressed may be an emotional display.

A feeling, though, is simply a feeling. And everyone, whatever his or her age, has feelings.

Feelings are our barometer, our way of keeping tuned in to how we're doing. Our feelings are intended to give us valuable information; in fact, some of them, like fear, help keep us safe and protect us from foolish actions. Paying attention to our feelings can help us decide what to do or let us know that we need to make changes. We access useful information when we tune in to the deeper message our feelings have for us instead of squelching them or reacting to them.

Teaching Children the Difference Between Feelings and Actions

IT'S IMPORTANT TO help children deal with their feelings and to express them in ways that don't involve hurting themselves or others. Children (and adults) need to learn that feelings are different from actions. Feelings are always okay—they're never right or wrong. On the other hand, our actions—the ways we choose to express our feelings—might be either appropriate or inappropriate.

Many adults struggle with acknowledging and expressing their feelings. It often seems easier—or more "polite"—to simply repress feelings (although those feelings often leak out in the form of anger or depression). This mistaken pattern of denying feelings may then be passed on to children. Consider this familiar exchange: An angry child says, "I hate my brother!" An adult responds, "No, you don't. You know you love your brother." It would be healthier to say to the child, "I can see how angry or hurt you feel right now. I can't let you kick your brother, but maybe we can find a way to help you feel better."

Young children often choose inappropriate ways to express their feelings, not because they're "bad" or malicious but because they're still learning what to do with those tidal waves of emotion that wash over them. Let's look at how we can teach children to accept and understand their feelings and to express emotions in ways that not only will help them feel better but will help them find solutions to the problems they encounter in life.

Learning to Feel

FEELINGS ARE THE language of energy. Energy can be positive or negative. We can't see energy or hear it, and for this reason some people try to ignore it (and teach their children to ignore it). This is unwise, because the energy of feelings can give us valuable information when we learn to trust it.

> Feelings are always okay—they're never right or wrong. On the other hand, our actions—the ways we choose to express our feelings—might be either appropriate or inappropriate.

Even when we want to, it is difficult to disguise completely the energy of what we're feeling: we express that energy on our faces, in our voices, and in the way we move or stand. We call this "nonverbal communication," and children are especially sensitive to it.

Three-year-old Kyle scampers into the kitchen where Linda, his mother, late for a meeting, is preparing dinner.

"Look, Mommy, look—I drew an airplane!" Kyle bubbles, waving his paper excitedly.

"That's great, sweetie. You're quite an artist," his harried mother replies quickly.

Linda undoubtedly means well, and there is certainly nothing wrong with her words; but Kyle notices that her hands never stop grating cheese for the casserole and her eyes never quite look at his airplane. What message has Kyle really received?

Five-year-old Wendy is helping her dad make lunch. Wendy's little brother is cranky, and Dad is trying to watch the football game on television while he makes the grilled cheese sandwiches. Wendy is valiantly pouring milk when the heavy carton slips from her grasp, sending a half-gallon of foamy liquid across the kitchen floor.

Wendy looks up timidly into her father's face. "I'm sorry, Daddy," she says. "Are you mad?"

Dad's eyebrows lower ominously, his jaw tightens, and when he speaks his voice is thin and tense. "No, I'm not mad," he says. When Wendy bursts into tears, he wonders why.

Ms. Santos is reading a nap-time story to her class of three-year-olds. She hasn't had a break because her replacement didn't show up and no substitute teacher is available. Little Allie looks at her teacher and asks, "Do you like this story?" Ms. Santos looks at Allie in surprise and answers, "Yes, of course I do. Why?"

Allie answers, "Because your face is all wrinkled up and you look mad."

The Power of Nonverbal Communication

AS OUR CHILDREN grow and develop, we need to be constantly aware of the messages we are sending them—and how frequently our words and our actions don't agree. A number of studies, for instance, have shown that saying "I love you" isn't the best way to communicate that important message to our children. Saying the words often (and meaning them) is important, but there are more effective ways to communicate this vital message to our young children.

Eye Contact

Try an experiment sometime. Stand back-to-back with someone and try to tell him or her about something that happened to you or explain how you're feeling. If you're like most people, you'll find yourself wanting to crane your neck and turn around to look your partner in the eye.

Eye contact signals attention. A good public speaker will catch the gaze of audience members and by doing so will involve them in what he or she is saying. In the same way, making eye contact with our children signals to them that they are important, captures their attention, and increases the effectiveness of our message.

THE BASICS OF EFFECTIVE COMMUNICATION

- Eye contact
- Posture and position
- Tone of voice
- Facial expression and touch

Unfortunately, most of us reserve eye contact primarily for certain occasions. Can you guess what those are? Adults tend to make direct eye contact with children most often when they are angry or lecturing them. We sometimes save our most powerful communication for our most negative messages.

In some cultures, eye contact is regarded as a sign of disrespect. Be sure to take this into account when communicating with families from such backgrounds. One teacher thought a child was avoiding eye contact out of a sense of "sneakiness" but changed her mind once she understood the respect this young child's lack of eye contact conveyed in his native culture. Her attitude shifted and she communicated far more effectively with this child and his family throughout the rest of the year.

Posture and Position

If we want to make eye contact with our children, we are responsible for making it possible. Remember that without help, young children tend to look us right in the knees! If you want to communicate with a child, get down on her level. Kneel next to her, sit beside her on the sofa, or (as long as you hold on to her) set her on a counter where her eyes can meet yours comfortably. Now, not only can you maintain eye contact while you speak to her, but you've eliminated the seemingly overpowering difference in size and height. Also, watch out for the signals your posture sends: crossed arms or legs, for example, can indicate resistance or hostility. Your child will be quick to notice. Here's an example:

Susan was trying to coax her daughter, Michele, into sharing what was upsetting her.

Michele hesitated, then said, "I'm afraid you'll get mad at me."

Susan replied, "Honey, I promise I won't get mad. I care about you, and I want you to be able to tell me anything."

Michele thought for a moment, then looked up into her mother's face. "I'll tell you if you promise not to look at me with those tight lips you get when you're trying to pretend you aren't mad."

Poor Susan—she was trying hard to be unconditionally accepting and loving. Her daughter, however, was able to read the body language that betrayed her true feelings. When Susan's words and her expression match, Michele will feel far more comfortable sharing her problems with her mother.

Tone of Voice

Your tone of voice may be the most powerful nonverbal tool of all. Try saying a simple sentence, such as "I can't help you," emphasizing a different word each time. How does the meaning change? Even inoffensive phrases like "Have a nice day" can become poisonous if we choose a particularly cold tone of voice. It is often the way we say something, rather than the words we use, that carries the message. Children are especially sensitive to the nuances of our nonverbal communications.

Facial Expressions and Touch

When you're feeling particularly blue, does it help when a friend smiles and gives you a pat on the shoulder or a friendly hug? The way we look and the way we use our hands can communicate very effectively without a single word being spoken.

Tommy is curled up on the couch under a blanket, suffering from a bad case of the flu. Dad walks by, adjusts the blanket, and gently ruffles Tommy's hair. Has anything been communicated? Chances are Tommy knows without words that his dad cares about him, wants to help, and hopes he'll soon feel better.

Let's go back to where we started. How might you say "I love you" now? Imagine how powerful it might feel to your child if you knelt in front of him, looked him directly in the eye, smiled, and in your warmest tone of voice said, "I love you, honey." Now the words and the nonverbal cues match up, and a hug might be on the way! Nonverbal communication, which most of us take for granted, teaches our children about communication, words, and the feelings that go with them.

The Art of Active Listening

ACTIVE (OR REFLECTIVE) listening is another effective tool of communication that you possess, one that will serve you well as you parent your children and (in the not-too-distant future) your adolescents. Active listening is the art of observing and listening to feelings, then reflecting them back. Active listening does not require that adults agree with children, but it allows children to feel understood—something all people need—and provides an opportunity to explore and clarify those mysterious impulses known as feelings.

> Children are especially sensitive to the nuances of our nonverbal communications.

Four-year-old Chrissy ran through the front door, slamming it so forcefully that the pictures rattled on the wall, and promptly burst into tears.

"Tammy took my ball," she wailed. "I hate her!" Then Chrissy threw herself onto the sofa in a storm of tears.

Her mom, Diane, looked up from the bills she was paying. "You seem pretty angry, honey."

Chrissy pondered for a moment, sobbing fitfully. "Mom," she said plaintively, sniffling a little, "Tammy is bigger than me. It isn't fair for her to take away my stuff."

"It must be pretty frustrating to be picked on by a big girl, Chrissy," Diane said gently, still reflecting her daughter's feelings.

"Yeah. I feel bad," the little girl said firmly. She sat quietly for a moment, watching as Diane licked a few stamps. "Mom, can I go play out in the backyard?"

Diane gave her daughter a hug—and a great deal more.

By responding with active listening, Diane refrained from lecturing, rescuing, or explaining, and she allowed Chrissy the opportunity to explore what was going on for her. In the process, Chrissy discovered a solution to her own problem. Some other time, Diane might be able to talk with Chrissy about avoiding the problem in the future—and, perhaps, ask her what she could do to express her anger instead of slam the door.

Diane also showed respect for her daughter's feelings. Parents often do not agree with (or completely understand) their children's emotions, but active listening does not require you to agree or completely understand. It invites children to feel heard and lets them know it's okay to feel whatever they feel. Validating a child's feelings with love and understanding opens the door for real communication and problem solving and works toward building a lifelong relationship of love and trust.

Pretend these statements are made by a child. How would you respond?

- "No! I won't take a nap!"
- "I want a bottle like the baby has."
- "I hate going to the doctor."
- "Nobody will let me play with them."

Parents can choose to respond with "adultisms" like these: "How come you never . . . ?" "When will you ever . . . ?" or "How many times do I have to tell you . . . ?" Or they can respond with active listening, which might sound something like this:

- "You look disappointed that you have to stop playing with your toys. You were having a lot of fun."
- "Sounds like you're feeling a little left out in all the fuss over your new baby sister. Is there more you can tell me?"
- "Sometimes I feel a little afraid of going to the doctor, too."
- "You seem pretty sad about being ignored by the older kids."

These responses make no judgments and open the door for children to go further in exploring their feelings. Asking "Is there more?" indicates a willingness to listen and may help a child discover deeper, buried feelings.

Like most adults, sometimes all children really need is for someone to listen and understand. Active listening will help your child learn about his own feelings (and the appropriate ways to express them) and will help you focus on what's really important.

What About Anger?
Dealing with Difficult Feelings

IT IS AMAZING how quickly some children learn that certain emotions aren't acceptable, that they must be softened somehow or buried completely. Yet as we've already discovered, our feelings don't always go away on command; sometimes they linger in dark corners, waiting to erupt in a moment when our guard is down. It is generally better for parents and children to find acceptable, positive ways of dealing with feelings—even the difficult ones.

> It is generally better for parents and children to find acceptable, positive ways of dealing with feelings—even the difficult ones.

Tantrums are one typical expression of preschoolers' anger. It is helpful to know, however, that there is more parents and caregivers can do to respond to a child's anger than simply deal with tantrums. We can help our children begin to understand why they get angry, to recognize how that powerful emotion begins in their hearts and bodies (anger is a deeply physical reaction), and to develop ways that help them cope with and overcome their anger.

Kelly was five years old when her anxious, frustrated parents brought her to the counselor's office. "Kelly just gets so mad," her mother said. "She throws things at us, she hits herself, and last night she banged her head against the kitchen door. We're frightened for her—and although we try to stay calm, we end up getting almost as angry as she is. What can we do?"

The counselor took Kelly to the play therapy room. As Kelly played with a doll's house, she asked Kelly how it felt to get so angry. Kelly fidgeted with a doll, then set it down and looked up at the counselor. "It feels like a monster crawls inside my skin," she said, "and I get all hot inside. It's really scary."

Many children experience anger as a scary emotion, something their parents often fail to realize. There is more to anger than challenge and fighting, however. Dealing with children's strong emotions can be a great opportunity to get into a child's world and to build closeness, understanding, and trust. Here are a few other ways you might help a young child explore and express strong emotions:

- Invite the child to draw a picture of how the emotion feels. Does it have a color? A sound?

- Ask the child to talk through rather than act out what he or she is feeling. Since most children are not consciously aware of their feelings, you might try asking simple yes-or-no questions about the feelings. "Sounds like you might be feeling hurt and want to get even." "Are you having a hard time holding your anger inside?" "When you don't get what you want, does it make you so angry you can hardly stand it?" When you are correct in guessing what their feelings are, children feel validated and experience the relief of being understood.

- Ask the child what she notices happening in her body when she gets really angry. Because anger triggers physical reactions (adrenaline is released, heart rate and respiration increase, blood vessels expand, and so on), most people actually *feel* anger physically. If your child reports that her fists clench, or she feels a knot in her stomach, or her face feels hot (all common responses), you can work together to help her recognize when she's getting really angry and provide ways to cool off before anger gets out of control. (Adults, too, can benefit from paying attention to their body's cues.)

- Provide an acceptable way to deal with anger. You might purchase a "bop bag" that a child can punch when angry (it helps to stay nearby to talk through those strong feelings as your child expresses them). Some preschools have an "anger box," a knee-high cardboard box where an angry child can go to stand, jump, or yell when upset. Sometimes the teachers use it, too! Screaming into a pillow, running a race around the playground, or playing with water or Play-Doh can also help vent emotions and restore calm.

- Invite the child to take a cooling-off, time-out period before acting on his or her strong emotions. This is effective only if the child understands the concept of positive time-out, as explained in chapter 13. You might go to time-out with your child, either as an extra display of support or because you need it too.

- Let children have the last word. Avoid trying to talk children out of their feelings or trying to fix things for them. Have faith in your children; let their feelings run their course and teach them to work things out for themselves.

Kelly and her parents discovered that anger became more manageable when she learned to tell her parents about her body ("My face is getting hot") and ask for a cool-off with Play-Doh to pound—and when all of them could talk about the anger and what caused it without letting it take over.

Anger isn't the only difficult emotion young children must learn to deal with. By practicing active listening, taking time to understand, and using some of the ideas above, adults can also help children deal honestly with jealousy, fear, sadness, and the other emotions that are a part of our human existence.

Preschools can have a "time-out corner" where children can go when anger or other strong emotions threaten the peace or a "cool-off basket" filled with soothing items such as a koosh ball or soft stuffed toys. These items are calming and have sensory characteristics that help a young child regain his equilibrium. (Because time-out is so often used in a punitive manner, we emphasize that it is effective *only* when used to teach, nurture, and empower).

Conflicts have a way of escalating quickly when many small children are involved. Teachers may find it helpful to practice ways of defusing anger or to

HOW TO HELP YOUR CHILD RECOGNIZE AND MANAGE FEELINGS

- Invite the child to draw a picture of how the emotion feels.
- Ask the child to talk through rather than act out what she is feeling.
- Ask the child what she notices happening in her body when she gets really angry.
- Provide an acceptable way to deal with anger.
- Invite the child to take a cooling-off, time-out period before acting on her strong emotions.
- Let children have the last word.

allow groups of children to play "Let's Pretend" about what can happen when they feel angry. Talking in advance about what to do when we feel upset can give everyone, children and teachers alike, a plan to follow when strong feelings erupt.

Practicing Emotional Honesty

PARENTS (AND TEACHERS) often wonder how much of their own feelings they should share with children. It can help to remember that, as with so many things in life, children learn best by watching their adult role models. If you deal with anger by yelling, you shouldn't be surprised if the young ones in your life do, too. If, on the other hand, you can find positive ways of expressing your own feelings, then not only will you reduce the chance of conflict, but you will also provide children with a wonderful example of how to deal appropriately with feelings.

As you have probably already discovered, sharing your world with a young child can stimulate all sorts of interesting emotions in you. In the course of a single day, a parent or teacher can feel love, warmth, frustration, anger, irritation, weariness, hope, and despair. Children are amazingly sensitive to the emotional state of those around them; their innate antennae and ability to read nonverbal cues often let them know what we're feeling even when we think we're acting "normal." So, how should adults explain and express their feelings to children?

> If, on the other hand, you can find positive ways of expressing your own feelings, then not only will you reduce the chance of conflict, but you will also provide children with a wonderful example of how to deal appropriately with feelings.

Emotional honesty is often the best policy. It is not only okay but may also be real wisdom to tell a child, "I'm feeling really angry right now." Blaming or shaming statements aren't necessary; simply explaining to your children what you're feeling and why can help you deal with your own feelings and teach your children about possible results of their behavior. Remember, too, that children often assume that whatever you're feeling is about them. Explaining your feelings and the reasons for them may save you and your children a great deal of misunderstanding and confusion.

One helpful way of expressing feelings is by using "I statements." An "I statement" is a simple formula (formulas come in handy when we're too emotional to think straight) that allows us to explain what we're feeling and why. An "I statement" might look something like this:

- "I feel worried when blocks are thrown in the playroom, because one of the other children might get hurt. Would it help you to take some time out until you have calmed down, or do you have another solution to solve this problem?"

- "I feel angry when cereal is dumped on the floor, because I'm tired and I don't want to clean up the mess. When cereal is dumped on the floor again, I'll know you've decided not to eat and you can help me clean it up."

- "I feel upset and frustrated because the car has a flat tire, and now I'm going to be late to work."

- "I'm so angry right now that I need some time out until I can calm down, so I don't do or say something I'll regret later."

Parents and teachers can also practice separating children from their behavior. That way, we can reassure children about their place in our affections and encourage their efforts to understand their world, while still telling them that certain behaviors or actions are not acceptable. For example:

- "I love you, and I can't allow you to kick me when you're angry."
- "I'm glad you want to learn about the kitchen, and you can't melt your crayons on the stove."
- "I appreciate your help, and you're not quite old enough to fix the vacuum cleaner."

How Much Honesty Is Too Much?

ADULTS MAY FEEL the need to shield children from sadness, loss, and the other unpleasant realities of life, but it is usually best to be as honest with your children as you reasonably can be. As we've mentioned before, children's emotional antennae usually let them know when something in the family is amiss, and without enough information, they may assume they have done something wrong. Children shouldn't be asked to shoulder burdens too heavy for them or to take responsibility for their parents' problems, but they can be given an opportunity to understand and share in whatever is going on. This draws children into the family circle and helps build in them a sense of belonging.

If a family member or loved pet has died, for example, it is best to include children and to provide them with information that will help them make sense of what has happened. It is tempting to tell a young child that Grandpa is "sleeping" or has "gone away," but that may lead a child to fear going to bed or to wonder whether Mom or Dad will also "go away" the next time they're out of sight.

Death can be explained in simple but honest terms, and children can be helped to grieve and to heal. You might choose to tell a child that when we die, we go to another, special place that some people call heaven. Just as we can't see someone who is in another city, we can't see someone who has gone to heaven. Remember that it isn't necessary to tell children more than they can comprehend. You may want to explain that many adults also have difficulty understanding death, and many have different beliefs about what it means and what happens afterwards. Including children in the rituals surrounding death, such as funerals, may actually be less frightening for them than being left out. Death is part of the cycle of life; treating it as such will make coping with death easier for parents and children alike.

In the same way, if the family is undergoing financial strain or other stresses, parents can give children simple facts to help them understand and then use active listening to explore and deal with their feelings. Be aware that children will have strong feelings and reactions to traumatic events in the family, such as divorce, and it is unwise to simply assume that they'll be "fine."

Take time to explain, without blaming or judging, what has happened and how it will affect your child. Be sure she knows that it wasn't her fault and that she is still loved and cherished. And stay tuned in; use active listening to check your child's perceptions and allow her to express her fears and feelings openly. (For more information on helping children cope with death or divorce, see *Positive Discipline for Single Parents,* Prima Publishing, 1994.) By including young children in the life of the family, parents help them learn about feelings and what it means to be human.

By exploring and respecting your children's feelings and by being honest about your own feelings, you will build communication and problem-solving skills that will last a lifetime.

It's Never Too Soon to Begin

"My parents just don't understand me."

"I want to talk to my kid about sex and drugs, but I don't know how."

"I worry that my teenagers are getting into trouble, but they don't seem to trust me . . . I just don't get it."

"I would never tell my parents what my friends and I do—they'd only lose it. We just never talk at all."

Many teenagers—and many parents of teenagers—wish things could be different; they wish they could understand and trust each other enough to talk openly about the choices and issues that face them. Yet regardless of how much they may love one another, they simply can't talk. They can't trust each other; they don't understand each other. While it's never too late to change, it certainly is harder the longer you wait.

If you're fortunate enough to be the parent of a young child, you have a golden opportunity. The best time to begin building a relationship of trust and openness isn't after your children have become adolescents and you suddenly realize you need to be able to talk; the time is now, while they're young. Time spent talking to your children, listening to their daydreams and thoughts and feelings, teaching them about life, and simply being human together is an investment in the future you will never regret.

Pay attention to children's feelings and help them to understand and express them; teach them to respect and understand yours. Take time to solve problems together, to learn, and to grow; discover together that being a family

> Pay attention to children's feelings and help them to understand and express them; teach them to respect and understand yours.

means making an occasional mistake, but it also means learning to value and respect the worth and uniqueness of each member.

If you are a preschool teacher, remember that the time your young students spend with you can shape the way they view their world—you truly do touch the future when you teach young ones. For parents and teachers alike, taking the time to understand feelings and to express them in positive ways will help you build relationships where love and trust can flourish.

PART TWO

Understanding Your Growing Child— and Yourself

There is no doubt that preschoolers can be utterly delightful young people. As you're beginning to see, however, this world of ours looks a great deal different when viewed from the perspective of a young child.

Parents and teachers frequently are baffled by the behavior of their small charges. Why do they fight with us—and with each other? Why do they seem not to understand the simple things we ask of them? Why are they so often charming and adorable for others, yet defiant and contrary at home? And why do the everyday tasks of life—eating, getting dressed, going to bed—sometimes become pitched battles?

As with so many things in life, information and understanding make a huge difference in the way we perceive life with preschoolers. In chapters 4 through 10, we will explore their fascinating world and discover why they do what they do. You will learn about their development, the tasks and concepts they are naturally meant to be learning, and why their normal development so frequently leads them in opposite directions from the adults in their lives.

You will explore how young children learn, what shapes their temperament, how they learn to get along with others, and how your own personality affects them. What you discover will help you enter the world of preschoolers to work *with* them rather than *against* them. Shaping your actions to their special gifts and abilities will make life easier and more enjoyable for everyone!

4

"I'm More Capable Than You Think I Am"

Nurturing Initiative, Not Manipulation

RAISING THREE-YEAR-OLDS WOULD be an easy task if they didn't have so many ideas of their own—and so much energy with which to implement them! Take this little fellow, for example:

Q. *My son doesn't walk anywhere—he gallops. He chases the birds at the beach, leaps into the wading pool for his swim lesson, and this morning I found him trying to saddle the dog. When I asked him why he had thrown a blanket over the dog's back, he explained that he wanted to ride him. I had to explain that dogs are not strong enough to carry people on their backs. He gave up the riding plan, but I know he will come up with something else any moment. He seems so fearless, and I worry that he will get hurt. I'm worn out trying to keep track of him. Should I allow him to do these things?*

A. If you've ever spent much time in the company of a three-year-old, your head is probably nodding vigorously at this moment. This parent sounds exhausted by the effort of supervising and guiding an active young child, and most of us have had moments when we wondered why God in His wisdom gave three-year-olds so much more energy and creativity than He gave their parents.

But think for just a moment: the young man in the example above is demonstrating a number of wonderful qualities. He is courageous and not afraid to try new things. He is obviously able to connect ideas and actions, and he hurtles through life with excitement and curiosity. The same traits that exhaust his parents may be just the traits that will make him a successful, capable adult.

Erik Erikson, a pioneer in understanding human development, tells us that from about the ages of two to six, children experience a crucial stage in their development that Erikson called "initiative versus guilt" (Erikson, Erik H. *Childhood and Society.* New York: Norton, 1963). In fact, some adults still struggle with life's challenges because they were never able to nurture and develop the sense of initiative that our young friend above is so ably demonstrating.

When we say that a child needs a healthy sense of initiative, we do not mean that he should be allowed to carry out every idea that pops into his head. We do mean that he needs secure boundaries and limits within which he can explore, experiment, and learn to develop his belief in his own competence and capability. Creating a balance between safety (and appropriate behavior) and creativity and courage is the essence of parenting a three-year-old.

> Creating a balance between safety (and appropriate behavior) and creativity and courage is the essence of parenting a three-year-old.

These are the years when parents are apt to hear a great deal of the phrase "me do it!" Children in the early preschool years want to try everything: they want to push the vacuum, wash the dishes, and dig holes in the garden. All too often, parents stifle their would-be helpers by telling them, "No, you're too little. You can't do it well enough. Wait until you're bigger. It is easier and faster for me to do it." It usually is easier (and less messy) for adults to do these tasks, but turning a child away may plant the seeds of guilt instead of initiative. And years later, those same adults may find themselves wondering why their child "just won't do anything!" The drive to develop initiative versus guilt and shame continues throughout the preschool years.

Again, we are talking about a *sense* of initiative—not actual ability. As in the first year children develop a sense of trust or a sense of mistrust and in the second year a sense of autonomy or a sense of doubt and shame, toddlers and preschoolers (ages two to six) begin to develop a sense of initiative—or a sense of guilt. Parents, preschool teachers, and caregivers who understand this important developmental stage can create an environment that enhances initiative instead of guilt, discouragement, or manipulation.

Initiative in Action

Michael's mom took him to a nearby park for an outing. Michael, newly turned three, was eager to play on the climber. He scrambled up the lower rungs easily enough, but halfway up he looked down—and his stomach did a flip-flop. Michael cried out, and his mom came to stand beside him. Michael whimpered for Mom to rescue him and lift him down, but Mom just smiled and placed an encouraging hand on Michael's back. She spoke reassuringly to her frightened little one, helping him find his way back down. When he was on the ground his mother gave him a big hug and congratulated him on getting down "by himself." Michael beamed a proud smile. Mom and Michael returned to the same park regularly, and by the end of the second week Michael was scampering up and down the climber with ease.

Margaret's mother faced the same dilemma but responded much differently. When Margaret, also three, cried out from the top of the same climber, her mother ran up and gathered Margaret into her arms. She cuddled her and told her firmly how dangerous it could be to climb up so high. Margaret cried a little, then went over to play in the sandbox. Even though they visited the park often, two months later Margaret still avoided the climber, clinging to her mother's leg whenever anyone invited her to climb it.

Preschoolers see the world as an exciting and fascinating place, especially as they develop more initiative and a greater physical and intellectual capacity to explore. At the same time, some children feel frustrated when adults get in their way, while others may give up and allow their anxious parents to overly protect them. In either case, their developing sense of initiative may be thwarted. Later, these children may experience guilt or shame when they find they do not have the skills or abilities to accomplish what they want to do.

A vicious cycle may be created when adults see a youngster's lack of skills and respond by rushing in to protect her from experiencing frustration, defeat, or bumps and bruises. Margaret's mother wanted to protect her daughter from injury but ended up convincing her to avoid the climber—and possibly any other potentially challenging activities. Children may respond to frustration by withdrawing and adopting a sense of guilt about their inability to "conquer the world." Adults can choose to encourage children as they face challenges, just as Michael's mom did. Michael's mom showed faith in his ability to master a new skill, and his experience told him "I am capable" in a way his mother's words never could. When Michael and Margaret face challenges and new responsibilities as they grow, how will they respond? What will they believe about their own abilities?

When children are discouraged from exploring the world around them, they may become frustrated and withdraw from the task of developing initiative. And discouraged children tend to misbehave. The need to develop initiative is inborn, whether parents and caregivers find it convenient or not. Even when they are frustrated, some children (the spunky, determined ones) keep fighting for their need to develop initiative. Adults usually call this behavior "defiance" and work to control, coddle, or overprotect the child. Yes, children must be kept safe and must be taught to behave appropriately—but this task is easier to accomplish when adults are also providing opportunities for preschoolers to experience initiative.

Initiative—or Manipulation?

A CHILD WHO is discouraged from developing initiative sometimes responds by developing manipulation skills instead. This is the child who withdraws into helplessness and insists that you do everything for her. She "can't" walk to the car; she "can't" put on her socks, and she "can't" pick up her toys. Whenever your child misbehaves, you might ask yourself, "Could it be that this behavior is founded in discouragement?"

Q. *My three-year-old daughter screams and cries when I say no. She never eats what we give her: she asks for peanut butter bread and only licks off the peanut butter, refusing to eat the bread. Then she will insist on putting more peanut butter on the bread. If I don't do as she says, she will start whining or crying. I don't always let her get away with it. She is not a very good eater but is very active. She's at child care during the day and is very well behaved there.*

Q. *I believe that "no" means "no" but my daughter doesn't realize that yet. I used to put her in a corner where she couldn't see us until she stopped crying, but it only worked for a while. Now my husband puts her in our small bathroom with the light off. I believe that this will make her claustrophobic, since it happens every day. She does sleep in her own bed, but she wets almost every night. Bedtime is a hassle, as she won't stay in bed. I have to pat her on the back until she falls asleep. I need* *help—this is driving me crazy. I hate the constant battle with my child, but she won't do what I say.*

Situations like this one are heartbreakingly common. So many of these battles could be eliminated if adults understood developmental and age appropriateness, the mistaken goals of behavior (see chapters 19, 20, and 21), and nonpunitive methods that create limits while inviting cooperation.

There is a better way. The first mother could choose appropriate moments to give in (such as letting her daughter experiment with the peanut butter and bread, and teaching her to clean up afterward) when her daughter is actively developing her autonomy and initiative. On the other hand, there are moments when it is wise not to give in (such as bedtime), because this behavior is demonstrating mistaken beliefs and actions (in this case, the need for special service and attention). This is the time for follow-through, kindly and firmly returning her to her bed every time she gets up, for as long as it takes.

> Children "listen" to kind, firm, and consistent action more than they listen to words.

Preschoolers need to know that we mean what we say and will follow through with kind and firm action (instead of lectures). Children "listen" to kind, firm, and consistent action more than they listen to words. Punitive time-out (such as locking a child in a dark bathroom) is another matter that is discussed in chapter 11.

Encouraging the development of initiative is a tricky task precisely because parents and caregivers find it so challenging and inconvenient. Still, adults at home and school can help develop preschoolers' confidence and initiative by providing a range of opportunities, time for training, and encouragement for the many things children can do. When supported in this way, children learn to trust in themselves and do not feel a sense of guilt or shame when they find they still have much to learn. When they can see themselves as capable and worthwhile, then not having a skill means only that they have yet to learn it, not that they can't do so.

Who said parenting was easy and wouldn't take much time? Too many parents want confident, courageous, respectful, resourceful, responsible, resilient children but don't want to invest time in methods that teach these characteristics. There are many ways to help children develop initiative rather than manipulation and misbehavior. Playing "Let's Pretend," stating clear expectations, offering limited choices, and following through, as well as other techniques that will be discussed later on, can be used to help children learn to behave appropriately at home and out in public, and will also encourage their developing sense of initiative.

Play "Let's Pretend"

Children love to play, so "Let's Pretend" can be a fun way to teach them skills and help them understand the difference between effective (respectful) and ineffective (disrespectful) behavior. Preschoolers are not too young to understand "Let's Pretend" when you make it simple.

One way to set up the role-playing (the technical term for "Let's Pretend") is to say to your child something like this: "You be the daddy, and I'll be the little boy. We are at the pancake house. How should I behave? Should I cry and run around and throw my food like this?" Then demonstrate crying and running around. "Or should I sit quietly in the seat and eat, or perhaps color quietly while I wait?" Then demonstrate by pretending you are sitting in the restaurant and have your child supervise your behavior. Reverse roles and let the child portray being both disrespectful and respectful. Be sure to engage your children in a conversation where they can see the benefits of respectful behavior!

State Clear Expectations

One of the oldest bits of parenting advice is still one of the best: Say what you mean, and mean what you say. How should we establish clear, appropriate expectations for young preschoolers? Let's listen in as Cody's father gives it a try:

Even though he is only four, Cody loves baseball. He's been collecting baseball cards since he was tiny, loves to play whiffle ball in the backyard with his dad, and knows the entire starting lineup of the San Francisco Giants. Tim, Cody's father, is planning to take his small son to his first real baseball game. Previous experience has taught him that in order to enjoy the day with his curious, active preschooler, some preparation and groundwork will be necessary.

First, Tim decides to take Cody with him to the local park for a Little League game. As they sit in the bleachers together, Tim asks Cody how he thinks they should act at the "big stadium." Cody considers this question thoughtfully, furrowing his small brow in concentration.

HAVE PATIENCE AND FAITH

The process of nurturing initiative is less painful when adults can make a slight attitude adjustment. Of course, preschoolers are too little to do things perfectly. But which is more important: perfection or helping your children develop healthy self-esteem and strong life skills? Of course it is easier and faster for you to do things. But which is more important: ease and speed or helping children develop confidence and an ability to learn from mistakes?

"We should sit still?" he offers tentatively, knowing this is a tough rule for him to follow.

"Well," his dad says with a smile, "we can stand up sometimes. And we can walk together to get a cold drink or a hot dog."

"We can do seventh inning stretch!" Cody shouts excitedly, and begins to sing "Take Me Out to the Ball Game."

Together, father and son explore the guidelines for the big day. Tim makes it clear that lots of people will be at the game, so Cody will have to hold his hand when they walk anywhere. Tim and Cody agree that Cody can have a hot dog, a cold drink, a snack, and one souvenir of his choice—as long as it costs ten dollars or less. And they agree that if Cody runs away or climbs on the seats, they will have to return to the car.

Tim knows his son well; when Cody's curiosity gets the better of him, a firm hand on his shoulder (without scolding or a lecture) draws him back to Dad's side. And when Cody decides to climb down a row (and over three people) to see better, Tim only has to ask him what their agreement about climbing was for Cody to plop quickly back into his seat.

Because Cody is four, his dad knows that the day will not be perfect. He also knows that Cody may not be able to follow the guidelines for nine full innings. But by setting clear expectations (in advance) and following through on these simple limits, Cody's first baseball game will be an occasion father and son will remember for years to come.

Offer Limited Choices and Follow Through

Parents sometimes believe that giving children what they want and not burdening them with rules will show them that they are loved. We want to stress that permissiveness is not the way to help children develop initiative. One alternative to permissiveness is offering limited choices with kind and firm follow-through. (We discuss many other discipline alternatives throughout this book.) Limited choices are effective when they are related, respectful, and reasonable.

Elena's family went to the zoo with another family from their neighborhood. Elena asked for cotton candy, snow cones, and everything she saw other children enjoying. Her father told Elena she could have either a snow cone or popcorn. Elena chose popcorn. Her father purchased the popcorn and then told Elena that if she continued to ask for other treats she would need to return to the car with him, where they would wait until the others finished viewing the exhibits.

Partway through eating the popcorn, Elena saw a child with a snow cone and began to ask for one. Elena was serious: she emphasized her demand by flinging the remaining popcorn down, spilling it all over the walkway. Her father calmly asked Elena if she wanted to hold his hand on the way to the car or be carried. (He decided to ignore the spilled popcorn, since the pigeons were already taking care of that problem.) When she refused to move, her father picked her up and left for the car. He did not scold, spank, or remind her why they were leaving. He treated her respectfully, and when she began to wail that she wanted to see the monkeys, he assured her that he was confident that next time they came to the zoo, Elena would make better choices—and would be able to visit the monkeys.

Giving a child a chance to try again is reasonable and encouraging. It is not reasonable to say, "I'm never taking you there again—or anywhere else, for that matter!" In addition, most parents do not follow through on such threats—which only teaches children that they can safely disregard both boundaries and rules.

Yes, it would be inconvenient for you to miss your family outing while using kind and firm follow-through. You also have a choice. Which is more important, a family outing or the self-esteem, initiative, and confidence your child will develop by learning appropriate social skills? When you follow through with kindness and firmness, you won't have to miss many outings before your child learns that you say what you mean and will demonstrate that you mean what you say. Of course, follow-through requires that adults think before they speak. If you can't do it, don't say it!

Positive Discipline in Action

Myrna and Lamar decided they would teach their son Mark to dress himself when he was three years old (excellent training for budding initiative). They purchased clothes that were easy for a small child to manage, such as pants with elastic bands, wide-neck T-shirts, and sneakers with Velcro fasteners. Mark was a willing student and pretty much mastered the art of dressing himself (even though he put his shoes on the wrong feet about half of the time).

Mark attended a preschool, and his job was to get himself dressed in the morning, help with breakfast, and be ready by 7:30, when his dad would drive him to school on the way to work. His parents decided to develop a morning routine to get more cooperation from Mark. Myrna and Lamar had been warned about the possibility that Mark might use his initiative to "test" the routine. In preparation, they worked out a plan with Mark in advance that included a limited choice and follow-through. Together they decided that any time Mark was not dressed in time to go, they would put Mark's clothes in a paper bag so he could finish dressing at school. They weren't sure how much Mark really understood about their discussion of choices and follow-through, but they had faith that he would learn if they ever had to carry out their plan.

Sure enough, after several weeks of smooth mornings, the day arrived when Myrna noticed Mark wasn't following his routine. When it was time for Lamar to leave for work, Mark was still in his pajamas. Myrna had prepared the sack of clothes, so Lamar kindly and firmly picked Mark up under one arm, took the sack of clothes in his other hand, and walked to the car through pouring rain—just as a neighbor was out picking up his newspaper.

Lamar sighed and reminded himself, "Oh well, taking time for training with Mark is more important than what the neighbors think."

Mark cried and complained that he was cold while they were driving to school. Lamar pointed to Mark's coat on the seat beside him and suggested he would be warmer if he put it on. He also assured Mark that he could get dressed as soon as they got to school. Mark hadn't finished testing, so he continued to complain. When they arrived at the school, Lamar took Mark into the preschool. Joyce, the preschool director, understood these moments well and smiled as the pair approached.

"Oh hi, Mark!" she said warmly. "I see you didn't get dressed this morning. That's okay. You can take your bag of clothes into my office and come out as soon as you are dressed."

Mark dressed in about five minutes. A month later, he decided further research was in order and tested the routine again. Lamar responded matter-of-factly, carrying the clothes bag to the car. When they arrived, Mark decided to continue checking out the adults' responses. His teacher invited him to get dressed, reminding him that he would need to be dressed for outside playtime. He refused, then walked into the classroom and began to play with the blocks, nattily attired in Mickey Mouse pajamas. Mark played happily until it was time to head outside. Mark's teacher assured him that as soon as he was fully dressed he could join his classmates in the play yard. After a moment of reflection, Mark decided that proving his point was not worth missing recess, and he scrambled into his clothes.

Mark's parents and teacher did not nag, lecture, or remind Mark about getting dressed. They simply did what they said they would do—carry his clothes to the car for him, limit his ability to play outdoors until properly dressed, and allow him to dress himself at school. (It's important to note that this plan would not be appropriate for an older child who might feel humiliated by arriving at school in pajamas. Adult actions that cause shame or embarrassment are unlikely to encourage respect or cooperation.)

Lamar could have made this experience humiliating to Mark by "piggy-backing," which means adding blaming or shaming lectures to his kind and firm actions. Lamar did not say, "It serves you right! Maybe next time you'll hurry up. You are making me late. All the kids will probably laugh at you for not getting dressed." Instead, Myrna, Lamar, and Joyce treated Mark kindly and firmly, which helped him learn the benefits of using his skills to help himself and cooperate with others.

"Oops, I Made a Mistake!"

BY NOW YOU might be afraid that you have to be a perfect parent to raise a perfect child. There are no such things. Isn't that wonderful? An important definition of human beings, adults and children alike, is that they never quit making mistakes—never! It doesn't matter how much we learn or how much we know. As human beings we sometimes forget what we know and get hooked into emotional reactions—or we just plain goof up. Once we understand this, we might as well see mistakes as the important life processes that they are: interesting opportunities to learn. Instead of feeling discouraged when we make a mistake, we can say, "Terrific! I've just been given another opportunity to learn!"

> Many children (and adults) short-circuit the lifelong process of developing initiative because they are afraid to make mistakes. Mistakes aren't the same as failures . . . and even so-called failures can provide opportunities to learn and grow.

Wouldn't it be wonderful if we could instill this attitude in our children so they wouldn't be burdened with all the baggage we carry about mistakes? Many children (and adults) short-circuit the lifelong process of developing initiative because they are afraid to make mistakes. Mistakes aren't the same as failures, although we often behave as though they are. And even so-called failures can provide opportunities to learn and grow.

One of the best ways to help children develop initiative is through family meetings or preschool class meetings, as discussed in chapter 15. By the time children reach the age of four, they can be excellent problem solvers. Asking "what" and "how" questions, instead of telling what and how, will help them develop this skill.

Asking "What" and "How" Questions

CHILDREN DO NOT develop a strong sense of initiative when parents and teachers spend too much time lecturing: telling children what happened, what caused it to happen, how they should feel about it, and what they should do about it. Telling may keep children from seeing mistakes as opportunities to learn. Telling instills guilt because it sends the message that children aren't living up to adult expectations. Perhaps most important, telling children what, how, and why teaches them *what* to think, not *how* to think. Parents are often disappointed when their children don't develop more initiative without realizing they are not using the kind of parenting skills that encourage initiative.

Children will develop thinking skills, judgment skills, problem-solving abilities, and initiative when adults ask them these kinds of questions: What happened? What were you trying to do? Why do you think this happened? How do you feel about it? How could you fix it? What else could you do if you don't want this to happen again?

When Mark (the child who wouldn't get dressed in the morning) complained about being cold in the car, his dad might have used it as an opportunity for asking questions. "Why do you think you are cold? What might you do to feel warmer?" These questions would have helped Mark make the connections between clothes, coats, and warmth. He might also have discovered why pajamas aren't a good choice when it is cold outside. Perhaps Mark does not truly understand this connection and would have answered, "Because I didn't eat all my toast." This would have given his dad an opportunity to help Mark learn the effect clothes have on whether we feel warm or not. Believe it or not, children do not always understand the reasoning that seems so obvious to adults.

> Believe it or not, children do not always understand the reasoning that seems so obvious to adults.

Helping Children Reach Their Full Potential

Joyce, the director of the preschool Mark attends, believes in the importance of giving children opportunities to develop initiative using all of the concepts discussed in this chapter. Her staff looks for every opportunity to let children experience how capable they are by taking time for training and then letting the children do many things that are usually done for them by adults.

For example, when Joyce goes shopping for groceries, she lets the children take turns going with her to help her put items in the grocery cart. When she returns to the child care center, she backs the station wagon into the play yard and calls the children to help take the groceries to the kitchen one item at a time. The cook helps the children remember where to put the items.

During lunchtime, the children dish up their own food. One little fellow named Matt would consistently take too much food. After about a week, his teacher helped him explore what was happening by asking, "What happens when you take too much food?"

Matt responded, "I can't eat it all and I have to throw some away."

The teacher continued: "What would happen if you took smaller helpings of food?"

Matt looked like he had made a great discovery as he said, "I could eat it all."

The teacher said, "I'm sure you could." Then she asked, "If you took less food, ate it all, and were still hungry, what could you do then?"

Matt beamed as he said, "I could take some more?"

The teacher asked, "When will you start doing that?"

Matt looked like he could hardly wait as he crowed, "Tomorrow!"

After lunch, the children each scrape their own food into a plastic dishpan, rinse their own plate in another dishpan, and then put the dish in the dishwasher. This routine is definitely more time-consuming than having an adult clean up after lunch. But Joyce and her staff of teachers are more interested in helping children develop their full potential than in getting chores done quickly. They also love the children, enjoy them, and feel privileged to be part of their growth and development.

There it is again: love and joy. The more we know about what is developmentally appropriate, how we can enhance the environment in which children grow, learn the skills that will encourage them to reach their full potential, and forgive ourselves when we make mistakes, the more we can relax and just enjoy watching our children grow, knowing that they're learning to trust their own abilities, to believe in the support of the adults in their lives, and to experience the wonder of life all around them.

5

Understanding Developmental Appropriateness

EACH HUMAN BEING is a work of art. Look at the variety we see in appearance alone: skin color, hair color and texture, shape of the nose, color of the eyes, height, weight, shape—each one of us is unique. And physical characteristics are only the beginning of our uniqueness. Temperament is as individual as a fingerprint. So is the rate at which we develop and grow. Understanding developmental appropriateness—the sorts of things children do, think, and are capable of at different stages—can help parents and teachers work effectively with children just as they are at the moment.

Windows of Opportunity

CHILDREN ARE, in many ways, similar. Johnny and Mary, for instance, will both be learning to walk in the first year and a half of life. Children are different, too. Mary doggedly pulled herself along the furniture and took her first steps at ten months of age, while Johnny was contentedly crawling at eleven months. By thirteen months of age, both children were walking, exploring their world on their own two feet. Similar, yet unique!

Picture a window in your mind. Although the window is framed on all sides, there is a great deal of space in the middle. In the same way, many behaviors and early experiences in our children's lives take place in just such a window. There are windows for physical, intellectual, and emotional development, and each child has his or her own individual schedule, neither exactly like nor completely unlike anyone else's.

Very few things in the world of parenting come in only black or white. This book is all about choices, windows, and possibilities. Understanding your child's individual progress—her development of trust, autonomy, and initiative; her temperament; her physical development; and her ability to interpret her experiences—will help you make the best choices for her, for yourself, and for your family or classroom. Let's take a look at some of the ways developmental stages influence children's perceptions and behavior.

Process Versus Product

IT'S A BUSY Friday evening, and you're off on a quick trip to the grocery store with your preschooler. You have a definite goal in mind, namely to grab the necessary ingredients for dinner in time to get home, prepare and eat it, and still be on time for your older son's soccer game. For you, going to the store means obtaining the desired *product.*

For your young child, however, the product just isn't the point. Children are firmly rooted in the here and now; they think about and experience life differently than adults do. A trip to the store is all about the *process*—the smells, the colors, the feelings, the experience. Being sandwiched into a busy schedule just doesn't allow time to enjoy the process!

Children do not share our goal-oriented expectations. It isn't always possible to go along with a child's relaxed approach, either. Sometimes we really do need to run in, grab the chicken, and run home again. But being aware of your child's tendency to focus on process rather than product can help you provide a balance. There may be times when you can take a leisurely browse through the store, enjoying the smell of flowers in the floral department, the colors of the fruits and vegetables, and the brightly colored magazines in the rack.

> There are windows for physical, intellectual, and emotional development, and each child has his or her own individual schedule, neither exactly like nor completely unlike anyone else's.

Children are miniature Zen masters, able to focus on the moment and enjoy it—an ability adults would do well to learn. (Most busy adults struggle to find a balance between enjoying the moment and getting everything done. What might we learn from our more relaxed offspring?)

When you must hurry, take time to explain to your child why you must shop quickly this time. You can explain that you want him to hold your hand and that you will have to walk past the toys and other interesting things. You can offer to let him help you find the chicken and carry it to the checkout stand. Then you will walk back to the car and drive home. Helping a child understand clearly what is expected and what will happen makes it more likely he will cooperate with you.

> Children are miniature Zen masters, able to focus on the moment and enjoy it— an ability adults would do well to learn.

When we understand that young children are more interested in process than in the final product, we can find many ways to use this knowledge.

Patsy Green arrived at the child care center one afternoon just in time to see Laura Anderson and her son carrying a huge, colorful painting out to the car. Patsy looked around eagerly to see what her son Paul had painted, but none of the pictures had his name on them.

Baffled, Patsy cornered the teacher and asked why Paul hadn't had a chance to paint that day.

"Well," the teacher said, "Paul was very interested in the paint—but not in putting it on the paper. He stirred the colors and experimented with the feeling of the paint on his fingers, then decided he'd really rather build with blocks." She smiled, for she understood that Paul was interested in the process, in texture and balance and fit, not in producing a product.

When Paul's mom can understand this as well, she'll be better able to help Paul benefit from the different experiences in his life.

Point of View

WHAT DOES THE world look like when you are under three feet tall? How might your choices, needs, and behavior be influenced by this particular point of view? Well, get down on your knees and take a look around. What does the painting six feet up the wall look like from this angle? How inviting is a conversation with adult knees? What kind of challenge does hand washing present when the sink begins a foot above where you end? Understanding a young child's physical perspective and limitations can help parents and teachers structure the environment so children have the greatest chance of success.

A child's point of view can actually add a unique perspective to the family's life together, if we let it.

On a bright Saturday afternoon, the Douglas family went out for a walk together. Mom, Dad, and the two older children were all busy admiring the brilliant colors of the autumn leaves, watching the birds in flight and commenting on the shapes of the clouds. It was three-year-old Melissa, whose vantage point was considerably lower, who noticed the tiny frog beneath the bushes. Without Melissa's excited exclamations, not only would the family have missed seeing the tiny creature, but they might have accidentally stepped on it!

"For Real?" Fantasy and Reality

CHILDREN OFTEN HAVE difficulty understanding that what they see on television and movie screens may not be real. For instance, even children as old as seven or eight usually believe the claims of television commercials—after all, if Michael Jordan says it, it must be true!

When Karen and Bill Jackson learned that the Disney classic Snow White and the Seven Dwarfs *was coming to their local theater, they were excited about the opportunity to share the movie with their three-year-old son, Philip. Philip was a bright, articulate child, and his parents explained to him carefully that the movie was fun but it did have some scary parts.*

"It isn't real," Karen told her small son. "You don't need to be afraid." Philip grinned and bounced up and down, too excited about seeing his first movie to pay much attention to his mother's warning.

Everything went well until the scene where the wicked queen drinks the potion that will turn her into a withered old hag. Suddenly, with a shriek like a teakettle boiling over, Philip leaped from his own seat into his mother's lap, where he huddled shaking. He stubbornly refused to return to his own seat for the rest of the movie, even though the fright eventually died away.

"Hey, kiddo, didn't we tell you the movie wasn't real?" Bill asked his small son on the way out to the car.

Philip looked up at his dad in amazement. "But Dad," he said slowly, "it was real. I saw it!"

Philip recovered quickly enough, learned the names of all seven dwarfs, and enthusiastically sang "Hi ho, hi ho" for the rest of the summer. But his

MAKING IT SAFE TO MAKE MISTAKES

Colin was not thrilled to find the broken egg on the kitchen floor. "Hey," he called, with exasperation in his voice, "who broke this egg?"

Four-year-old Sammy replied calmly, "An alligator did it."

Now Colin knows there aren't any alligators in Kansas. Can he find a way to handle the situation that both solves the egg problem and teaches Sammy the importance of telling the truth? Let's look at a couple of possibilities.

Colin could join in the pretending with his son. "An alligator!" he exclaims. "Was it orange? I think I just saw it in the driveway." Sam grins and agrees that it was an orange alligator.

Colin smiles too, then says, "You know, I'm just pretending that there was an alligator. I know we don't have alligators around here. Isn't that right, Sam?"

Sam happily admits that there are no alligators. Colin suggests that they clean up the broken egg together, knowing there will be opportunities to talk as they work.

"Sam, were you afraid I would yell at you about the egg?"

Now Sam drops his eyes and nods slowly.

Colin makes his voice warm and gentle as he says, "I know it's tempting to blame things on an alligator or to make up something that didn't really happen. But it's important for you to know that you can tell me the truth, even when you feel scared. Do you know why it's important to tell the truth?"

parents learned that the best lectures in the world don't change the fact that a child's definition of reality is far broader than an adult's.

"Tell Me the Truth!" Young Children and Lying

Q. *I'm a mother of three little ones, ages four, two, and seven months. My question is how do I deal with my four-year-old's lying? She lies about even little things.*

Sam shakes his head.

Colin continues, ruffling his son's hair as he speaks. "I want to be able to trust what you tell me, buddy. I love you very much, and I want to know that when you tell me something, it's what really happened."

Sam looks up now and says slowly, "I love you, too, Daddy. I was just pretending."

Colin says, "Yes, I know we were pretending. And it's fun to pretend sometimes. It's important to know that we can tell the truth, though. We're pretending when we make up a story together. We're lying when we use a story to avoid admitting we've made a mistake."

Sam will probably have to learn this lesson more than once. His dad could also simply have asked Sam if he felt scared. Or he could have asked the original question in a less threatening way, saying "Sam, this broken egg made a mess. How can we solve this problem? Can you clean it up by yourself, or would you like me to help?"

Removing the sense of fear and getting the message of love through to our children (or even participating in a bit of nonsense with them) can help them learn to tell the truth. It is probably wise to remember, too, that few adults can claim to be completely truthful all of the time. Realistic expectations and acceptance will help your child learn trust and truthfulness.

I can't let her get away with such behavior. Please offer some advice on how I should handle this delicate situation.

A. Children can "lie" for all sorts of reasons. Sometimes they're not lying; they're indulging their imagination and active fantasy life. Sometimes they do lie, because they've learned it isn't safe to tell the truth.

Your statement about letting her "get away with it" gives a clue about your attitude. At four, most children can understand that their behavior has consequences, but they still need far more teaching than they do "discipline." In fact, the origin of the word "discipline" is actually "to teach," not "to punish." If your daughter suspects that wrong choices and mistakes will earn her punishments or lectures, of course she'll lie. Most children (and most adults) lie from time to time. If we want our children to be truthful, we must be willing to listen, to refrain from shaming or punishing, and to work together to find solutions to problems. We also need to find ways to enter our children's worlds and to understand why their perceptions may be different from our own.

Children are not born understanding the difference between truth and lies, and they will not automatically value honesty. Parents should plan to do some teaching on why trust and telling the truth are important. Mistakes are inevitable—especially when you're four—and if they're viewed as opportunities to learn rather than sins or failures, they're not as scary. A good way to avoid lectures (which often cause children to shut down instead of to listen) is to ask, "What do you think might happen when you don't tell the truth?" (This is effective only if you are truly curious about your child's opinion, instead of trying to disguise a lecture with a question.)

Continue helping your child explore the consequences of her behavior with other "what" and "how" questions: "How do you feel when someone lies to you?" "What do you think is the reason children might be afraid to tell the truth?" "What ideas do you have to help you feel safe to tell the truth?"

When a child does not tell the truth and is spanked, sent to time out, or shamed, she probably will learn unintended lessons. Punishment only *appears* to work, and often it creates side effects, such as children who lie, are fearful, and try to wriggle out of taking responsibility for their actions. It is also true that children are more likely to value honesty when they see the adults around them practicing it. In other words, your children will not learn to be truthful if they hear you calling in sick to work because you've decided you would rather go skiing!

WAYS TO RESPOND TO LYING

- Join in, pretending with the child by exaggerating the story. If a child claims "the alligator did it" pretend you saw it too—"a big orange one!"

- Focus on solutions rather than on blame. Instead of asking who broke the egg, ask if the child needs help cleaning up the spill. Or ask if the child has other ideas about how to solve the problem.

- When you suspect a lie, state it: "That sounds like a story to me. I wonder what the truth is?"

- Empathize with a child. Ask if he feels scared to admit to making a mess. Assure him we all feel scared at times.

- Explain the need to accept responsibility for his actions: "We all make mistakes, but blaming others, even imaginary people, does not take away responsibility for what we did."

- Talk about the meaning of trust. Help a child see the connection between telling the truth and having others trust what he says.

As we've already discovered, children don't have the same grasp on fantasy and reality that adults do, nor do they automatically understand the difference between acceptable and unacceptable behavior. Lying is often a problem for parents with children around the ages of four or five, and developmentally it makes some sense. After all, a child is only vaguely beginning to understand the difference between things that are real and those that are unreal. Lying needn't provoke horror and punishment; parents and teachers can help children tell the truth by making it safe for them to do so and by understanding why they sometimes do not.

Children and Stealing

YOUNG CHILDREN DON'T make the same assumptions about property rights that adults do. And because children learn by watching adults, they sometimes make surprising decisions about what they've seen.

Jason goes into the supermarket with his mom. He watches Mom pick up a copy of the free local paper and place it in her purse. Further down the aisle a woman is offering samples of cookies. Mom takes one for herself and offers one to Jason, who munches on it happily as they complete their shopping.

When they arrive at the car, Mom lifts Jason into his car seat and discovers a bulge in her son's pocket. Further examination reveals a candy bar.

"You stole this," Mom exclaims, shocked.

"What on earth is 'stealing'?" Jason wonders.

It's not really surprising that Jason is confused; what difference is there between the paper, the cookies, and the candy bar? These are the moments of truth parents face each day, and they can be either occasions for disappointment or opportunities for teaching.

If Mom is paying attention, she may realize that the problem is not one of dishonesty but of differing perceptions. She may remember picking up the newspaper and the cookies. And she may choose to help her little boy understand why we can take some things out of the supermarket but not others.

If Mom lectures Jason, shames him, and makes him feel guilty and afraid, he may be more likely to believe that right and wrong are a matter of getting caught. He may also be less able to apply what he has learned to a future situation.

Understanding the developmental limitations in your child's thinking will help you focus on his underlying beliefs and invite real thinking and learning to take place. Discipline is meant to teach, and mistakes are opportunities to learn. We can't say it often enough!

"Who Am I?" Discovering Gender Identity

Alice Billings walks into the preschool shaking her head. She prides herself on being a "no frills" sort of person: she wears no makeup, pulls her hair back simply, and usually dresses in jeans and T-shirts. Right behind mom is her daughter, Sally— and Sally is a sight to behold. She is wearing a lacy pink dress, ribbons in her hair, her best shiny shoes, and a jangly assortment of bracelets on her arms.

Alice looks at the teacher in despair. "Where does Sally get this 'Barbie doll' taste in clothes?" she laments. Sally's teacher laughs as she welcomes them for the day.

As it happens, Sally is four years old and is making a very big discovery. Sally, it seems, is a girl. Not only was she born a girl, but she will remain one for the rest of her life, despite her earlier declaration that she would become a boy after her next birthday. Sally may not always insist on ruffles and bracelets. She is simply exploring all the aspects of what it means to be a girl from her perspective as a four-year-old.

Sex role identification takes place even when parents are careful to minimize gender stereotypes. On playgrounds everywhere games emerge during the preschool years that focus on gender. "No boys allowed," say the girls. "Girls, ick," reply the boys with equal fervor.

Although we understand this natural phase, we can still teach young children to respect all people. Children naturally learn that they are either male or female, but this learning process needn't involve the learning of prejudice or gender-based limitations. Girls can play army and boys can play with dolls with no particular implications for the future; both can learn to develop their own special abilities, regardless of sex.

Children will also begin to notice physical differences between boys and girls and often will ask what they mean. In these days of explicit television and advertising, questions may come earlier than ever before (an excellent reason for staying tuned in to what your child is watching on the tube). A little boy may want to touch Dad in the shower. Watching Mom nurse a baby brother or sister may lead to all sorts of interesting questions. As much as possible, try to remain calm, relaxed, and "askable."

Children don't need a great deal of detailed information about sexuality (in fact, their eyes will probably glaze over if you try), but most experts agree that it is wise to answer questions or offer explanations in simple, accurate terms. There are a number of wonderful, illustrated books available for young children. Being open helps establish an atmosphere of comfort and trust and will enable your children to seek further information later on, when they really need it.

Children who are raised in homes where mutual respect flourishes will feel good about being who they are. Their tastes in clothing will change, as will their desire to have same- or opposite-sex friends.

Gender roles are a topic of much debate and controversy in our society. Be sure you let your children know that being a boy or a girl need not place restrictions on the opportunities life offers. Treating both boys and girls with respect, encouraging their unique abilities, and giving them access to a variety of life skills will produce children with healthy self-esteem. Limiting children to

sex-typed roles, expecting play or work to fall into male or female compart-
ments, or discouraging abilities on the grounds that they are "too feminine,"
not "masculine" enough, or not "ladylike" may cause children to stifle skills and
interests that would help them become healthy and happy as they grow up.

Racial Identification

CHILDREN NATURALLY NOTICE differences between themselves and others. The conclusions they draw about those differences can vary, depending on
what they're taught.

> *Randy is the child of biracial parents. When he was three, the black couple next
> door announced that they were expecting their first child. With the innocence of
> childhood, three-year-old Randy wondered aloud whether the baby would be black
> or white. To him, anything was possible. By the time Randy was four-and-a-half,
> he had noticed that his skin looked different from some of his playmates. What deci-
> sions will Randy make about who he is?*

Wouldn't life be boring if we all looked the same? Parents and teachers
have the opportunity to teach children to value differences, not condemn
them, and to enhance development with experiences and information that celebrate the diversity and worth of all humanity. Prejudice, whether it concerns
race, religion, or nationality, is learned. Even young children can learn to respect differences in race, age, gender, and physical ability. And because children of this age are learning so much about themselves, it is vital that they
learn about others in ways that are respectful and positive.

Adoption: "Should We Tell Our Children?"

ADOPTION IS A wonderful thing, providing many children with safe and
loving homes that they might not have had otherwise. Still, as with anything
that is perceived as "different," most adopted children (and most adoptive parents) will have questions: How much should children be told about their birth
parents? Will our adopted child truly feel like a part of our family? When
should we tell our child that he is adopted?

Adoption research does not give a clear answer to the question of when a child should be told about his or her adoption. Some research says that too much information before age six or seven only confuses a child. Other researchers believe that the older a child is when told, the more upsetting the news may be. Much of human behavior relates to our feelings of "belonging." As children put together the unique puzzle of who they are, questions about adoption ("Where did I come from?" "Why did my parents give me away?") are to be expected.

An adopted child who is racially different than his adoptive parents will begin to notice this difference by the age of four or so. Knowing that a child is becoming aware of race may help parents know when to tell her that she is adopted.

There are important cultural considerations as well. Children adopted from different cultures often enjoy participating in special cultural classes during their preschool years. For example, Tory, Sarah, and Anna, who were born in Korea, are all adopted into American families. Each summer the three girls attend a special Korean cultural camp where clothing, food, and Korean art and language skills are taught. Their parents want them to enjoy the richness of their birth culture. These girls knew of their adoption from their earliest years and proudly have worn Korean outfits to preschool whenever they wished to do so.

Another family brought treats to their daughter's preschool to help their daughter celebrate her "adoption day," much as birthdays are enjoyed. Her parents explained the idea of adoption to all of the children in her class. Her classmates benefited from learning about the different ways families come into being.

> Behaving as if there is anything disturbing, secretive, or mysterious about adoption invites distrust, fear, and anxiety.

Attitudes toward adoption vary widely. The families described above treated the issue of adoption as important. Adoption was another version of their definition of a "normal" family. This attitude encourages children to feel safe, trusting, and comfortable with adoption. Behaving as if there is anything disturbing, secretive, or mysterious about adoption invites distrust, fear, and anxiety.

All children need to feel that they truly belong. If your family includes both adopted and natural children, be aware that eventually everyone will have questions. As with so many other issues, your attitude is the key. If you treat all of your children with respect and teach them to treat each other (and themselves) that way, then the inevitable questions will not feel threatening. We encourage families with adopted children to focus on giving children many opportunities to experience belonging and to know that they have worth and significance.

All the World's a Stage

PARENTS CONSTANTLY HEAR the words "It's just a phase." There's a great deal of truth in the concept: children usually are in one stage or another. It is also true that no two children grow and develop exactly alike. Remember that children can't help being children and that experiments and mistakes are not the same as misbehavior. Understanding your child's development will enable you to deal effectively with behavior and will help you shape your child's world into a place where he can love, be loved, and learn about himself and others.

6

The Miracle of a Young Child's Mind

Preschoolers, Learning, and Brain Development

*R*obbie is five years old. His older sister goes to school with the other "big kids" and Robbie can hardly wait until he's old enough to join them on the big yellow bus. He has heard his mother telling her friends that in the fall he will be starting something called "kindergarten"; when he asks her about it, she tells him that kindergarten is a special school for younger kids, to help them get ready for first grade.

Robbie wants to start school. He loves his books, knows his letters and numbers, and can write his own name and that of his dog, Comet. Robbie is eager for the next important part of his life. Robbie's mom, though, has mixed emotions. She knows it will be hard to let her "baby" go; she and Robbie have always been especially close. And while Robbie enjoys learning and displays an avid curiosity about the world around him, his mom worries a bit. Robbie is shy and sometimes has trouble getting along with other children his age. He clings to his mom in public places. And sometimes he draws the few letters he knows backwards. Robbie's mom worries that he isn't really ready for school.

"What should I do?" she asks her next-door neighbor, whose three children all attend the nearby elementary school. "Should I enroll him in a prekindergarten program to get him ready? Maybe I should get some flash cards and teach him to read. Or maybe I should keep him back for a year. I don't want Robbie to fail—but

I don't want to disappoint or discourage him, either." Robbie's mom shakes her head in confusion and concern.

The How, When, and Why of Learning

THE LATE PRESCHOOL years are an unnerving time for many parents— and for their children. As preschoolers approach the age of five or six, the prospect of school and formal learning looms on the horizon. The world broadens beyond the home and family to include friends and teachers, all of whom will take on greater significance in a child's life as the years go by. It isn't always an easy transition for parents or for children.

Most parents realize that ours has become a highly competitive world. Most of us have read the newspaper stories detailing the decline in academic performance of American children. And because we love our children and want them to succeed at whatever they do, we wonder: What should we be teaching them, and when should we start? How much should children know about reading, writing, and arithmetic before they enter school? How well developed should their social skills be? And how do children learn, anyway? What happens in their growing brains that enables them to absorb and use knowledge and skills? Why are some children better at it than others?

There is a great deal that parents and caregivers can do to prepare children to learn and thrive, and most of it isn't nearly as complicated as we sometimes try to make it. Over the past few years, our understanding of how the human brain grows and develops has changed dramatically. We now understand that the first three years of a child's life are critically important in the formation of thinking and reasoning skills—and in the actual "wiring" of the brain itself. The brain continues to grow and learn throughout the preschool years, and the way parents and caregivers interact with children is crucial.

Not too many years ago, we believed that babies were born with brains that were more or less developed; all that remained was to fill the waiting brain with the necessary information. Brain scans and sophisticated imaging techniques now allow researchers to peer inside the living brain, to observe its structure and to discover how it uses energy, blood flow, and special substances called neurotransmitters to think, to perceive, and to learn. What those researchers have discovered is extraordinary.

The human brain begins life as a small cluster of cells in the fetus. By the fourth week of pregnancy, these cells have begun to sort themselves out according to the function they will one day perform and, to the wonder of researchers, have begun to "migrate" to the part of the brain they are destined to occupy. Nature provides the fetus with more cells than it will need; some do not survive the migration, but others join together in a network of connections called synapses.

This network continues to grow even after the baby is born. By the time a child is two years old, his brain has the same number of synapses as an adult's; by the age of three, he has more than one thousand trillion connections—twice as many as his parents and caregivers! The human brain is "under construction" for the first three years of life, and what a child learns and decides about himself and the world around him becomes part of the "wiring" of his brain. By about the age of ten, a child's brain begins to prune away the synapses that haven't been used enough. By adolescence, half have been discarded.

> The human brain is "under construction" for the first three years of life, and what a child learns and decides about himself and the world around him becomes part of the "wiring" of his brain.

While the brain is amazingly flexible and is able to adapt to change or injury, there are windows early in a child's life during which important learning (like language development) takes place. If those windows are missed, it becomes much more difficult for a child to acquire those abilities. Brain development is a "use it or lose it" proposition—and what is used (and kept) depends on the adults who shape a child's world.

Nature or Nurture?

PERHAPS YOU ARE wondering where your child gets his or her particular, unique combination of traits and qualities—and why, if you have more than one child, they can be so amazingly different! Popular magazines, books, and research journals are filled with new studies on human genes and their importance in how we live and who we become. Researchers now believe that genes may have an even stronger influence on temperament and personality than we previously thought; many researchers believe that genes determine such qualities as optimism, depression, aggression, or even whether or not a person is a thrill-seeker—which may come as no surprise to parents whose preschoolers thrive on gymnastics, hurl themselves at the ball in soccer, and climb trees faster than their harried parents can say abracadabra! (We will discuss temperament in chapter 7 and personality in chapter 10.) Parents may find themselves wondering just how much influence they have on their growing child. If genes are so powerful, does it really matter how we parent our children?

The answer is that it matters a great deal. While a child inherits certain traits and tendencies through her genes, the story of how those traits develop hasn't been written yet. Your child may have arrived on the planet with her own unique temperament, but how you and her other caregivers interact with her will shape the person she becomes. As educational psychologist Jane M. Healy puts it in her book, *Endangered Minds: Why Children Don't Think and What We Can Do About It* (Touchstone, 1990), "Brains shape behavior, and behavior shapes brains."

It is no longer a question of nature versus nurture: a child's genes and her environment engage in an intimate, complicated dance and both are part of who she will become. We adults, fragile and imperfect as we are, bear the responsibility for shaping our children's environment. We shape the very structure and wiring of their brains; we shape the people they become and the future they will have.

College for Kids?

OCCASIONALLY A NEWSPAPER will carry the story of a precocious preschooler who, at the age of four or five, has finished grade school and is ready for higher learning. Then there are children like Robbie, whose parents worry that their beloved children may not be ready to learn at all.

Should parents begin teaching academics at an early age? If brains are growing, shouldn't we be putting in as much information as we can? The truth is that we don't yet know whether it works to "teach" academics to young children and we don't know the real effect that lots of early stimulation has on their growing brains. Some researchers believe that it may even be harmful to force children to learn too quickly or to absorb concepts that their brains are not yet mature enough to handle. If the brain isn't ready to learn abstract concepts (math, for instance), it may patch together a pathway of connections that is less effective than the one that would have been used later on—and the less effective pathway becomes "wired" in place.

Forcing children to learn before they are ready may also have psychological effects. Children may believe they are inadequate when they can't live up to the expectations of their parents or caregivers, when the truth is that their brains just are not ready to absorb certain concepts.

There are few absolutes: each human brain is unique and special, and it is impossible to generalize about what is right or wrong for an individual child, but some scholars like Jane Healy believe that our fast-paced modern culture (and some of our "educational" television shows) may be affecting children's ability to pay attention, to listen, and to learn later on in life. Young children learn best in the context of *relationships,* and what they most need to learn in their preschool years isn't found on flash cards (or on television).

> Young children learn best in the context of *relationships,* and what they most need to learn in their preschool years isn't found on flash cards (or on television).

Many early childhood educators report that preschoolers these days seem to have more difficulty sitting still and paying attention to class lessons or stories. At the same time, many of these children appear to be sophisticated beyond their years because they have acquired a large (and sometimes disturbingly adult) vocabulary from television. Perhaps all learning isn't "good"; parents need to pay close attention to what their young children are exposed to and make sure that character and values are taught along with vocabulary and skills.

Encouraging Healthy Growth and Learning

REMEMBER ROBBIE? His mother wanted to know what she could do to help him succeed in school. Actually, parents can begin setting the stage for learning from the day a baby is born—not by using mobiles, flash cards, or "superbaby" programs but by responding to their child in ways that foster healthy brain growth, build trust and loving relationships, and encourage a love of learning.

Parents and caregivers can apply what we've learned from recent research in the first three years of life. While four- and five-year-old brains may not be actively forming synapses, the principles that work early in life continue to be important as children enter the preschool years.

How can adults help young children "grow" a healthy brain?

Demonstrate Affection, Interest, and Acceptance

A child never outgrows the need to feel a sense of belonging and significance—and the connections in the brain that are "fired" most frequently are the ones your child will keep for life. It is not enough just to love your child; that love must be demonstrated daily.

Research has shown that children who receive warm, consistent, loving care produce less of the stress hormone cortisol, and when they do become upset, they are able to "turn off" their stress reaction more rapidly. On the other hand, children who suffer abuse or neglect early in life are likely to feel more stress more often—and with less provocation.

Hugs, smiles, and laughter are wonderful parenting tools and will mean more to your child in the long run than the most marvelous toys and activities.

HOW TO DEVELOP A HEALTHY BRAIN

- Demonstrate affection, interest, and acceptance.
- Practice the art of conversation.
- Read, read, read!
- Encourage curiosity, safe exploration, and "hands-on" learning.
- Limit television time.
- Use discipline to teach, never to shame or humiliate.
- Recognize and accept your child's uniqueness.
- Select child care carefully—and stay involved.
- Take care of yourself.

Spending special time with a child, showing curiosity in his activities and thoughts, and learning to listen well will show your child on a daily basis that he is accepted and loved and will shape and strengthen the development of his brain.

Practice the Art of Conversation

Contrary to popular belief, children do not learn language from "educational" television shows; television is passive and requires no response from its audience. Children develop language by having the opportunity to speak and be spoken to by real humans.

Conversation with preschoolers truly is an art, requiring both humor and patience. Most young children pass through the phase when every other word is "why?" or "how come?" One weary mom, bombarded by questions from her curious three-year-old son, told him she was tired of answering questions for one day and suggested that he keep quiet for a while. The boy looked at his mom with puzzlement and informed her, "But Mom, that's how little boys learn!" And he is absolutely right.

Adults sometimes speak to young children in ways that do not allow for much response. Questions like "How was preschool today?" or "Did you win your tee-ball game?" can be answered with a single syllable or even with a grunt. One wonderful way to invite conversation with a preschooler (and to develop language skills in the process) is to ask "what" and "how" questions. "What did you like about school today?" or "How do you think you might solve that problem?" invite a more thoughtful response and give a child the opportunity to practice vital reasoning and language skills. Some researchers believe that simply inviting real conversation and problem solving can actually raise measurable IQ by several points!

Read, Read, Read!

There is no substitute for reading when it comes to growing healthy brains and preparing for formal learning, and it's never too soon (or too late) to start. Books open new worlds to children. And because the setting and characters must be created inside a child's mind, books also stimulate thinking and learning. Babies and toddlers almost always love colorful picture and "board" books; as children grow, they enjoy reading "chapter" books and no longer need pictures to maintain their interest. Many families find that reading time is a favorite shared activity well into the elementary school years and long after children learn to read well themselves.

When you read, make the story come alive: Change your voice to play different characters, and stop to talk about the story or the pictures. Preschoolers often memorize favorite books and want to "read" to you themselves, turning the pages at all the right spots. Adults usually tire of favorite books and stories long before children do, but be patient: preschoolers learn by repetition. Children who grow up with books often develop a love of reading and learning that lasts a lifetime—and sets the stage for success in school. Your local librarian or bookseller can recommend age-appropriate books and series; you may be surprised to learn that you enjoy reading time as much as your child does!

Incidentally, storytelling also is a wonderful way to stimulate learning. Sharing stories from your family's history or experiences you had when you were your child's age builds closeness and trust as well as encourages listening and learning skills. The memories you make in these shared moments will last a lifetime.

Encourage Curiosity, Safe Exploration, and "Hands-On" Learning

Preschoolers develop their sense of autonomy and initiative throughout these busy years, and they need lots of opportunities to practice. This is a time when young children are discovering themselves and are eager to explore and experiment with their own interests and abilities.

Parents and caregivers can provide lots of safe opportunities to run, climb, jump, and explore. Honor your child's interests: young children rarely appreciate (or learn from) being forced into activities they do not like or that actually frighten them. There are, however, many wonderful ways preschoolers can get acquainted with sports, the arts, and a world of exciting ideas. It is not always necessary to sign up children for organized activities, either; they can learn to paint, play baseball, sing, or plant a garden by working alongside welcoming adults.

Preschoolers usually want to *do* rather than just watch, so be prepared for a few messes along the way. Remember, too, that some children demonstrate curiosity and talents at this age that are very real and that will be important for the rest of their lives.

Christopher was only four when he asked his mother for a violin. His mom's first impulse was to laugh, but then she remembered that her grandfather had played beautifully. When Christopher asked again a few days later, his mother honored his interest, rented a miniature violin, and found a teacher willing to work with a very young pupil.

Christopher's love for the violin was genuine—and was backed up by considerable talent. He outgrew his first teacher in just a few years, and by the time he entered first grade he was setting his own alarm clock so that he could get up early to practice before school. Christopher also enjoyed soccer and in-line skating, but music would remain his first love. While he never became a concert artist, Christopher played the violin for the rest of his life and never lost his enjoyment of music. His mother never regretted renting that first tiny instrument.

Of course, not all preschool interests reveal lifelong talents. Still, providing reasonable opportunities for children to experiment with a variety of activities will give them ways to build a sense of self-esteem and self-confidence and to develop into healthy, active people.

Limit Television Time

Walk into many living rooms today and you will notice that one item has the place of honor. Centrally located in the entertainment center, supported by satellite, cable, and sophisticated remote controls, the television has become the center of family life in many, many homes. Our "family time" is illuminated by the flickering blue light of the screen—and the bigger the screen, the better!

Unfortunately, there is much we do not fully understand about the way television affects growing brains, and what we do know is not encouraging. Most young children spend a phenomenal amount of time in front of the TV, watching favorite shows and videos—or whatever the adults are watching. How does this affect their brains, their capacity to learn, and their ability to pay attention?

Researchers and educational psychologists like Jane Healy believe that excessive television may actually be changing the way the brain functions.

CHILDREN AND TELEVISION: WHAT SHOULD YOU DO

- Watch television and videos with your children. Be aware that children may not be able to differentiate between reality and fantasy; be sure you provide some guidelines, especially where violence and advertising are concerned.
- Ask "what" and "how" questions to invite critical thinking, such as "What would you do if you were in that situation?".
- Pay attention to what children are learning from what they watch. If, for instance, you hear your child chanting "Jer-ry, Jer-ry, Jer-ry," it may be wise to turn the television off more often.
- Decide what *you* will do. Be sure that videos and shows your children watch match your values and beliefs. If you aren't sure, check them out. Be prepared to talk with children about why some shows aren't okay.
- Encourage reading and active play. Yes, this takes time that busy grown-ups may not feel they have, but the television is a dangerous baby-sitter. Books, games, and shared activities are undoubtedly healthier for your young child.

Watching TV and videos is essentially a passive activity; there is little or no critical thinking going on in the mind of a young child propped in front of the tube. Even so-called educational shows such as *Sesame Street* may not be helpful; the flashy, frantic format does not encourage sustained attention, and some studies indicate that children begin school expecting entertainment and special effects like those they've seen on TV and are bored by classroom teaching. Many teachers report that attention spans, comprehension, and language skills are declining rapidly.

In addition, children who watch lots of TV tend to have more weight problems and show less creativity in their play. There is growing evidence that violent computer and video games, television shows, and movies warp a child's ability to understand the real consequences of violent acts; children do imitate what they see on television, especially if there appears to be no negative result.

Is it necessary to take your big-screen TV to the dump? Of course not. But it is undoubtedly wise to exercise judgment where preschoolers and television are concerned.

The following are some suggestions.

Use Discipline to Teach, Not to Shame or Humiliate

Remember, the synapses your child will keep are the ones that are used most often, and shame, punishment, and humiliation can shape the way a young child's brain is wired. The best sort of discipline is teaching. Children respond well to loving, effective discipline and will be healthier for having it. Isn't it good to know that your Positive Discipline skills are also encouraging healthy brain development?

Recognize and Accept Your Child's Uniqueness

Young children learn about themselves and the world around them by watching and listening; what they decide about themselves (and about us) depends in large part on the messages they receive from parents and caregivers. Learning to accept your child for exactly who she is not only builds her sense of self-esteem and worth, it supports her healthy brain and encourages her to value her own special qualities and abilities and to have the courage to try new things—the best insurance policy there is against the challenges and pressures she will face as she grows into adolescence and adulthood.

Select Child Care Carefully—and Stay Involved

Child care is critically important. Many, many children spend all or part of each day in the care of someone other than their parents. It's crucial that child care providers and teachers also know how young brains grow and that they do their best to foster health and learning. It is a sad and alarming statement that the same study that reported the results of the new brain research also reported that half of American children are in child care settings that jeopardize healthy brain development (Shore, Rima. *Rethinking the Brain: New Insights into Early Development.* New York: Families and Work Institute, 1997). We will explore ways to select child care in chapters 22 and 23. For now, realize that choosing your child's care provider is as important as choosing the way you will parent your child.

Take Care of Yourself

You may wonder what taking care of yourself has to do with your child's brain. But think for just a moment: nurturing and shaping a growing, learning preschooler is hard work—and a full-time job. Parents and caregivers need every ounce of energy and wisdom they possess, and all too often the well runs dry just when the crisis occurs.

You will do your best work as a parent when you are rested and reasonably content. Yes, weariness and stress seem to be an everyday part of life with young children, particularly if you also have a partner or job to deal with. Still, caring for your own needs must be a priority.

> Keeping yourself healthy isn't selfish: it's wisdom.

Take time on a regular basis (no, once a year isn't enough!) to do things you enjoy. Get some exercise, eat healthy foods, and do your best to get enough sleep. Spend time with your partner; have a cup of coffee with a friend. Sing in a choir, take a class, read a book—anything you do to refill the well will benefit your children. They will learn respect for you (and for themselves) when they see you treating yourself with respect. And they will find a calm, rested, happy adult much easier to respond to than an exhausted, grumpy, resent-ful one. Keeping yourself healthy isn't selfish: it's wisdom.

Off to School: "Is My Child Really Ready?"

Kate had sworn she wouldn't cry. Other moms did that; she was going to celebrate with Sarah on the first day of kindergarten, and then go get the shopping done without any interruptions. Somehow, though, the morning didn't work out the way she'd planned.

Oh, Sarah was fine. A bit nervous, maybe, but excited and happy. She had dressed herself with care in her new outfit, combed her hair neatly, and packed a few articles into the brand-new backpack that marked her new status as a "school-age kid." Kate and Sarah had visited the classroom the week before school began, explored the playground, and met the teacher, an energetic, friendly young woman who remembered everyone's name.

Everything was fine—until Kate watched Sarah, looking suddenly very small, filing into the classroom with the other children. As she turned to walk back to her car, she discovered that some sort of fog seemed to have descended on the neighborhood—she couldn't see a thing. She realized with a shock that she was crying. A dad walking nearby grinned at her. "Gets to you, doesn't it?" he said. "It certainly does," Kate replied, shaking her head. "It certainly does."

A child's first day of "real" school is a landmark event. The world will never again consist just of a small circle of family and friends; it has suddenly expanded to include other adults and children who may spend more time each day with our youngsters than we do ourselves. Many parents wonder how they will know if their children are ready—intellectually and emotionally—for the wider world of school.

It is important to recognize that all children (and all schools) are different. By the time a child is ready for school, parents have had years to get into that child's world and understand the way he thinks, feels, and sees the world. Most school systems group children by chronological age, but age is not a true indicator of a child's development. Many children are eager for school to begin and head off on their new academic career with hardly a backwards glance. Others hover at the fringes or seem to struggle with even the simplest tasks. While assessing learning disabilities or psychological problems is beyond the scope of this book, there are things parents can consider that will help them feel comfortable sending their children to school.

Know Your Child

NO ONE KNOWS a child as well as an attentive, loving parent, especially one who has made the effort to understand development and acquire effective parenting skills. Most school districts offer "readiness" interviews to help parents and teachers decide if a child is ready to begin kindergarten or would benefit from waiting a year.

Remember that school success involves more than just academic skills; children also must be able to tolerate time away from parents, respond to a teacher, and make friends with other children. There is no disgrace in waiting to begin school; in fact, children do better with academic learning when they are emotionally and socially ready to be away from home. It is less upsetting for everyone to delay the start of school rather than to be held back later on.

Considering a few simple questions may help you assess your child's readiness:

- Does your child enjoy learning? Is he curious about the world around him?

- Does your child tolerate separation from you reasonably well?

- Is he eager to make friends and open to peer relationships?

- Is he able to pay attention to a task for an age-appropriate length of time?

- Does he express interest in school, or does he seem more fearful than you would expect?

Taking time to visit the school and meet the teacher usually resolves most of a child's anxieties. It is also helpful to talk about feelings (remember your active listening skills) and to share with your child that most people get "butterflies in their tummies" when they do something new. The more parents can stay tuned in, both to their child and to the teacher, the happier the school experience will be. You and your child may feel more comfortable if you have time to volunteer in the classroom and attend school events and parent-teacher conferences. School will be part of your lives for years to come; getting off to a good start is worth the effort it takes.

Learning Takes a Lifetime

IT HAS BEEN said that "learners inherit the earth" and "the truly educated never graduate." And there is always something new and wonderful to learn, for us and for our children. The outside world isn't always kind or welcoming; as children move away from our sides they will experience hurts and difficulties, and we will not always be there to smooth the way. There are many important lessons that we teach our children in their preschool years, however. We can teach them that we are always on their side, that we will always listen, and that we believe in their ability to learn, to grow, and to thrive. Regardless of what happens as they grow up, our children can trust that we will always have faith in them and will always welcome them home.

7

Temperament

What Makes Your Child Unique?

W E ' V E A L L H E A R D it; we've probably done it ourselves, privately if not publicly. We compare our children to those around them: the others girls and boys at the preschool, the neighbors' kids, our nieces and nephews. And comparisons usually lead to judgments: Bobby is "such a good boy"; Miranda is "a little monster." We've already seen that preschoolers are passing through some interesting developmental stages; we know that experimenting with autonomy and initiative can lead them to behave in ways that adults perceive as "bad." Is there such a creature as a "perfect child"? Would we really want one?

The Myth of the Perfect Child

A " P E R F E C T C H I L D " is often pictured as the one who quietly obeys his parents, doesn't fight with his brothers or sisters, does his chores without complaining, saves his money, does homework without being reminded—and who gets good grades, is athletic, and is very popular. Does this mean that a child who doesn't fit this description is "imperfect"?

Frankly, we worry about the child who fits this fantasy description. This is usually the child who does not feel secure enough to test power boundaries and find out who she is apart from her parents and teachers, who is afraid to make mistakes or risk disapproval. We say usually, because a few children do fit the fantasy description yet still feel secure and aren't afraid to make mistakes. They are called "easy" children.

Drs. Stella Chess and Alexander Thomas investigated the miracle of personality in their longitudinal study of the nine major temperaments found in children. These temperaments—the qualities and characteristics that contribute to individual personalities—serve to describe three types of children: the "easy" child, the "difficult" child, and the "slow to warm up" child. All are good; some are just more challenging than others. We will discuss these nine temperaments, but for more information we highly recommend *Know Your Child* (Basic Books, 1987) by Stella Chess and Alexander Thomas.

The Berkeley Studies

SCIENTIFIC INVESTIGATION OF temperament theory began in the late sixties and seventies with the Berkeley Studies, a longitudinal study of two basic temperaments, active and passive. This study revealed that these two temperaments were lifelong characteristics; in other words, passive infants grew up to be passive adults, while active infants grew up to be active adults. Actually, activity levels can be measured in the womb. Chess and Thomas expanded the temperament theory significantly, even though their nine temperaments all fit under the general headings of active and passive. A major benefit of being aware of temperament differences is that parents and teachers can better understand their children and students, learn to respond to them in ways that encourage development and growth, and learn to appreciate and accept them as they are. With understanding and acceptance, parents and teachers are equipped to help children reach their full potential rather than trying to mold them into perfect fantasy children.

The Nine Temperaments

THE NINE TEMPERAMENTS ARE: activity level, rhythmicity, initial response (approach or withdrawal), adaptability, sensory threshold, quality of mood, intensity of reaction, distractibility, and persistence and attention span. All children possess varying degrees of each characteristic. The following sections will describe what they look like in real life (you may want to think about children you know as we examine these aspects of temperament).

Activity Level

Activity level refers to a child's level of motor activity and the proportion of active and inactive periods. A high-activity preschooler might delight in energetic running games, while a low-activity child chooses something quiet, like drawing or looking at a book.

> With understanding and acceptance, parents and teachers are equipped to help children reach their full potential rather than trying to mold them into perfect fantasy children.

Q. *My three-year-old son doesn't know what the words "Wait, please!" mean. He never slows down. I am worn out. I sometimes wish I could push a button on his forehead and run him on slow speed instead of fast forward. My sister's child seems so much calmer. Am I doing something wrong?*

A. Have you ever noticed how often parents and teachers of preschoolers use the phrase "worn out"? Most preschoolers have a high level of physical energy—after all, there's so much they have to do and learn each day—but some youngsters seem to have far more than their share. If you have one of these highly active little ones in your home, rest assured: there is nothing wrong with you or your child. We are all born with different temperaments. An active child is not "bad"; he does not jet around out of a desire to wear you out. He simply is busy being who he is. The key to living peacefully with your active preschooler is to find a way to meet his needs without abandoning your own. Here are some suggestions:

- Plan ahead with your child's needs in mind. Provide him with space, challenging activities, and opportunities to run off excess energy. Take him to parks, enroll him in swim classes or gymnastics, or provide plenty of time for energetic play. It may also be wise to skip, for now, the ballet class, the music recitals and plays, and the four-course restaurant meals. Set yourselves up for success. Remember to match your expectations to your child's abilities.

- Schedule time for yourself. Get a sitter, enroll your child in preschool or other classes to give yourself a break, or ask a friend or partner to spend time with your child on a regular basis. This is not selfishness; it's wise parenting. You need lots of energy to deal calmly and effectively with an active preschooler, and you need time to rest and refresh yourself.

- Learn to love your child for who he is. He did not choose his temperament. Rejoice in his strengths. There is much he can accomplish later in life with his abundant energy!

Monica has learned to plan her days with her twins' different temperaments and activity levels in mind. One Sunday afternoon at the community swimming pool, three-year-old Ned and Sally keep Mom company while their older sisters take swimming lessons. As the hour progresses, Ned plays happily with the bag of plastic animals that his mother has brought along. He takes them over to the drinking fountain and gets them wet, then pretends they are eating a koosh ball sea urchin. The entire hour passes with Ned happily absorbed in his play.

Twin sister Sally is a different story. She begins coloring in the book her mother has brought along, but within ten minutes has marked up all of the pages and wants her mom to read to her. Halfway through the story, Sally decides she is thirsty, so Monica takes her to the drinking fountain. Then Sally begins to climb on the bleachers. Before half an hour has passed, Sally has colored, heard a story, gotten a drink, and explored the bleachers. Monica knows her daughter well and is already expecting to take a walk to the swings—and she knows they'd better be ready to leave the minute lessons are over.

Ned has a low activity level, while Sally's is high. Monica used to feel frustrated by the differences between her twins, especially since she thought she treated them the same way. Information about temperaments helped her understand them better. She decided she might as well relax and simply enjoy (and plan for) the uniqueness of each child.

Rhythmicity

Rhythmicity refers to the predictability (or unpredictability) of biological functions, such as hunger, sleeping, and bowel movements.

The Silvertons could set their clocks by the routine of their younger son, three-year-old Martin. He woke up at 6:30 every morning; he wanted the same lunch every day, always chose to play with the same toys, and went to bed every night at the same time.

Martin provided a needed rest for the Silvertons after their experience with his five-year-old brother Stanley, who was as unpredictable as his younger brother was predictable. They wondered what they did "wrong" with Stanley and what they did "right" with Martin, until they learned about temperament and realized they couldn't take credit or blame for the basic personality of their children. However, they could learn to be more patient with Stanley and avoid showing preference for Martin's style. They got both boys involved in planning morning and bedtime routines (even though Martin didn't need one). Stanley found it helpful to follow routines that he had helped create. They also took time to involve both boys in planning for mealtime menus and teaching them to help out with meal preparation and household tasks.

The Silvertons found that Stanley was less cantankerous about not "liking" his meals when he had helped plan the menus. He was more accepting of the meals that others preferred when he was in-volved in the planning process and learned to give and take— and when he knew that his favorite foods would be on the menu tomorrow.

Understanding rhythmicity can help parents and caregivers plan a child's schedule in ways that ease conflict and stress for everyone.

Fred knows that his four-year-old daughter still gets weary and welcomes a nap precisely at 1:30 each afternoon. He makes sure that her weekday caregiver under-stands this, and he leaves space in his weekend schedule to help her get her rest.

Fred has discovered that respecting his daughter's temperament and need for regular naps helps prevent those endless afternoons with a cranky, tired child.

Initial Response

This temperament describes the way a child reacts to a new situation or stim-ulus, such as a new food, toy, person, or place. Approach responses are often

The following nine temperaments shape a child's personality and approach to life:

1. Activity level

2. Rhythmicity

3. Initial response (approach or withdrawal)

4. Adaptability

5. Sensory threshold

6. Quality of mood

7. Intensity of reactions

8. Distractibility

9. Persistence and attention span

displayed by mood expression (smiling, speech, facial expression) or motor activity (swallowing a new food, reach-ing for a new toy, joining a new playmate). Withdrawal responses look more negative and are expressed by mood (crying, speech, facial expression) or motor activity (running away, spitting food out, or throwing a new toy). Learning to parent your unique child means recognizing these cues and responding in encouraging, nurturing ways.

Older preschoolers reveal this temperament in the way they cope with new experiences, either running to join a new group or hovering on the sidelines a while to check things out.

Amanda came to her new child care center when she was three years old. Whenever the children gathered for a group activity, Amanda would hang back and refuse to join in. Because her teacher was sensitive to her temperament, she did not insist that Amanda join the group, although she made sure that Amanda knew she was welcome. For two weeks, Amanda held back, watching what happened and gradually moving closer. By the third week, she was happily playing with the others. Amanda's initial response was withdrawal, and her teacher wisely honored this aspect of her temperament.

Again, temperament is inborn, and research indicates that these deeply in-grained personality traits are not easily changed by anxious parents.

Bonny worried about her five-year-old son, Jason: she feared that his shyness would keep him from ever having happy relationships or enjoying the activities that she and his father had always loved. Bonny's love for her son gave her the clues she needed; however, she found that when she pushed him forward, urged him to speak to or play with someone new, or signed him up for a sport or activity, he only re-treated further, hiding behind her leg and burying his head against her side.

When Bonny realized that Jason might always be wary of new situations, she decided to accept her son for who he was—and to find ways to help him feel more comfortable and confident. She learned to provide opportunities for Jason to watch other children playing tee-ball before signing him up. She learned not to push him to speak to new acquaintances but to carry on a friendly conversation herself, keep-ing a gentle hand on her son's shoulder as reassurance.

Bonny made time to stay a while with Jason in new situations, accepting that he felt comfortable more quickly when she was with him. Most important, she offered him acceptance and encouragement without requiring that he "get over" his shyness.

Jason may always be slow to warm up to new people and circumstances, but his mother's patience and loving encouragement will help him to believe in—and accept—himself.

Adaptability

Adaptability describes how a child reacts to a new situation over time—her ability to adjust and change. Some children initially spit out a new food but accept it after a few trial tastes. Others accept a new food, a new article of clothing, or a new preschool far more slowly, if at all.

When three-and-a-half-year-old Maria's parents decided to file for divorce, her dad found an apartment a few blocks away. Any child finds divorce painful, but Maria's "slow to adapt" temperament increased the stress associated with such a major change. Although both parents agreed to share parenting duties, with Maria spending several nights each week with her dad, they decided to take a gradual ap-proach at first.

When Maria's dad moved out, he invited her to help him carry things to his new apartment. Over the next few weeks he took Maria to his apartment several times, increasing the length of these visits. After three weeks, Maria was spending full days with Dad and eating dinner at his new apartment but returning to her familiar bedroom at the family home to sleep.

Gradually, Maria and her dad set up a bedroom for her at his new home, picked out some furniture, and selected clothes she could move to her new room. Despite her own pain and disappointment, Maria's mom refrained from criticizing Dad and did her best to ease the transition for her daughter. After all, she figured, as long as they shared Maria they would need to find some way to work together, and she was relieved that Maria's father still felt deeply committed to his little girl.

A month had passed before Maria and her parents felt comfortable with overnight visits at Dad's apartment. It would not have been appropriate for Dad to ask Maria if she wanted to spend the night at his house. This would have placed too great an emotional burden on a young child who was already experiencing a sense of upheaval and divided loyalties.

Maria's parents put her needs first and gave her time to adjust to this change. (For more information on divorce and single parenting, see *Positive Discipline for Single Parents*, Prima Publishing, 1994.)

Many children would benefit from this gentle, gradual approach. If your little one struggles with rapid transition and change, then recognizing and allowing for her temperament may save you both discomfort and unhappiness.

Sensory Threshold

Some children wake up from a nap every time a door opens, no matter how softly, while others can sleep through a hurricane. Some children complain about tight clothes or rough sheets, while others scrape their knees or thump their heads without even slowing down. The level of sensitivity to sensory input varies from one child to the next and affects how they behave and view the world.

Alice was celebrating her fourth birthday. She opened a present containing a beautiful flowered dress and smiled in delight. The smile changed to dismay, how-

ever, when she noticed that the puffy skirt was held in place by a layer of stiff nylon net. "Do I have to wear this part?" she asked in alarm. "It'll scratch my legs."

Such minor details didn't faze Andy. He loved to walk barefoot and took off his shoes at every opportunity. His parents would point with concern to the gravel playground or exclaim about the hot pavement, but textures and temperatures didn't bother Andy. His little feet padded along undaunted, while their owner enjoyed the feeling of each toe wiggling freely.

Quality of Mood

Have you ever noticed how some children (and adults) react to life with pleasure and acceptance while others can find fault with everything and everybody? One child might favor her family with sunny smiles, while another feels compelled to pout or scowl, just "because."

Parents of less sunny children can take heart. If your child wears a "frowny face" more often than you would like, remember that those scowls are not in response to you or your parenting skills. Be sensitive to his mood, but take time to stroke the shoulders and back of your sober little fellow, and share your own sunshine with him.

It can be discouraging for parents and teachers to deal with a child who always looks on the dark side, but there are ways to both accept this temperament and help a child to face life more positively.

Stephen Ellis came home from his parenting class with a new idea: he would ask his four-year-old son, Carl, about the happiest and saddest moments of his day. Stephen looked forward to making this a part of their bedtime routine and having a chance to get into his son's world. When Stephen asked Carl about his saddest moments, he often had a long list of troubles to relate, but when asked about his happy moments, he couldn't think of any. Stephen began to feel real dismay that Carl was so miserable.

In fact, Carl simply has a negative mood temperament and sees the world from that perspective. When Stephen learned about temperament, he was able to stop getting hooked by Carl's negative mood. He would listen to his son's list of troubles, then share some of his own sad moments. Then he would share his happy moments. As Stephen continued to show Carl that it was okay to see both negatives and positives, Carl started sharing happy times too. He still sees lots of negatives, but he is learning to see the positive things as well.

Intensity of Reaction

Children often respond to events around them in different ways. Some smile quietly or merely take a look, then go back to what they were doing; others react with action and emotion. For instance, the tantrums of your high-intensity child can be heard throughout the apartment complex, while your neighbor's son only retreats into quiet when faced with disappointment.

Veronica Peters was getting ready for art time with her class. While the children played quietly, Mrs. Peters set out paper, markers, pastels, and scissors. She was carrying the box containing the trays of water colors and brushes when she tripped over a forgotten block, and the box of painting supplies crashed to the floor.

The group of children reacted in a number of interesting ways. Some looked up, startled, then returned to playing. Little Steffi and Adam began to cry loudly. Mark got up to poke through the debris with his toe, while Angie ran around the room giggling.

The children responded differently to the same situation because their intensity levels were different. Understanding that children react to stimuli with varying degrees of intensity can help both parents and teachers deal with behavior more calmly.

Distractibility

"If my daughter decides she wants to go out and play but it's lunchtime," one mom says, "she'll fuss and fuss and won't get involved in anything else." "My little guy knows when he's hungry, and he follows me around the kitchen until I have his lunch ready," says another. They may not realize it, but these parents are actually talking about their children's distractibility, the way in which an outside stimulus interferes with a child's present behavior and his willingness (or unwillingness) to be diverted.

It is nap time at the child care center when Melissa makes the unfortunate discovery that her special teddy bear has been left at home. The teacher holds her, talks with her, and offers one of the center's toys as a substitute, but nothing helps. Melissa spends the entire nap time sitting on her mat whimpering for her teddy.

Melissa has low distractibility, which will be a real asset someday when she's hired to be an air traffic controller or the president's bodyguard. But for now, Melissa is not a child who should be brought to child care without her precious teddy. In fact, it might be wise to have two teddys, one for home and another for school, so this sort of crisis can be avoided.

Aaron, on the other hand, is perfectly happy to curl up with whatever toy is available. Today he has forgotten his stuffed dinosaur, but when his teacher offers a blue rabbit, Aaron smiles and contentedly drifts off to sleep.

Later on in life, Aaron may prove to be an easygoing person who can do many things at once, an invaluable asset to a busy corporate office. It is encouraging to adults and children when parents and teachers remember to focus on the assets of a child's temperament.

Persistence and Attention Span

Persistence refers to a child's willingness to pursue an activity in the face of obstacles or difficulties; attention span describes the length of time he will pursue an activity without interruption. The two characteristics are usually related. The toddler who is content to tear up an old magazine for half an

> It is encouraging to adults and children when parents and teachers remember to focus on the assets of a child's temperament.

hour at a time has a fairly long attention span, while another who plays with ten different toys in ten minutes has a short one. A child who is threading beads on a string might give up if a bead doesn't go on immediately; another will try again and again until she succeeds. These children are demonstrating different levels of persistence. Again, no temperament is necessarily better than another; they're simply different and present different challenges in parenting and teaching.

Mitchell has been tracing a map from his children's atlas every morning for a week. He has carefully continued his work, adding details and humming contentedly to himself as he draws. Mitchell's best friend, Erica, comes over to play, and she sits down to help him—for a while. Within half an hour, Erica has three hastily completed drawings and turns her attention to Mitchell's new Play-Doh. Someday Erica may be discovering new strains of bacteria and new medications with her ability to detect and investigate new things, while most of us would be very comfortable with the future Dr. Mitchell performing our six-hour open-heart surgery!

It is important to understand that a child with a short attention span and little persistence does not necessarily have the condition known as attention deficit disorder (ADD), with or without hyperactivity. ADD is a very real neurological condition that should be diagnosed by a pediatric neurologist or a pediatrician trained to recognize its special symptoms. It is not usually wise to act on a "diagnosis" offered by another parent or a caregiver—although such suggestions may be worth investigating with your child's physician.

Most physicians are reluctant to diagnose ADD until a child is at least five or six years old; before that time, impulsive behavior, high activity levels, and short attention spans may be due to temperament or developmental differences. If you're concerned, check with your child's pediatrician or a child therapist trained to evaluate young children. Medication is an option, but one to exercise very carefully (more about special needs in chapter 24). In either case, understanding development and temperament, a willingness to be firm and kind, and using Positive Discipline skills will help both you and your child succeed at home and at school.

Temperament: Challenge or Opportunity?

IF ASKED, MOST parents and teachers would probably prefer children with a long attention span and high persistence; they're much easier to teach and entertain. However, few children fit this ideal description. In fact, most families include children of different temperaments, while teachers can find themselves working with quite an assortment.

Teachers may need to provide information about temperament to parents, too. An understanding of temperament can help both parents and teachers encourage acceptance instead of unrealistic expectations. Each child—and every temperament—possesses both assets and liabilities, strengths and weaknesses. None are "good" or "bad," and as we've already seen, comparison and judgments can lead to discouragement, distance, and disappointment. Effective parenting and teaching will help each unique child build on her strengths and manage her weaknesses, providing opportunities to learn skills that will last a lifetime.

All parents must eventually recognize and accept the ways in which their children's dreams and temperaments are different from their own.

BECOME YOUR CHILD'S ADVOCATE

Parents who understand their child's temperament can be knowledgeable consultants to teachers and other people who may be working with that child. For example, if your child is slow to adapt, ask for a conference and explain to the teacher that your child adapts slowly but responds to patience and kind firmness. If your child has a short attention span, find a teacher who appreciates creativity and provides a variety of experiences during the day. Avoid authoritarian teachers who require children to spend a great deal of time sitting still and who punish children who do not conform to expectations. Be sure that it is your child's temperament and not your own that motivates you. You should always be your child's best advocate and supporter.

Evan's parents are very artistic people who design beautiful wall hangings and nontraditional clothing. They became concerned that Evan wasn't being given ample opportunity for artistic expression at his preschool, as Evan never came home with paint on his clothes or clay under his fingernails.

In fact, Evan had many opportunities to explore the world of art. He just wasn't interested. Evan was a precise, orderly youngster who preferred to work quietly putting together puzzles or exploring counting materials. He didn't like the slippery feel of paint on his hands or the gooey mess of clay. Evan's parents were viewing their son in light of their own temperaments, not his. When Evan's teacher explained the facets of his temperament, his parents were very grateful. Now they could begin to accept Evan for the unique person he is and encourage him to follow his own dreams, not theirs.

Goodness of Fit

CHESS AND THOMAS emphasize the importance of "goodness of fit," the depth of understanding parents and teachers have of a child's temperament and their willingness to work with that child to encourage healthy development. Children experience enough stress in life as they struggle for competency and belonging. It does not help to compound that stress by expecting a child to be someone he is not.

Understanding a child's temperament doesn't mean shrugging your shoulders and saying, "Oh well, that's just the way this child is." It is an invitation to help a child develop acceptable behavior and skills. For instance, a child with a short attention span will still need to learn to accept some structure and stay focused. Offering limited choices is one way to be respectful of the child's needs and of the "needs of the situation" (behavior appropriate for the present environment).

Working out a match between parents and children that meets the needs of both is critical to goodness of fit. If your child has difficulty adapting to new situations while you are the life of a party, you have a poor fit. The key is to find the balance. Your child may not make friends quickly, but she can learn social skills that will help her find one or two good friends. She will find it very discouraging if you "push" her to be like you but will find it encouraging if you gently teach her that it is okay to take her time while being open to the friendly overtures of other children. Finding the balance between your needs and those of your child can take some time and practice, but learning to accept and work with the individual, special temperament of your child will benefit you both as the years go by.

Needs of the Situation

AN AWARENESS OF temperament in children helps us understand why different methods are more effective with some children than with others. There are some universal principles, such as everyone's right to dignity and respect, but this doesn't necessarily mean that we can just demand our children treat us with dignity and respect—or that children will automatically know how to do so.

In school, for example, the needs of the situation are that learning must take place and children should respect themselves and one another. Giving a child a limited choice of more than one way to learn or do an activity would fit the needs of the situation, take the child's temperament into account, and still be respectful to everyone concerned. A child with a long attention span may need encouragement to expand her horizons to include a variety of interests and activities.

Each individual must learn to take personal responsibility for his own dignity and respect. You may not be able to demand that your child treat you with respect, but you can treat yourself with respect. If your child is behaving disrespectfully, you can choose to leave the room or find another Positive Discipline method to deal with the behavior. It is neither effective nor respectful to withdraw love or acceptance from a child because her behavior needs work.

> An awareness of temperament in children helps us understand why different methods are more effective with some children than with others.

Marty did nothing in half measures. His mother described her four-year-old son as "passionate," an admirable trait—in the right circumstances. One afternoon, Marty's mom told him it was time to put away his crayons. Marty did not want to stop coloring. His face scrunched up in anger, his jaw jutted out, and in a burst of anger he launched his crayons at his mother. Marty's frustration may be understandable, but his feelings and his intense temperament do not give him permission to mistreat others. Marty's mother took a calming breath to control her own anger, then proceeded to leave the room without any comment.

Marty continued to complain. His mother remained calm, going to her own room. A few minutes passed, and Marty began to realize that tantrums feel pretty silly when there is no one around to witness them. Marty wandered off in search of his mother.

When he found Mom in her room, Marty climbed onto the bed with her and snuggled wordlessly against her side. Now Mom has a choice: she can lecture Marty about his unacceptable behavior and march him into the next room to pick up the crayons, or she can respond to his desire to be close. Marty's mom chose to give her small son a hug.

Mom told Marty that it was okay to feel angry sometimes, but it was not okay to throw things at her or anyone else. He snuggled closer to her and nodded that he knew he shouldn't throw things. After a few quiet moments, Mom asked whether he wanted help picking up the crayons that he had thrown or if he could do it on his own. Marty bounced off the bed and with one more hug dashed off to gather his crayons.

Did Marty "get away with" misbehavior by throwing crayons at his mother? Actually, Marty's mother chose to deal with the situation in a manner that allowed for both her own temperament and her son's. Had she yelled, demanded immediate compliance, or punished Marty, the situation would likely have grown passionate on both sides. Instead, she respected her needs by removing herself as a target, modeling self-control, and taking her own cool-off moment. She let Marty know that he was still loved by returning his hug, then invited him to correct the situation by picking up the crayons when he had calmed down.

> Temperament and strong emotions are not an excuse for inappropriate actions.

Both Marty and his mom learned powerful lessons about how to deal with their own intense temperaments. Temperament and strong emotions are not an excuse for inappropriate actions. Taking into account a person's natural tendencies simply provides perspective, guides our responses, and reminds us that children always need our love, especially as they struggle to improve their life skills.

Positive Discipline Skills for Parents and Teachers

MANY OF THE skills we suggest are appropriate for children of all temperaments, because they invite children to learn cooperation, responsibility, and life skills. However, an understanding of temperament helps us understand why different methods may be more effective, depending on the temperament and needs of an individual child.

For example, time out, when properly used, can be an encouraging way to help children who need time to calm down and cool off (see chapter 13). Family meetings and class meetings are essential to help all children learn problem-solving skills and cooperation (see chapter 15). Positive Discipline skills help children who are misbehaving redirect their energy in useful ways. Asking "what" and "how" questions encourages children to focus on personal accountability as they explore what happened, what caused it to happen, how they feel about it, and what they might choose to do differently next time. Parents and teachers can help children develop into the best people they can be when they understand and respect differences, individuality, and the creativity of each child.

Individuality and Creativity

PARENTS AND TEACHERS may not be aware of how they squelch individuality and creativity when they buy in (often subconsciously) to the myth of the perfect child. It is tempting for adults to prefer the "easy" child or to want children to conform to the norms of society. Our egos often get involved; we worry about what others think and fear that our competency may be questioned if our children aren't "good" in the eyes of others.

One of the primary motivators for Chess and Thomas' study of temperament was the desire to stop society's tendency to blame mothers for the characteristics of their children. Chess and Thomas state, "A child's temperament can actively influence the attitudes and behavior of her parents, other family members, playmates, and teachers, and in turn help to shape their effect on her behavioral development." In this way, the relationship between child and parents is a two-way street, each continuously influencing the other.

Harry Chapin's song "Flowers Are Red" beautifully (and sadly) illustrates how we can kill the individuality that makes our children special in our desire to make them "fit in." The music to this song is delightful, and we hope you will make the effort to find *Living Room Suite* by Harry Chapin. Here are the words (reprinted with the kind permission of Elektra/Asylum Records):

The little boy went first day in school; he got some crayons and he started to draw. He put colors all over the paper, for colors was what he saw.

And the teacher said, "What're you doing, young man?" "I'm painting flowers," he said.

She said, "It's not the time for art, young man; and anyway, flowers are green and red.

"There's a time for everything, young man, and the way it should be done. You've got to show concern for everyone else for you're not the only one."

And she said, "Flowers are red, young man, and green leaves are green. There's no need to see flowers any other way than the way they always have been seen."

But the little boy said, "There are so many colors in the rainbow, so many colors in the morning sun, so many colors in a flower, and I see every one."

The teacher said, "You're sassy. There's ways that things should be. And you'll paint flowers the way they are; so repeat after me."

And she said, "Flowers are red, young man, and green leaves are green. There's no need to see flowers any other way than the way they always have been seen."

But the little boy said, "There are so many colors in the rainbow, so many colors in the morning sun, so many colors in a flower, and I see every one."

The teacher put him in a corner. She said, "It's for your own good. And you won't come out till you get it right and are responding like you should."

Well, finally he got lonely. Frightened thoughts filled his head. And he went up to the teacher, and this is what he said:

And he said, "Flowers are red, and green leaves are green. There's no need to see flowers any other way than the way they always have been seen."

Time went by, like it always does, and they moved to another town. And the little boy went to another school, and this is what he found. The teacher there was smiling. She said, "Painting should be fun. And there are so many colors in a flower, so let's use every one."

But the little boy painted flowers, and he drew them green and red. And when the teacher asked him why, this is what he said:

And he said, "Flowers are red, and green leaves are green. There's no need to see flowers any other way than the way they always have been seen."

It is easy for us to say, "Oh, I could never be that mean!" We don't believe parents and teachers discourage individuality or creativity intentionally. Even the teacher in the song truly believed "it was for his own good." Hopefully, an awareness of temperament and of the immense value of individuality and diversity will help us avoid the "meanness" that comes from a lack of information and understanding.

Work for Improvement, Not Perfection

EVEN WITH UNDERSTANDING and the best intentions, most of us will struggle occasionally with our children's temperaments and behavior when we get caught up in a lack of patience or our own ego, or we simply get hooked into reacting to behavior instead of acting thoughtfully. Both we and our children are all too human: we will have good days and days when we're just cranky. Awareness and understanding do not mean we become perfect; mistakes are inevitable. However, once we have had time to cool off after we make a mistake, we need to resolve it with our children. They're usually more than willing to hug and offer forgiveness, especially when they know you'll do the same for them. It is important to help our children work for improvement, not perfection; we can give this gift to ourselves as parents and caregivers as well.

Kindness and Firmness

RUDOLF DREIKURS BELIEVED it was most effective for parents and teachers to use kindness and firmness with children. An understanding of temperament shows just how important this is. Kindness shows respect for the child and his uniqueness; firmness shows respect for the needs of the situation. By understanding and respecting your child's temperament, you will be able to help him reach his full potential as a capable, confident, contented person. And there's a bonus: you will probably get a lot more rest, laugh more, and learn a great deal about yourself and your child in the process.

> Kindness shows respect for the child and his uniqueness; firmness shows respect for the needs of the situation.

8

"You Can't Come to My Birthday Party!"

Social Skills for Preschoolers

WILL YOU BE my friend?" Every preschool teacher has heard that plea. The first years of life are filled with so much growth, and that growth can be traced in the development of friendships. The acquisition of social skills happens in predictable phases, and it happens much less painfully when adults understand and can work with their children's ability. Understanding adults provide training, patience, and encouragement during this period of social skill development, a time sometimes fraught with tear-streaked faces, thrown toys, and grim tugs-of-war.

Just what does friendship mean to a young child? When a child is younger than two years old, his friends are most likely to be classmates at child care, the children of his parents' acquaintances, or neighbors with whom he is plopped down to "play" while the adults socialize. Between the ages of two and three, children begin to interact more with their peers. There is no greater statement of friendship from a preschooler than "you can come to my birthday party." She is saying, "I like you enough to share the most important day in my world: the celebration of me!"

Jenna is three and a half years old. It is June and her birthday is not until December. Even so, hardly a day goes by that Jenna does not invite—or uninvite—someone at her preschool to her birthday party. When a parent wandered in to discuss enrolling her daughter, Jenna immediately went up to her and said, "I'm going

to be four. You can come to my party." Jenna is a generous soul and includes every-
one she meets in this grand event.

A short while later, however, when Jenna's friend Ilsa won't share the dress-up
clothes, Jenna sticks out her lip and announces in a voice of doom, "You can't come
to my birthday!" Ilsa trembles at such a threat and quickly hands over one of the
dress-up scarves.

For young children, birthday invitations (or the threat of their withdrawal)
are an early social tool. They represent an offer of mutual companionship and
acceptance—or momentary rejection. As children mature and develop a less
self-centered view of the world, they learn to interact in different ways.

Playtime: A Stage for Socialization

CHILDREN'S PLAY IS actually a laboratory
where intensive research about human relationships
is taking place. Playing is an activity that will form
the foundation of their future interactions with
others—it definitely is not meaningless or wasted
time.

Still, there will be rough spots, and most parents and caregivers can tell stories like this one.

> Understanding adults provide training, patience, and encouragement during this period of social skill development, a time sometimes fraught with tear-streaked faces, thrown toys, and grim tugs-of-war.

Four-year-old Sharon came home with a scraped and bleeding knee one after-
noon; her "best friend," Jamie, had pushed her off the swing. Her mother's first in-
stinct was to call the preschool teacher and complain. After all, weren't they
supposed to be watching the children?

Fortunately for Sharon, her mom was more interested in helping her learn life
skills than in blaming others for social conflicts. She sat down next to Sharon and
asked, "Honey, can you tell me what happened?"

"Jamie got off the swing and I got on. She wasn't using it anymore," Sharon
added defensively.

Mom suppressed a smile, suddenly realizing where this story might be going.
"Do you know why Jamie got off the swing?"

"To get her jacket," was the calm response.

As Mom suspected, when Jamie came back with her jacket she found Sharon on "her" swing and pushed her off. Mom took a moment to validate her daughter's feelings.

"I'll bet it was scary when Jamie pushed you. Maybe you felt that she wasn't your friend anymore."

Sharon's lip quivered. "Uh huh," she said, and burst into tears. When her crying had subsided and she felt better, Sharon and her mom explored what happened. Mom asked if Sharon might have done something other than get on the swing when Jamie got off. Sharon thought for a moment and decided that she could have held the swing for Jamie until she got back.

"What might have happened if you held the swing for Jamie?" Mom asked.

"Jamie would have gotten back on," Sharon said.

"Would Jamie have pushed you off?"

Sharon shook her head. She could see that the results would have been different if she had behaved differently. Mom agreed that it was wrong of Jamie to push Sharon and helped her daughter understand that she could have told Jamie clearly, "No pushing." Mom has helped Sharon understand that she has choices that can affect the outcome of a situation. In other words, Sharon has power and influence. By talking this through with Sharon rather than rushing in to rescue her, Sharon's mother has helped her to feel capable.

> It is important that parents avoid training children to see themselves as victims, helpless to change or affect what happens to them.

It is important that parents avoid training children to see themselves as victims, helpless to change or affect what happens to them. This mother could have rushed to call (and blame) her daughter's preschool, and in the process might have encouraged her daughter to develop a "victim mentality." Sharon might need some help, but not through sympathy, blaming others, and being rescued. Help children learn to see problems as opportunities for learning. Help a child explore for herself what is happening, how she feels about it, what she is learning from it, and what ideas she has to solve the problem. It is in this way that children learn that they are not powerless and that the choices they make in life affect what they experience. This is valuable knowledge for all of us to acquire.

Special Friendships

THREE- AND FOUR-YEAR-OLDS often focus on one special playmate with whom they have a special relationship.

Sergio and Kenneth are best buddies. Each watches for the arrival of the other at the child care center in the morning. They greet each other by rolling around on the floor in mock combat, or they quickly run off to begin a new Lego tower. They want to sit next to each other at group time, and their teacher sometimes has to remind them that if they can't sit together quietly, they will have to sit apart. Sergio and Kenneth are together all through the day; theirs is a wonderful and important early friendship.

Five-year-old children are at the peak of being social and love to play elaborate and complicated games, trying on dress-up clothes and many different roles. They may have one special friend or a special circle of friends.

Lauren, Erin, and Allie are all five-year-olds. They choose the same activities to do together each morning, and at playtime they are engaged in elaborate games of "Let's Pretend" with lots of dress-up props. Their friendship goes beyond individual play—they form a special group of their own.

Erin runs up to the teacher with something in her fist. "I found a potato bug," she announces. "Lauren wanted me to find one for her and I did. Allie wanted me to find one for her, too, but it was nap time." This is typical of the older preschooler's "one for all and all for one" style of friendship.

Catastrophe often threatens when one member of a special group links up with another, excluding the third. Lauren's parents will hear anguish in her voice when she tells them that Erin and Allie are going swimming together; being left out is very painful. But by the next day, the hurt feelings are usually resolved and the friendship continues to thrive.

Hal, Aaron, and Shelley are also pals. They chase one another around the playground and are an inseparable team. Shelley is the clear leader of this threesome; she is frequently the one who chooses the game to be played and makes the rules. The wise teacher knows that if he wants to get these three interested in a new activity, the one to convince is Shelley.

Special friendships form important foundations for many of life's relationships and provide a way for children to experiment with different roles. Just because Aaron chooses to follow Shelley's lead now, for instance, doesn't mean he will never be a leader. It's just one of the roles he's trying on for size.

Social skills do not come without practice, and there will be many yelps of complaint and tearful faces. But if adults can focus not on playing the rescuer or referee but on nurturing healthy children who feel influential and capable and who can achieve a sense of belonging, then they will be helping children acquire the social skills they need to thrive in a world of relationships.

"But Nobody Likes Me"

AS WE'VE MENTIONED, children's friendships are social skills laboratories—and not all of their experiments turn out well. Scraped knees and hurt feelings come with the territory. When we can help children learn from their mistakes and we can avoid playing superparent or superteacher, we will be teaching them to feel capable and competent.

Marla is another four-year-old. She says she doesn't want to go to preschool because she has no friends and no one likes her. Marla's parents and teachers must figure out what is really happening. If, in fact, Marla does not have playmates, the adults in her life can help her understand why. A child who is hurting others or who refuses to cooperate in games is not a welcome playmate, but such children can be taught more effective ways of relating to their peers.

Children who are successful at social relationships often learn to watch a game in progress and then join in by creating a role for themselves. Angela, for instance, spends a few moments watching her playmates play "house," then offers to bake cookies for the others. She smoothly blends into the game in progress.

Erica is less skilled at doing this. She bounces over to a group of children and says, "Can I play?" She is often told "no" because the others don't want to be interrupted by having to create a role for Erica. Helping a child develop social skills can help her find success at belonging to her peer group, a need that, if not met, can result in the "mistaken goal" behaviors of attention, power, revenge, and inadequacy (more about these in chapters 19, 20, and 21).

A child like Marla may actually be a welcome playmate who simply does not see herself that way. Class meetings may be helpful in dealing with this situation at preschool; a parent confronted with this dilemma might try a different approach.

Try asking simple questions. Marla's dad might ask her "What makes you believe that the other children don't like you?" or "What do you think it means to be someone's friend?" Together they can explore Marla's perceptions of friendship and then examine her experiences. "I noticed that today Adrian asked you to play on the swings with him. Why do you think he did that?" Marla now has an opportunity to compare her perceptions with what has actually happened. Teachers may also be able to offer information about positive experiences that happened during the day.

> Helping a child develop social skills can help her find success at belonging to her peer group, a need that, if not met, can result in the "mistaken goal" behaviors of attention, power, revenge, and inadequacy.

Inviting a child over to play is often a way of establishing a connection between home and school. Children feel a greater sense of kinship when they share times together in different settings. Marla's parents can invite one of her schoolmates to go to the zoo with them or perhaps to spend a Saturday afternoon playing with Marla's new playhouse. The increased closeness that results will often translate itself into increased playing at the preschool as well.

The Less-Than-Lovable Friend

SOMETIMES YOUR CHILD will actively dislike another child—or you may not care for the way your own child behaves when with a particular playmate. If your child's friendship results in exceptionally rowdy behavior or aggressiveness, it is helpful to set clear expectations.

Ben just loved to play with Marty, who lived down the street. Marty was a wild little guy who was very physical. The two four-year-olds inevitably wound up running recklessly around the house or wrestling on the lawn, and more than once Ben returned scraped, bumped, and bruised.

Ben's mother wasn't very happy about this friendship, especially since Marty was the only child with whom this sort of play occurred. Ben's mom decided not to rescue Ben but to establish clear guidelines about what she would allow when the boys played at her house.

One quiet morning, Mom sat down with Ben and explained her problem and her concerns for the boys' safety. She then clearly explained her expectations to Ben, gently having him repeat them back to her to be sure he understood.

She established three rules: no bad names, no laughing at people, and no sticking out tongues.

Mom and Ben agreed that when Ben or Marty chose not to follow the rules, Marty would have to go home. Marty would wait in the den and Ben would wait in his room until Marty's mother could come to get him.

The plan was discussed with Marty and his mother, who agreed with the rules. Now both moms needed to plan ways to follow through when necessary. It is the nature of learning (and young children) that Ben and Marty would need to check it out and see if the plan was for real. They might play nicely once or even twice, but eventually the rules would have to be tested.

Sure enough, the day came when Ben joined Marty in climbing on the countertop. Ben refused to get down when his mother asked him and threw in a "You're a butthead" for good measure.

Ben was given the choice of walking to his room or being carried there. Mom pointed kindly but firmly to the sofa, where Marty could wait for his mother. There was no reminder or warning necessary, since both boys knew the expectations and consequences. Marty's mom arrived at the front door quickly and escorted Marty home. Now both boys had learned that their parents really meant what they said and that their behavior would have to change. If it didn't, Ben and Marty would lose the opportunity to play at one another's houses.

"Hey, Look at Me!" Showing Off

SOME CHILDREN SEEM to have some "peacock genes." They act as though strutting their stuff is the best way to succeed with others.

Q. *My four-year-old son seems to totally forget everything we have taught him when he gets together with his peers. He is so excited to be with them that he tries to* *show off by misbehaving intentionally in their presence. He turns a deaf ear to all grown-ups and will only stop goofing off if we raise our voices very loud. What action can we take to stop this behavior?*

A. It would probably be a good start to stop using the very loud voice. When you want your son's attention, kindly and gently take him aside, get down to his eye level, and establish eye contact. Explain the problem, what you would like him to do, and what you will do. In other words, explain that the yelling indoors must stop. If it continues, you will have to take him home. If you are not willing to actually leave, perhaps you can go into another room with him where he can calm himself before rejoining the play.

This plan will work only if you can speak to him respectfully and privately, so that he is not tempted to continue misbehaving out of embarrassment. Your son is becoming more interested in interacting with his peers than in paying attention to adults. As with so many aspects of a preschooler's behavior, his development and temperament have a strong influence on his behavior. Understanding this fact will help you decide how to respond to your young "show-off."

"Where Do I Fit?"
The Importance of Birth Order

THE FAMILY IS often the laboratory where children first experiment with social skills—and brothers and sisters are the guinea pigs! Where children "fit" in their families is one factor in how they approach relationships with each other, and with the wider world outside the family.

The preschool years are when children are making many of the decisions about themselves and others that will influence the rest of their lives. They are asking themselves, "What must I do to find belonging and significance in this family—and with my friends? Am I cute and adorable, or less than lovely? Am I good enough or must I keep trying harder—or should I just give up?" Preschoolers will carry the answers to those questions with them into the world around them, and they will practice what they are learning as they explore social relationships.

While birth order is certainly not a reliable predictor of a child's abilities or behavior, it (along with temperament and perception) does affect the way children see themselves and the way they define where they belong in their world. Following are some characteristics that children of different birth orders might share.

Only Children

Carrie is five years old. On the wall of her beautifully decorated bedroom hangs a poster depicting a princess sitting on a bejeweled throne, waving a golden scepter. Above the princess' head are the words "It is good to be queen."

Carrie would certainly agree; she enjoys being the undisputed ruler of her small realm. Carrie was born late in life to parents who had longed for a child for years. There will be no brothers or sisters, so all her parents' stored-up love is poured out for their small daughter. At five, Carrie is too young to understand that the rest of the world is not as willing to bow in worship as are her own parents.

Carrie spends three days a week in a prekindergarten program. Her parents told the director on her first day that they don't want her to be alone too much and know that she must learn to get along with other children. So far, however, Carrie and her new companions are finding the process a bit painful.

The other children don't agree that Carrie should be queen. Carrie isn't used to noisy groups of children and finds it hard to blend into their games. She isn't used to sharing or to going along with another child's wishes, and the teachers often find her alone in a corner, curled up with a book or playing quietly with a toy. The other children try to be friendly, but when Carrie doesn't respond, they leave her alone. After two weeks at school, Carrie announces to her parents that she doesn't want to go there anymore; she'd rather stay at home.

Carrie's predicament is not unusual for an only child making her first foray into the world of social relationships. Only children are the recipients of their parents' undivided love and attention. They are often highly motivated, sometimes lonely, and occasionally slow at learning to share and be flexible. They also may be more comfortable than other young children with "alone time" and more focused on the world of adult relationships. Occasionally, though, it is easier for them to learn to share because they have not been forced to share before they were ready.

Firstborn Children

Firstborn children are first to be born and often are treated as the "best" child that was ever born. Like only children (which they are for at least a while), they live in a world populated by adults. They often acquire language quickly and are more articulate than children born later. Firstborn children may have more privileges in the family—but much is expected of them, too. How many oldest children have heard the words, "Share with your baby sister! You're older; you should know better!"

Some firstborn children become perfectionists, always trying to do things "right." Some succeed in their quest for excellence and become high achievers. Sometimes, though, firstborn children feel so pressured to live up to expectations that they give up instead. In candid moments, many parents will admit that their firstborns were their parenting "experiments" and that they loosened up considerably by the time other children came along.

Youngest Children

Youngest children are the "babies." One little boy just entering kindergarten declared to his classmates that it was fun to be youngest because "we get the most toys and stuff!" Youngest children often do find that the rules have relaxed for them. Their siblings, however, may perceive youngest children as spoiled—and sometimes they are! Many youngest children decide "I belong and am significant only when others take care of me."

> While birth order is certainly not a reliable predictor of a child's abilities or behavior, it (along with temperament and perception) does affect the way children see themselves and the way they define where they belong in their world.

These children may develop manipulation skills that are irresistible and with which they charm others into serving them. Other times, youngest children tire of being "last in line" and try to rush the process by keeping up with older siblings. (Remember, these decisions are made subconsciously; however, if you observe carefully, you can see them being acted out in a child's behavior.)

Middle Children

Middle children sometimes feel lost in the family and may turn to peers and siblings for support and encouragement. One researcher found that middle children have the fewest photographs in their family albums. They may try to define a special place for themselves by choosing a role or identity that is distinctly different from the children who have come before. If the older child is interested in sports, for example, the middle child may choose music; that way, she doesn't have to compete with her firstborn sibling.

Middle children can be in an uncomfortable spot. They don't have the privileges of the oldest, but neither do they receive the special treatment of the youngest. They sometimes feel they are treated unfairly and may become rebels (with or without a cause) in their efforts to create a place of belonging.

Watching young children at play together is a wonderful opportunity to observe how all the different aspects of who they are fit together to make a whole. Understanding that children are learning and making decisions about themselves and their world will help parents and caregivers guide and shape that world so that each child learns to value himself and to feel that special sense of significance that each of us needs.

A parent with arguing children can use one of the following three options:

- "Beat it." You can choose to leave the area. It is amazing how many children stop fighting when they lose their audience. Don't be surprised if they follow you. This is why Rudolf Dreikurs suggested that the bathroom is the most important room in the house—the only room with a lock on the door. If your children pound on the door, you may want to jump into the shower or stuff your ears with Kleenex while you read a good novel. If you choose these methods, it is a good idea to tell your children, in advance, that this is what you will do when they fight. Also, you may want to discuss fighting and problem solving at a family meeting.

Sibling Fights

ARE BROTHERS AND sisters a blessing or a curse? Most children occasionally wonder. We do know that brothers and sisters are forever; most of them will outlive their parents, and children usually learn their first lessons about friendship through their relationships with their siblings.

It is heartwarming to see eighteen-month-old Timmy go up to his four-year-old sister and say, "Wuv you, Bef." It isn't so heartwarming to watch Timmy pull Beth's hair when she tries to rescue her favorite book from his clutches. When children are two or three years old, sibling fighting is the result of their immature social skills and the reactions of the adults involved. Social skills training is important for siblings, especially because of the unique aspect that sharing (and vying for) a parent's love and attention brings to their conflicts. (Keep in mind that sibling fighting is not the same as sibling rivalry. Sibling rivalry is about the decisions each child in the family makes based on his or her birth order and role in family life—and can be a hidden basis for sibling fights. For an excellent discussion of sibling rivalry, see chapter 3 on birth order in *Positive Discipline* by Jane Nelsen (Ballantine, 1996).

- "Bear it." This is the most difficult option because it means staying in the same room without jumping in to stop the fight or fix the problem. When children are fighting in a car, "bear it" may mean pulling to the side of the road and reading for a while, telling your children, "I'll drive as soon as you are ready to stop fighting." The hard part is keeping your own mouth shut until they say they are ready.

- "Boot 'em out." You can send both children to cool off somewhere, or they can go outside if they want to continue their fight. Or they can "end the bout," an option they have at any time.

Corsini, Raymond, and Genevieve Pointer. *The Practical Parent.* New York: Simon & Schuster, 1984.

It is helpful when parents learn to see sibling fighting for what it usually is. Young children sometimes tussle as they investigate their relationship with each other. Parents can stay out of the "rescuer" role by simply leaving the room. Taking a quiet moment elsewhere eliminates the audience—and sometimes the struggle.

If the noise level and fear of mayhem is too great to ignore, try giving the children a big hug. "What?" you may say, "Reward them for fighting?" Not exactly. If your children are competing for your attention, try giving it in an unexpected way. While hugging them, say, "I bet the two of you would like my attention right now. Next time, try telling me with your words instead of hurting one another." Acting in an unexpected way can cause children to pay more attention to your words—and it's always great to be hugged!

Since both children are involved, treat them the same way. Even toddlers can be placed in their rooms to cool off. Don't try to be judge and jury; worry about "whodunnit" when you read a mystery, not when you raise a preschooler. When your children are ready to get along, they can come out. You have shifted the message from "who is loved more" to "hurting each other is not okay."

Of course, fighting is not limited to siblings, and there are other options for dealing with fighting.

Mr. Conners found another creative way to deal with fighting when he saw two five-year-olds wrestling with each other at their preschool. He grabbed a toy microphone, rushed up to the boys and said, "Excuse me. I'm a reporter for the six o'clock news. Would you each be willing to take thirty seconds to tell our listening audience your version of what this fight is all about?" He handed the microphone to one boy and told him to look into the make-believe camera.

The boy caught the spirit of the game and started telling his story. When thirty seconds were up, Mr. Conners took the mike and handed it to the next boy. When his thirty seconds were up, Mr. Conners looked into the imaginary camera and said, "Well folks, only you can decide. Tune in tomorrow to find out how these boys solved their problem."

Then Mr. Conners turned to the boys and said, "Would you boys be willing to come back tomorrow and tell our listening audience how you solved this problem?" With big grins on their faces, both boys agreed and went off together to work on a solution—which was reported the next day to the imaginary camera. Mr. Conners turned fight time into playtime that distracted the boys into learning some social skills.

The Social Skill of Sharing

SHARING ISN'T EASY. Most of us know adults who struggle with the concept, and for preschoolers, sharing is an ongoing challenge in the development of social skills. We expect little people to take turns, to welcome new siblings, to give up playing with a favorite toy. These expectations accelerate during the late preschool years. Older preschoolers are only beginning to suspect that they are not the center of the universe—and the idea is not entirely welcome.

Many adults do not have much patience with children who have not mastered the social skill of sharing, as the following frustrated parent reveals. Helping children learn to get along is easier when we understand that learning to share is an ongoing, developmental process that requires skill training, lots of practice, and lots of patience from adults.

Q. *My three-year-old has been acting up lately in child care. He is fighting with the other kids. He doesn't hit them, but he can't agree about sharing toys. He is not listening to his teacher. One day he seems okay, but the next day he just loses it. How can I get him to understand that what he is doing is not acceptable behavior?*

A. It sounds like you have a very normal little boy. Three-year-olds are learning how to share, and sharing is a difficult skill to master. Most of us are unhappy when we do not get to have what we want when we want it.

MORE POSSIBILITIES FOR PEACEMAKING

- Invite children to put the problem on the family or class meeting agenda.

- After a cooling-off period, use "what," "why," and "how" questions to help children explore what happened, how they feel about it, what they learned from the experience, and how they can solve the problem now.

- Teach children to use their words. This means that adults act as coaches—not lecturers or referees!

A child needs clear and firm guidance, and he needs teaching rather than lectures or punishment. Remember, he does not yet know how to negotiate, compromise, and discuss problems with others. When children argue over a toy, adults frequently take the toy away from both children. There is more, however, that parents and caregivers can do to help children learn this important skill.

> A child needs clear and firm guidance, and he needs teaching rather than lectures or punishment.

Children need to learn how to use words to ask for what they need. The adult can take two children aside after a dispute. When everyone is calm, try practicing how to ask to play with a toy. For instance, a child may ask, "May I use the blocks?" One possible response to a playmate's request is, "I am not done with them yet." You can then teach negotiation skills: "You can play with them in five minutes" or "Would you like to play with me?" Such training is vital to learning to share.

Quarreling

HAVE YOU EVER watched a litter of puppies wrestle, nip, and fight? We laugh at puppies and see their aggressive behavior as normal and even cute. When children argue and fight, however, we're a bit less enchanted. Yet testing limits and disagreeing are as normal for young children as for puppies.

When children between the ages of three and a half to five years of age quarrel, it may be helpful to ask them to sit quietly for a few minutes, not as punishment but as an opportunity to cool off and calm down. Later you can then ask them to explore and name their feelings, and invite them to identify ways they could handle the situation next time. It is usually not helpful for adults to lose their own tempers, offer blame, punishment, and lectures, or leap into the fray themselves.

Teaching social skills with the same attention we give to other types of skill development will produce children who can play together peacefully—at least most of the time. When children experience continuous modeling and training, they can learn to get along quite well with other members of the world around them.

Recognizing and Naming Feelings

FOR PRESCHOOLERS, a big part of learning social skills involves learning about feelings. It helps to know that children often hit because they are acting upon their feelings of frustration and anger. After all, there are so many people who get in the way of a child's impulses and urges. This can be a good opportunity to teach that there is a difference between a feeling and an action, and to help a child learn to identify and cope with his feelings (see chapter 3).

Three-year-old Jack was on a rampage. He had been hitting the other children at the preschool, knocking over their towers of blocks, and kicking gravel on the playground. One afternoon, Jack got angry when another child ran in front of him. He pushed her down, causing her to scrape her knee.

Miss Terry, Jack's teacher, gently led the raging Jack away from the other children and toward the book corner. As Jack calmed down, he looked over and noticed that one of the books had a picture of a sad-looking boy on the cover.

"Why does he look like that?" Jack asked Miss Terry.

"Well," his teacher replied, sitting down to look at the picture, "he looks sad to me. Why do you think he might be sad?"

Jack began to explain that the boy in the picture was sad because his favorite baby-sitter had gone away and he wasn't going to see her anymore. Miss Terry asked Jack if he would like a hug, and he scrambled gratefully onto her lap. "That little boy must feel very lonely and sad," she said. Jack began to cry in his teacher's arms.

When Jack's sobs had slowed to sniffles, Miss Terry asked if he could think of a way to help the child he had pushed feel better again. "I bet she's sad, too," Jack said. "Maybe I could play a special game with her and help her put away her lunch stuff."

Miss Terry wrote a note to Jack's parents explaining what had happened and mentioning Jack's sadness over the loss of his baby-sitter. Jack helped by making a mark at the bottom to serve as his signature.

Jack had an opportunity to explore his feelings in safety. He also learned that he was responsible for his behavior toward other children. Identifying and accepting feelings can help children learn effective social skills.

Hitting and Aggression

OLDER PRESCHOOLERS WHO are hitting or pulling hair should be firmly separated. A parent or teacher can say, "I can't allow you to hurt others" and can help the combatants explore other ways of acting when they feel angry or frustrated. It is important to understand that behavior often contains a coded message about how a child is feeling; while some behaviors are inappropriate or hurtful, the feelings themselves are not wrong. As we will learn in chapter 19, interpreting the beliefs a child has about himself will provide clues about how parents and teachers might respond.

It will take more than one such occasion to teach children to play cooperatively together. Patient repetition, modeling, and guidance will help children learn more quickly the pleasures of getting along; it won't turn them into angels! Remember that social skills "mistakes" can always be turned into opportunities to learn.

When Children Hurt Adults

SOMETIMES A CHILD'S aggression and anger aren't directed only at other children. Some preschoolers have learned to hit, kick, bite, or yank the hair of their parents and caregivers when life doesn't go their way. And even little fists and feet can hurt! Parents often do not know what to do with an aggressive child and may inadvertently reinforce the very behavior they are trying to change.

Q. *I'm the mother of a three-and-a-half-year-old boy. My son has been calling me names and hitting me when he doesn't get what he wants. I think he picked this up at his preschool. We've always tried to use the most humane methods of discipline; we don't hit, yell, or humiliate him in any way. We always try to reason with him. I'm at a loss in this situation. Please tell me the best way to deal with such behavior.*

A. It is unlikely your child "picked up" this behavior at preschool. Preschool simply exposes him to more children and adults with whom he must share, to whom he sometimes has to defer his demands, and over whom he

STOPPING VIOLENT BEHAVIOR

Q. *How do you handle a child who feels that violence is the only way to solve a problem?*

A. This question raises several more: What is going on in this child's life? Where is this child learning violence? Too much television? Too many video games? Too much punishment? A child's environment and the role models he encounters provide many clues about that child's violent behavior.

As a wise person once said, if you want to understand the fruit, take a look at the tree. Children do indeed learn what they live, and changing angry, aggressive behavior is best accomplished through kind, firm teaching about respect, nonviolent ways of solving problems, and watching adults practice what they preach.

tries to establish his right to territory. At home he may simply redouble his efforts to get his way, where the odds are a bit more to his liking.

There are several things a parent can try to help a child change his behavior. The following sections provide suggestions; choose the one that fits you and your child.

Decide What You Will Do

Let your son know that every time he hits you or calls you a name, you will leave the room until he is ready to treat you respectfully. After you have told him this once, follow through without any words. Leave immediately.

Hold the Child Kindly and Firmly

If you are concerned that your child will tear up furniture, break things, or hurt herself, try sitting down and holding her firmly so that she cannot hit or kick, without lecturing or yelling, until the moment passes. Rocking gently may help her to calm down more quickly.

Share Your Feelings

Tell him, "That really hurts (or that hurts my feelings). When you are ready, an apology would help me feel better." Do not demand or force an apology. The main purpose of this suggestion is to give a model of sharing what you feel and asking for what you would like. People don't always give us what we would like, but we show respect for ourselves by sharing our feelings and wishes in nondemanding ways.

Design a Positive Time-Out Area

The time-out area could include teddy bears, books, and a soft cushion. When your child hits or hurts, ask, "Would it help you feel better to go to the time-out place for a while?" While designing the area, it is important to teach that people do better when they feel better and that sometimes we need time to calm down and cool off. If your child doesn't want to go, you might model for him by say-ing, "I'm very upset right now. I think I'll go to a quiet spot until I feel better." (More about this in chapter 13.)

Use "What" and "How" Questions

"What" and "how" questions help a child explore the consequences of his be-havior. "What happens when you hit people or call them names? How does it

WHEN CHILDREN SPEAK OR ACT DISRESPECTFULLY TO ADULTS

- Decide what you will do.

- Hold the child kindly and firmly.

- Share your feelings.

- Design a positive time-out area.

- Use "what" and "how" questions.

- Put the problem on the family or class meeting agenda.

make you feel? How does it make others feel? What could you do to help them feel better? How else could you get what you want?" Be sure to ask these questions with a sincere desire to hear what the child has to say. Don't turn the conversation into a lecture.

Put the Problem on the Agenda

When the problem of hitting and name calling appears on the family or class meeting agenda, it can be discussed during a regular family or class meeting when everyone is feeling calm. Everyone can work together for solutions. (More on meetings in chapter 15.)

Disruptive Behavior in the Classroom

IT IS ESPECIALLY important in group settings to provide opportunities for learning about social skills. Teachers face the ripple effect of behavior daily: Everyone sits down to group time and one child starts to make "raspberry" noises; within moments, the entire group is buzzing and spitting.

Sit quietly until the class calms down. Model the behavior you want. Some teachers decide to join in the noise making, which usually makes everyone laugh—and which may be the easiest way to help children settle down. When disruptive behavior causes repeated problems, ask the children for help.

Use a class meeting to explain that it causes a problem for you when children continue to make noise after the group gathers together. Discuss what happens, invite the children to comment on what they notice, and then come up with a proposed solution. A hand signal, clapping pattern, or lights out might be decided upon as a way to indicate that classroom noise should stop.

Class meetings can be used to explore many possible problems. Ask "What would you do if . . . ?" or describe a situation and ask the children what they think went wrong. Storytelling, flannel boards, and books are other ways to introduce social skills. Help children identify the skills you are teaching, and take time to discuss what happened and why.

Social Interest

ALFRED ADLER DESCRIBED "social interest" as a real concern for others and a sincere desire to make a contribution to society. As children enter into the lives of their families and schools, they want very much to feel that they belong. And one of the most powerful ways to achieve a sense of belonging is to make a meaningful contribution to the well-being of others in the family or group. When adults can help preschoolers care about and participate in their community, everyone benefits. In the family or preschool, a wonderful way to encourage social interest is by sharing chores or the work the family does together.

For young children there really is no difference between play and work, so adults can use play as an opportunity to teach social interest.

While Charlene Clark fixed the hamburger patties, three-year-old Sean happily unwrapped cheese slices and placed them on the buns. When the family sat down to dinner, imagine how pleased Sean felt when the family mentioned how good their cheeseburgers tasted, thanks to Sean's efforts.

Five-year-old Becky reminded her grandma to use her eye drops every evening during her visit. When Grandma returned home, Becky wanted to call her every night so she could continue to remind her. That is social interest at work; it is meaningful involvement that benefits others.

There are any number of tasks that preschoolers can do that not only build skills and cooperation but also give them opportunities to practice getting along with others. Invite your child to help you with one of the tasks in Table 8.1.

Relationships: The Ties That Bind

LIKE IT OR NOT, relationships form the fabric of our lives. We live in families; we go to school with peers; and eventually, we work, live, love, and play with other people. Helping our young children get along prepares them to experience the best that life can offer: connection and contentment with friends and family. Disagreements and conflict are inevitable, but children can learn to handle those, too, with dignity and mutual respect. Taking the time to teach and encourage social skills now will pave the way for a happier life as your child grows and matures.

TABLE 8.1 Age-Appropriate Tasks

	SELF-CARE	FOOD	HOUSEHOLD
2–3 years	Undress self; wash hands; feed self; put on coat; take off shoes	Wash vegetables; pour milk from small pitcher; oil potatoes for baking; peel and slice bananas with butter knife; stir batter; slice hard-boiled eggs in special slicer	Set table (napkins and silverware); serve fruit and cookies; pick up toys; put own clothes in hamper; dig in garden; rinse lettuce
4 years	Select clothes; dress and undress self; put on shoes	Squeeze fruit for juice; grate cheese; butter toast; scrub mushrooms; knead dough; measure water for juice	Straighten bedcovers; arrange cut flowers; harvest berries and other garden produce; stack newspapers and crush cans for recycling; set table; wash car; sort laundry
5 years	Help pack lunch; comb/ brush hair; wash hair (with help)	Slice fruit or vegetables; roll out dough; make a cake mix; spread peanut butter and jam on crackers or bread; "smash" cooked potatoes with masher	Fold washcloths; help care for pet; put away laundry; wash windows; help plan menus; help grocery shop; polish shoes

For more information on age-appropriate tasks, see *Chores Without Wars* by Lynn Lott and Riki Inter (Prima Publishing, 1997).

9

"My Child Just Won't Listen to Me!"

The Continuing Saga of the Developmental Process

PRESCHOOLERS DON'T THINK like adults, they don't act like adults, and they don't have the same priorities as adults. This may sound obvious, but many parents forget these facts when they feel frustrated by the challenges their young children's behavior presents.

Q. *I have a five-year-old who will not listen to me at all. She talks back to me all the time and does not respect me. I have tried everything from time-outs to grounding, and nothing works. She even has taught her baby sister to say "no!" I need some help. What should I do?*

A. When adults say, "I've tried everything," they usually mean they've tried every punishment they can think of. Children will not learn respect when they are treated disrespectfully. Punishment is very disrespectful. Most children don't listen because parents talk too much, lecture too much, and don't get into their children's world to understand their developmental process.

Later in this chapter, we will discuss more nonpunitive methods that invite respect, listening, and cooperation, but first we need to discuss the developmental issues that surround a child's understanding of the word "no."

What Does Your Preschooler Really Know About "No"?

CHILDREN UNDER THE age of four do not understand "no" in the way most parents think they do. (And a full understanding of "no" doesn't occur magically when the child turns four. It is a developmental process.) "No" is an abstract concept that is in direct opposition to the developmental need of young children to explore their world and to develop their sense of autonomy and initiative. Preschoolers are in a growing individuation process, which means they are continually experimenting to find out who they are separate from their parents.

> Preschoolers don't think like adults, they don't act like adults, and they don't have the same priorities as adults.

Your child may "know" you don't want her to do something. She may even know she will get an angry reaction from you if she does it. However, she cannot understand "why" in the way an adult thinks she can. Why else would your preschooler (who desperately wants your approval) become sneaky (or defiant) and do what she "knows" she shouldn't do?

Researchers like Jean Piaget discovered long ago that preschoolers lack the ability to understand cause and effect (an excellent reason not to try to lecture and argue a young child into doing what you want). In fact, higher order thinking, like understanding consequences and ethics, may not develop until children are as old as ten.

Parents, preschool teachers, and child care providers might respond very differently to defiance and sneakiness if they understood what their children were trying to do. Children need to test their initiative, experiment, explore, and find out what they can do and what they can't do. Adults need to realize that preschoolers may not "understand" in the way we sometimes think they can.

Understanding Age Appropriateness: How to Teach and Empower

AROUND THE AGE of one, children enter the "me do it" stage. This is when they develop a sense of autonomy (as opposed to a sense of doubt and shame), as discussed in *Positive Discipline: The First Three Years* (Prima Publishing, 1998). The ages of two through six herald the development of a sense of initiative (rather than a sense of guilt). This means it is a child's developmental job to explore and experiment. Can you imagine how confusing it is to a child to be punished for what he is developmentally programmed to do? He is faced with a real dilemma (at a subconscious level): "Do I obey my parents, or do I follow my biological drive to develop autonomy and initiative by exploring and experimenting in my world?"

This process does not stop when children enter the preschool years. When they enter the stage of developing initiative (as discussed in chapter 4), it is their "job" to initiate activities and to enjoy achievement and competence. Their developmental struggle at this stage occurs when they feel unable to control their newly acquired power. Punishment—a typical adult reaction to new and challenging behavior—leads to a sense of guilt and shame.

These stages of development do not mean children should be allowed to do anything they want. It does explain why all methods to gain cooperation should be kind and firm at the same time instead of controlling and/or punitive. This is a time of life when your child's personality is being formed,

INTELLECTUAL DEVELOPMENT

The following illustrates why children can't understand some concepts (such as "no") as soon as adults think they can.

1. Take two balls of clay that are the same size. Ask a three-year-old if they are the same. Make adjustments by taking clay from one ball and adding it to the other until the child agrees that they are the same size. Then, right in front of her, smash one ball of clay. Then ask her if they are still the same. She will say, "No," and will tell you which one she thinks is bigger. A five-year-old will tell you they are the same and can tell you why.

2. Find four glasses: two glasses that are the same size, one glass that is taller and thinner, and one glass that is shorter and fatter. Fill the two glasses that are the same size with water until a three-year-old agrees they are

and you want your child to make decisions about herself that say, "I am competent. I can try, make mistakes, and learn. I am loved. I am a good person." If you are tempted to help your child learn by guilt, shame, or punishment, you will be creating discouraging beliefs that are difficult to reverse in adulthood.

The Child Power of "No"

TODDLERS AND PRESCHOOLERS are experiencing individuation, learning to see themselves as separate, independent beings. It's a natural and healthy process, but one that is frequently trying for parents and teachers. It doesn't take long for a young child to learn the power of the word "no" or that by using it he can provoke all sorts of interesting reactions. Adults can't always avoid these confrontations, but changing your own behavior and expectations can lessen their impact. There are actually three types of no: the ones you can avoid saying, the ones you can avoid hearing, and the ones that you just learn to live with.

the same. Then, right in front of her, pour the water from one of these glasses into the short, fat glass, and the other one into the tall, thin glass. Then ask her if they are still the same. Again, she will say, "No," and will tell you which glass she thinks contains the most water. A five-year-old will tell you they contain the same amount and can tell you why.

Both of these examples demonstrate thinking abilities identified by Piaget. When we understand that perceiving, interpreting, and comprehending an event are so markedly different for young children, our expectations as adults alter. The meaning children attach to their experiences does not match the meaning adults attach to the same experiences.

How Not to Say No

"SOMETIMES I LISTEN to myself talking to my son," one mom confided to a group of friends, "and all I hear myself saying is 'no' and 'don't.' I sound so negative, but I don't know what else to do." There are actually a number of ways adults can avoid saying the "no" word themselves.

- *Say what you* do *want.* Arthur is four, and he loves to run around the tables at the restaurant. He stops to stare at several tables and watch the other people eating. His aunt keeps bringing him back to his chair, wagging her finger in his face and saying, "No running. Don't bother the other people. If you keep acting this way, there will be no dessert!" (She couldn't resist throwing in a "helpful" threat.) Poor Arthur. He now knows he is not supposed to run or "bother" others. What should he do instead? He decides to try climbing the back of the booth where they are seated. Just before he manages to get his leg over the top, his aunt catches him again. Who feels more frustrated, Arthur or his aunt? It is probably a close call.

  Arthur needs some clues about what he *can* do in this situation. His aunt might say, "Arthur, please sit in the chair and keep your feet on the floor (or at least pointed in that direction). What would you like to do after we've finished eating?" She could also offer him some choices. "Would you like to color on your place mat, or shall we play 'I Spy'?"

- *Say yes instead.* Sometimes it seems parents are programmed to respond with an automatic no. Before acting on this instinct, ask yourself, "Why not?" Jennifer wants to put mustard on her pancakes. Just before you crinkle your nose and say "Yuck, no way!" stop and ask yourself, "Why not?" Mustard isn't going to stunt her growth. You don't have to try it yourself. What is the harm of letting her experiment? She might find out for herself that she doesn't like it, which is a much more valuable lesson than a lecture—and much easier on everyone concerned!

  Sometimes we say no when yes is possible. Imagine that your five-year-old has just asked you if she can watch television. Your response might be, "No, you haven't cleaned your room." You might be surprised to learn that you can say yes and still communicate the same message. "Yes," you tell your daughter, "you can watch TV just as soon as your room is clean." If your daughter responds, "But I want to watch TV right now!" you can simply smile and say, "You can watch when your room is clean. Which program did you want to see?" Eventually your daughter will figure out that she can choose to either clean her room or not watch television.

- *Use questions or statements instead of saying no.* It's art time at the child care center, but two of the boys have a better idea than making collages. Chris and Peter are having a marvelous time throwing the pieces of colored paper around the room. When the teacher comes over, she can say, "Stop throwing the paper around!" Or she can say, "Who can show me what to do with these colored papers?" Or even, "There is collage paper on the floor." These responses give the boys an opportunity to demonstrate their knowledge of appropriate behavior and to clean up the mess. They can do this without experiencing shame or humiliation—and without receiving undue attention.

- *Agree to discuss the subject.* Family or class meetings are an excellent place to explore situations that provoke a lot of no's (see chapter 15 for more information). If you find yourself saying no frequently when in the vicinity of the candy rack at the store, you may want to place "candy buying" on the agenda for your next family meeting. A child three years old or older can usually help make an agreement about when you will or will not buy candy. Once everyone has agreed, you can follow through with kind and firm action.

- *Draw a picture.* Simple pictures can help a child understand what is expected of him, especially if that child hasn't yet mastered language. Some children respond better to visual clues than auditory clues. For instance, a child who struggles with bedtime may enjoy helping her parents make a chart illustrating her bedtime routine. (Remember, preschoolers thrive on predictability and consistency.) Future disputes can be resolved by asking, "What's next on your chart?" The chart becomes the boss, and parents can refrain from excess no's, lectures, and threats.

Pictures are useful in other ways, as well. Andy had brought his favorite toy fire engine to the child care center and was busily creating havoc with it. Max, his teacher, told Andy that he needed to put the engine on the shelf until it was time to go home. Andy reluctantly complied, but a few minutes later Max noticed that Andy had taken it down and was running through the playroom with his "siren" on.

Max approached Andy again and was met with a scowl as the boy clutched his toy tightly. Max paused for a moment, then picked up a pencil and a piece of paper. He drew a simple picture of the fire engine sitting on a shelf and said, "This is the shelf with your fire engine on it." Andy was fascinated. Then Max drew the figure of a little boy running. "This is Andy," he said, "playing outside without a fire engine."

Andy looked at the pictures for a moment, then calmly went to the shelf to put away his fire engine and headed out the door to play. Max was astonished, but Andy had simply needed the additional visual clues and encouragement the picture gave him to choose the right behavior. (There's also something to be said for doing the unexpected!)

INVITING CHILDREN TO LISTEN

If you find yourself complaining bitterly about children who "won't listen," consider the following suggestions:

- Don't talk. Act! Children "hear" kind and firm action much more than words. Kindly and firmly take your child by the hand, and lead her to what needs to be done.
- Have regular family or class meetings where children have an opportunity to feel listened to, be taken seriously, and have their thoughts and ideas validated.
- Create routine charts together, then let the routine chart be the boss.

Another teacher decided to try the picture approach with Jenna, a three-year-old who refused to stay on her cot during nap time. The teacher drew a simple stick figure of a little girl lying in the center of a rectangle. She showed the picture to Jenna and said, "This is Jenna lying on her cot." Amazingly, Jenna went over to her cot and lay down. Drawing a picture may not work for every child every time, but it can be very helpful for children who are helped by receiving visual clues.

How to Avoid Hearing the "No" Word

WOULD YOU PREFER that the youngsters in your life say no a bit less often? Try asking fewer questions that allow for a yes or no answer. Asking "Are you ready to eat?" invites a yes or no answer. Giving limited choices, such as "Would you like milk or apple juice with your dinner?" can avoid the entire problem.

Instead of asking, "Did you have fun today?" ask, "What was the happiest time of your day?" You're inviting thoughtful answers instead of single-syllable ones.

- Work on solutions together. This can be done during family meetings or one-on-one. Children are motivated to follow solutions and guidelines they help create.
- Ask instead of telling: "What did we decide to do about that?" "What is next on our bedtime (morning, dinner, etc.) routine chart?"
- Ask for help. This is very appealing to most children. You might say, "I really need your help. How could you help me now?"
- Use nonverbal signals: point without saying a word. (Do smile, though!)
- Use one word: towels, toys, bedtime, and so on.
- Use your sense of humor: "Here comes the tickle monster to get children who haven't picked up their toys."

Another good way to avoid hearing "no" is to look for cooperation instead of giving orders and commands. If your boss stomps in and tells you, "Get over there and finish that job!" most adults would be tempted to respond with something stronger than a simple "no." Children are no different. Most of the time, if you invite their help and cooperation in a friendly way ("Let's work together. I'll pick up the books, and you can put the dominoes in their container."), they will respond. Try it and see.

The No's We Live With

THERE ARE TIMES, of course, when we must say no. Children need safe, secure boundaries as they develop and grow, and they will respect adults who can gently and respectfully draw those boundaries (even if a temper tantrum comes first). Children, too, will say no from time to time. In fact, the ability to say no and mean it can prove important, especially as a child grows up and faces peer

HE JUST WON'T LISTEN

Q. *I have a five-year-old son. Lately he has refused to listen to his mom or me. It drives us nuts! We tell him to pick up his toys when he is finished playing or to hang up his coat—just simple tasks. He does not do it. We must ask him three times or more. For punishment he goes in time-out, and if that doesn't work we take privileges away (such as computer time or favorite videos). This isn't working as well as I want it to. Do you have any new ideas?*

A. Have you ever thought about *why* your son doesn't listen? Answering the following questions might give you some insights. What kind of model do you give him? Do you listen, or do you talk (lecture)? What would you do if someone was always ordering you about? Would you resist in any way you could? If you were punished for this, would you dig in your heels and resist more?

The good thing about what you are experiencing is that your child's resistance shows he still has enough self-esteem to care more (at a subconscious pressure about drugs, sex, and other serious issues. (Many adults wish they could learn to say no comfortably, especially when asked to serve on yet another committee or help with yet another fund-raiser.)

Give your children an opportunity to practice saying no in acceptable ways. Ask your child, "Do you want more milk?" "No," especially with a "thank you" attached, is a fine answer. Model saying no in a calm way—not as an invitation to battle.

Listening Is a Two-Way Street

IF CHILDREN COULD verbalize their subconscious feelings, they might ask, "Why don't adults listen to me?" Could it be that asking why children don't listen is the wrong question? When adults ask, "How can I do a better job of listening to my children?" they will find ways to listen and to invite listening. Children will listen to you when they feel listened to!

level) about his developmental process than avoiding punishment. And you are learning why punishment does not motivate a child who is discouraged and displays his discouragement through power struggles. Punishment only deepens the discouragement and increases the power struggles.

To reverse this cycle of discouragement (yours and his), show him what listening is really like. Start by getting into his world to see things from his perspective. The best way to encourage and to invite cooperation is to drop all punitive methods and use respectful methods. In addition to the suggestions above, try creating a plan together where toys not picked up go on a high shelf. Then all you need to say is, "Do you want to pick up your toys, or do you want me to?" If he refuses, follow through by picking up his toys. These can be kept in a box on a high shelf for a day; then he can be invited to try again. If you are kind (avoiding lectures) and firm (acting decisively), it won't take him long to learn that cooperating pays off because you say what you mean and mean what you say.

10

Personality
Yours and Theirs

It is bedtime at the Jasper house. Bedtime routines are too much bother for Mrs. Jasper; she would rather wait until the children fall asleep on the floor and carry them to bed than create stress for herself by arguing. She prefers avoiding emotional pain and hassles in life, and she thinks that letting her children "do their own thing" is one way to keep things comfortable.

Mr. Jasper, however, does not agree. He believes it is very important for the children to have a schedule, and he is willing to take responsibility for it. He walks the children through every step of their routine, making sure they are in their pajamas, have their teeth thoroughly brushed, and are in bed by 7:30 P.M. He believes that being in control of himself, of situations, or of others is a way to avoid humiliation and criticism.

Mrs. Jasper avoids situations that she believes will take her out of her comfort zone. We call this a comfort lifestyle priority. Mr. Jasper controls situations to avoid criticism and humiliation. His lifestyle priority is called control. The Jaspers act differently in situations that appear potentially stressful to them.

What do we mean by lifestyle priority? Why were such different people attracted to each other? How will their lifestyle priorities affect their parenting and their relationship?

Before answering these questions, let's peek into the Sanchez home and look at two more lifestyle priorities.

It's bedtime here, too. Mrs. Sanchez believes it is good for children to be in bed on time and tries to convince her children by lecturing them about their responsi-

bility to do what is "right." She is constantly frustrated that the children find her lectures meaningless. They hardly listen while she talks. What an insult! Meaninglessness is the one thing in life she wants to avoid, and she believes doing things "right" is one way to make life meaningful.

Mr. Sanchez has a very different approach. He just wants his children to be happy and bedtime to be easy. To make things pleasant, he tries "loving" his children into bed. He plays games with them to get them into their pajamas and to brush their teeth. He reads them stories; he fetches glass after glass of water and returns for endless "last" hugs. He feels he can win their love and avoid rejection by making bedtime fun and by doing what he thinks will please the children.

Mrs. Sanchez has a significance lifestyle priority. Mr. Sanchez has a pleasing lifestyle priority. They, too, are very different.

> What a challenge it can be to unravel all the actions and interactions of family members with very different personalities, beliefs, and private logic.

What attracted these couples to each other? What problems are they having now that the honeymoon is over? How will their lifestyle priorities affect their parenting styles and influence the personality development of their children? What a challenge it can be to unravel all the actions and interactions of family members with very different personalities, beliefs, and private logic.

These are extreme examples. Few parents with a comfort lifestyle priority actually wait for their children to fall asleep on the floor (although one of us admits that she did that before she learned effective parenting skills). However, most parents can recognize a few of their tendencies in these examples, which illustrate the concept of lifestyle priorities.

Lifestyle Priorities

SO FAR, WE'VE spent a great deal of time looking at how children grow and develop and at the influences that shape their behavior. In this chapter we will focus on parents' behaviors, originally defined by a theory called "impasse/priority" developed by Israeli psychologist Nira Kefir, which we have refined as "lifestyle priorities." It can be helpful for parents and teachers to know how their priority choices influence their parenting and teaching styles—and thus, the lifestyle choices of their children.

We will expand on the assets and liabilities of each style and discuss effects they might have on children. With understanding, we can learn to build on the assets and avoid getting hooked into the liabilities of our style (at least some of the time). But the first step, as always, is to understand.

What Are Lifestyle Priorities?

ADULTS HAVE ACCUMULATED a wealth of subconscious decisions from childhood that combine to form their lifestyle priorities. Lifestyle priorities do not describe "who you are." They do define the accumulated decisions you have made throughout your life that affect the way you choose to behave in certain circumstances. The information in this chapter will help you identify your primary priority (what you may do when stressed) and your secondary priority (your usual method of operation when not under stress).

We have already identified the four lifestyle priorities: comfort, control, pleasing, and superiority (see Table 10.1). Each priority has both assets and liabilities. Most people want to claim the assets of each priority and reject the liabilities. For example, most people like to have some control of their life and dislike humiliation and criticism. However, humiliation and criticism are more difficult for a person with the control lifestyle priority to endure than they are for people with the other priorities. A person with a control lifestyle priority believes that the best way to avoid humiliation is to maintain control. Remember, this is a personal belief, not necessarily reality. Another person may laugh at a situation that would seem humiliating to someone with a control priority.

Many people want significance (in the form of excellence) and would be uncomfortable with meaninglessness and unimportance. However, meaninglessness and unimportance are to be avoided at all costs for a person with the significance priority.

Just about everyone wants comfort in his or her life and wants to avoid emotional and physical pain and stress. However, trying to avoid pain and stress can be the concern that motivates the behavior of a person with the comfort priority. People with other priorities may have just as much difficulty with pain and stress, but they don't base their actions on trying to avoid them.

TABLE 10.1 Lifestyle Priorities

Priority	Worst Fear	Believes the Way to Avoid the Worst Fear Is to:	Assets	Liabilities	Unknowingly Invites from Others	Creates Then Complains About
Comfort	Emotional and physical pain and stress; expectations from others; being cornered by others	Seek comfort; ask for special service; make others comfortable; avoid confrontation; choose the easiest way	Easygoing; few demands; minds own business; peacemaker; mellow; empathetic; predictable	Doesn't develop talents; limits productivity; avoids personal growth	Annoyance; irritation; boredom; impatience	Diminished productivity; impatience; lack of personal growth
Control	Humiliation; criticism; the unexpected	Control self and/or others and/or situation	Leadership; organized; productive; persistent; assertive; follows rules	Rigid; doesn't develop creativity, spontaneity, or social closeness	Rebellion; resistance; challenge; frustration	Lack of friends and closeness; feeling uptight
Pleasing	Rejection; abandonment; hassles	Please others; active—demand approval; passive—evoke pity	Friendly; considerate; compromises; nonaggressive; volunteers	Doesn't check with others about what pleases them; doesn't take care of self	Pleasure at first and then demands for approval and reciprocation	Lack of respect for self and others; resentment
Significance	Meaninglessness; unimportance	Do more; be better than others; be right; be more useful; be more competent	Knowledgeable; idealistic; persistent; social interest; gets things done	Workaholic; overburdened; overresponsible; overinvolved	Feelings of inadequacy and guilt; "How can I measure up?"; lying to avoid judgments	Being overwhelmed; lack of time; "I have to do everything"

Few people enjoy rejection and being left out. However, trying to avoid rejection is a primary theme and the basis for behavior when the person with the pleasing lifestyle priority feels stressed.

An interesting twist is that the behavior motivated by each priority often creates the opposite of what the individual intends. For example, the pleasing person may fail to please someone because he forgot to check out what the other person actually finds pleasing. He also creates conflicts by trying to avoid them. The comfort person may create more stress by avoiding steps that seem uncomfortable at the time but could create greater comfort in the future. Control people often invite criticism and humiliation when they attempt to control their feelings or the feelings of others, and significance people may create meaninglessness by trying too hard and getting caught up in "busy work." Awareness and humor can help all of us get beyond our self-defeating beliefs and behaviors.

Discovering Your Primary Priority

In chapter 19 we discuss how children make subconscious decisions that become beliefs and how those beliefs motivate behavior. Personality priorities are developed when children perceive their world, make decisions about it, and come to some basic conclusions that include a "therefore, I must . . ." belief. The following examples illustrate the different decisions children might make based on the same circumstances.

- "I'm little; others are big. Therefore, I must get others to take care of me." (Comfort)

- "I'm little; others are big. Therefore, I must maintain control of myself and situations so I don't feel humiliated." (Control)

- "I'm little; others are big. Therefore, I must please others so I will be loved." (Pleasing)

- "I'm little; others are big. Therefore, I must try harder to catch up, and do even better." (Significance)

These thought patterns represent different decisions—and lifestyle priorities—that many different circumstances may invite from individuals. Children are in the process of making such decisions throughout the early years of their lives. The results of those decisions lie in the future. Adults have already made these decisions long ago—they just do not consciously recall having done so. Because such decisions form our beliefs about the world, we as adults act upon them as though they must be true axioms of life.

If you are still having trouble deciding which lifestyle priority is yours, choose the statement that fits you best:

- "I feel best about myself when I and those around me are comfortable. I feel worst about myself when there is tension, pain, and stress." (Comfort)

- "I feel best about myself when things are orderly and organized and I am in control of myself and the situation. I feel worst about myself when I feel embarrassed and humiliated or criticized about something I think I should have known or done." (Control)

- "I feel best about myself when I can please other people and avoid conflicts so that life is fun, not difficult. I feel worst about myself when I feel rejected, left out, or overwhelmed by the difficulties of situations." (Pleasing)

- "I feel best about myself when I am the best, when I'm number one, or when I'm achieving. I feel worst about myself when I feel worthless, meaningless, and stupid." (Significance)

The statement that is truest of you in times of stress is your primary priority. "In times of stress" is an important factor in understanding lifestyle priorities. When not under stress, we are not worried about humiliation, rejection, meaninglessness, or pain. During peaceful times in our lives, we are usually not hooked into old childhood decisions, patterns of behavior, and beliefs. It is only when we perceive stress or feel threatened in some way that we are catapulted into priority lifestyle behaviors.

We say "perceived" stress, because that is what stress is. What is stressful to one person may not be stressful to another—only our thinking makes it so. You can find more information on this important concept in Jane Nelsen's *Understanding: Eliminating Stress and Finding Serenity in Life and Relationships* (Prima Publishing, 1997).

Discovering Your Secondary Priority

You may say, "Well, I certainly want to avoid humiliation and embarrassment, but I don't think I try to control others or situations. In fact, I usually try very hard to please others." If that is the case, you have just identified your secondary priority. This means that your usual method of operation, or "style," is pleasing. This is your secondary priority because it is what you usually do when you are feeling secure. It is only when you feel insecure or pressured that you may fall back into your "must have" beliefs. Then you may give up pleasing and use your control methods to avoid perceived humiliation.

Many of us choose one priority as our method of operation (or secondary priority), which we use on a daily basis when we feel secure. When we feel stressed or insecure, we tend to fall back on our primary priority.

All the priorities may serve as operating priorities to be chosen at various times under various conditions (for example, when we're happy and content as opposed to when we're frustrated and stressed). In other words, under different conditions and in different situations we will use behaviors from different priorities, but it is always for the purpose of maintaining our "must have" priority. For example, a control priority person may please others to obtain control, strive for excellence to obtain control, or make people or situations comfortable to obtain control.

> When we understand the possible liabilities of our lifestyle priority, we can develop strategies to overcome them.

Your priority identifies what you need in order to think well of yourself and maintain your self-esteem, and what you need to avoid feeling insignificant. Remember, all of us need to feel a sense of significance and belonging; beginning early in our childhood, we find many different ways to obtain it.

Lifestyle Priorities and Parenting (and Caregiving)

THE MANY ASSETS and liabilities of each priority affect how you behave as a parent. It is not our purpose to create stereotypes, but we have found that increased understanding and awareness help us make informed choices instead of being blind victims to perceptions we had and decisions we made as children then subsequently "forgot." When we understand the possible liabilities of our lifestyle priority, we can develop strategies to overcome them. We can take more responsibility for what we create with our choices and behavior instead of acting like victims. We can also enhance our assets with more confidence and purpose through increased awareness.

Comfort

ON THE ASSET side, comfort priority adults may model for children the benefits of being easygoing, diplomatic, and predictable. Their children may truly learn to enjoy simple pleasures in life and take time to "smell the roses." Positive Discipline skills can help these adults understand their tendency to be too permissive with their children because it seems easier at the time. Comfort-seeking adults often choose a laissez-faire, permissive style, which may create a tendency toward "spoiled brattiness." Comfort priority adults can become more effective when they get their children involved in creating routines, setting goals, and solving problems together.

Mrs. Carter's priority is comfort. She often left too many decisions to her children and was too quick to give in to their demands because it seemed "easier." But oddly enough, taking the easy way out didn't always make life easier. She began to suffer a great deal of stress and discomfort (as did her children) because the only way they knew to get along was through emotional tyranny (whining or throwing tantrums until their mom gave in). Instead of making them comfortable, Mrs. Carter had unwittingly created a family atmosphere of great tension.

Mrs. Carter was excited to learn how understanding priorities could help her emphasize her assets instead of her liabilities. She started taking time to teach her children life skills and providing opportunities for them to practice what they were learning. She gave them allowances, discussed saving and spending, and then allowed them to experience the consequences of their choices.

When the children made demands, she put their requests on the family meeting agenda to be discussed later. During the family meetings, she invited discussion and brainstorming on various ways the children could get what they wanted through their own efforts. They created morning and bedtime routines, decided on plans to accomplish chores, and planned simple family outings.

Mrs. Carter learned that she needed to make many decisions, such as choosing a suitable preschool, determining safety issues, and setting clear and consistent boundaries and expectations for behavior, herself. It was not appropriate to ask her children whether it was okay with them if she took the freeway instead of the slower route home, whether they wanted baths at night, or whether she could offer to baby-sit their cousin over the weekend. Such decisions were her responsibility. Once she quit burdening them with such choices, the children felt far more secure.

Clear expectations give children a feeling of safety, whereas Mrs. Carter's previous behavior invited anxiety, the opposite of the comfort she sought.

Mrs. Carter was grateful to realize that she was more comfortable, there was less tension in the home, and the children were more comfortable, having learned skills to get their needs met.

No one wanted their child to be in Miss Sheila's class at the child care center. She constantly looked exhausted, and no wonder—the toddlers in her class didn't do anything for themselves. She helped them eat; she put on, then buttoned everyone's coat carefully. She thought no one could put shoes on properly either, and every child seemed to constantly have a runny nose and no clue how to wipe it himself. If children objected to the snack that was served, Sheila would hurriedly offer several other items to prevent tantrums (she lived in terror of tantrums).

Learning about her comfort priority gave Sheila insight, and she realized that her unwillingness to deal with conflict was running her life. Sheila decided that she needed to pay some attention to her own comfort. When a child would demand yet another story or a different color Play-Doh, she learned to tell him that was all for now. She also instituted a training plan so that within a month all of the children had learned how to put on their own coats and shoes. What a relief it was not to be trying to do it all! Sheila found the children in her class began to show more and more interest in learning to do things on their own. And she went home with enough energy to go out to a movie in the evening. Not surprisingly, parents began to request Miss Sheila as their child's teacher.

Control

ON THE ASSET side, control priority parents and teachers may be very good at helping their children learn organization skills, leadership skills, productive persistence, assertiveness, and respect for law and order. Positive Discipline parenting skills can help parents with a control priority curb their tendency to be too rigid and controlling of their children. Excessive control invites rebellion or resistance, instead of encouraging children to learn the skills these parents want to teach. Control priority adults may be more effective if they make an effort to recognize their need for excessive control and practice the skills of letting go, offering choices, asking "what" and "how" questions, and of getting their children more involved in decision making.

Mrs. Jones's lifestyle priority is control. She used to tell her children what to do, how to do it, and when to do it, and she certainly didn't allow any "back talk" from them. She truly believed that this was what responsible parents were supposed to do. Her controlling behavior was actually counterproductive to the goal of helping her children learn self-discipline, responsibility, cooperation, and problem-solving skills. Two of her three children were in constant rebellion, doing as little as they could get away with and always testing the limits until they were punished. This made Mrs. Jones feel "out of control," the very thing she was trying to avoid. She was in a perpetual power struggle with these two children.

Her other child was becoming a "pleaser." He tried to live up to his mother's expectations and to gain her approval by pleasing her. However, instead of developing the life skills he needed to be a happy, successful citizen of the world, he was losing a sense of what pleased him and lived with the fear that he would never be able to make people happy enough. He was becoming an approval junkie.

Learning about priorities helped Mrs. Jones emphasize her assets instead of her liabilities. She started using family meetings with her children to involve them in solving problems. She learned to risk asking "what" and "how" questions to help both herself and her children discover the consequences of their decisions and to learn from their mistakes in an atmosphere of unconditional love. She stopped needing to be in charge of everything and invited suggestions and discussions about solving problems. She was grateful when she realized that as she let go of her need to be in control, she and the children all felt more in control.

Mrs. Jones also taught in a preschool. Her control style was sorely tested by the three- and four-year-olds in her classroom. Potty accidents, tears over a parent not waving good-bye, or the onset of an ear infection could sabotage her carefully orchestrated lesson plans. Mrs. Jones focused on the learning and activity portion of her teaching and felt annoyed when the children in her group forced her to deviate from her plan.

When Mrs. Jones began to understand her control priority, she realized that she found nurturing and dealing with the physical needs and limitations of the children the most challenging part of her job. She began to shift her focus by getting into the children's world more effectively. When she did this, she was able to feel compassion for the child with the spilled milk rather than impatience and a desire to take over. She began to see that learning life skills was the most important task of the children in her care. She became less concerned about completing the activities or games that she had prepared and more willing to let the children's needs set the pace for the day.

Pleasing

ON THE ASSET side, pleasing priority parents and teachers may be very good at helping their children learn friendly, considerate, nonaggressive behavior. They are often peacemakers because of their desire to make everyone happy. They are good at compromising and often volunteer to help others. They are champions of the underdog. Unfortunately, excessive pleasing may invite resentment and depression when pleasing adults work too hard to please children or partners at their own expense (and when others don't return the courtesy). And recipients of the pleasing may feel resentful because of the expectations placed on them that they should appreciate what is done and are now expected to return the courtesy. Positive Discipline skills can help these adults curb their tendency to go overboard in trying to make everyone happy.

Pleasing priority parents can be more effective when they stop focusing exclusively on others' needs and invite joint problem solving. They need to have faith in their children's ability to please themselves and teach them the skills of emotional honesty. Both adult and child will benefit from learning to express what they think, feel, and want without expecting anyone else to think the same, to feel the same, or to give them what they want—easily said, but not so easily done! Learning to value everyone's needs—including their own—is crucial to fostering mutual respect.

Mr. Smith's lifestyle priority is pleasing. He expended huge amounts of energy and effort trying to make his children be nice to each other, the neighbors, their grandparents, the members of their church, and their teachers. He was more concerned with how they treated others than with helping them with their own feelings. At other times he would give them too much special service when they whined or cried. For example, he would try to please them when they demanded snacks or more stories before bedtime. Then he would get angry when the snacks and stories didn't satisfy them enough to make them go to bed cheerfully. All too often, everyone went to bed upset. No one was pleased!

TABLE 10.2   How Lifestyle Priorities May Influence Parenting and Caregiving

PRIORITY	POSSIBLE PARENTING ASSETS	POSSIBLE PARENTING LIABILITIES	MAY NEED TO PRACTICE
COMFORT	Models for children the benefits of being easy-going, diplomatic, predictable, and enjoying simple pleasures	Permissiveness, which may invite children to be spoiled and demanding. More interest in comfort than in the "needs of the situation"	Creating routines; setting goals; solving problems together; teaching life skills; allowing children to experience the natural consequences of their choices; family meetings
CONTROL	May teach children organizational skills, leadership skills, productive persistence, assertiveness, respect for law and order, time management skills	Rigid; controlling. May invite rebellion and resistance or unhealthy pleasing	Letting go; offering choices; asking what and how questions; involving children in decisions; family meetings
PLEASING	May help children learn to be friendly, considerate and non-aggressive, peacemakers, compromisers, volunteers, and champions of the underdog	Doormats, keep score (now you owe me). May invite resentment, depression, or revenge	Having faith in children to solve their own problems; joint problem solving; emotional honesty; learn to give and take; family meetings
SIGNIFICANCE	Models success and achievement; teaches children to assess quality and motivates to excellence	Lecture, preach, expect too much; invite feelings of inadequacy and failure to "measure up"; see things in terms of right and wrong instead of possibilities	Letting go of need to be right; getting into child's world and supporting needs and goals; unconditional love; enjoying the process and developing a sense of humor; holding family meetings where all ideas are valued

Adapted from *Positive Discipline for Preschoolers Facilitator's Guide* by Jane Nelsen, Cheryl Erwin, and Roslyn Duffy (available from Empowering People Books, Tapes, and Videos: 1-800-456-7770).

It was also important to Mr. Smith that his children like him and approve of him as their father. It seemed only logical to him that his children would also want to please him. He couldn't understand it when his children complained that he didn't care about their feelings. It was a vicious circle; he was sure they didn't care about his feelings, even after "all he did for them."

Mr. Smith wasn't sure whether or not he believed the information about lifestyle priorities. But when he started using family meetings with his children to involve them in joint problem solving, he couldn't help but notice the changed atmosphere in his family. Mr. Smith and his children learned to use emotional honesty to express their feelings. They discussed the idea of "separate realities" and the fact that people perceive situations in different ways (none of which are necessarily wrong), that different things please different people, and that it is respectful to ask instead of to assume.

He discovered that it was important to take his own needs into consideration, as well as the needs of the situation. He learned to respond to his children's bedtime demands by kindly and firmly saying, "It is bedtime now." At first he had to repeat that simple statement several times. However, once his children learned he meant what he said, they gave up trying to manipulate him.

Mr. Smith eventually realized that when he tried to please his children without first discovering what pleased them, he wasn't really pleasing anyone. This family began listening to each other, asking for what they wanted, and being honest about whether or not they would grant each other's wishes. When Mr. Smith learned about priorities and Positive Discipline parenting skills, his children began to enjoy being his children and Mr. Smith began to truly enjoy being a parent. Everyone was pleased—at least, most of the time.

Marnie also had a pleasing priority. She taught a group of five-year-olds in the Sunday school at her church. It was very important to her that the children learn how to behave correctly. She approached children in conflict by insisting that they apologize to one another. When the children forgot to say please or thank you, Marnie rushed in to supply the correct words for them. Yet somehow the children in her class weren't "getting it." There were more and more fights, and rudeness was rampant. When the pastor came to visit her class, Marnie was mortified when some of the children forgot to call him Sir.

When Marnie learned about priorities, she also realized how much time she spent worrying about others' opinions and how little time she spent actually enjoying herself. She began to allow herself to smile at the children's attempts at good manners and to feel encouraged by their small successes. She also started to ask the children what they were fighting about rather than insisting they offer each other insincere apologies. When they began to seek solutions together, much to her surprise Marnie found that the children were willing to apologize when they hurt another child—when an apology was their idea. The atmosphere in the classroom became much more pleasant and encouraging for everyone.

Significance

SIGNIFICANCE PRIORITY PARENTS and teachers may be very good at modeling success and achievement. They often are able to judge and encourage quality and seem to have a knack for "motivating to excellence." Their children, however, sometimes see this as "badgering to perfection" and feel inadequate to meet the high expectations of their parents or teachers.

Positive Discipline skills can help these adults curb their tendency to expect too much from children. Excessive significance often invites feelings of inadequacy instead of the desire for achievement these adults want to inspire. Significance priority adults will be more effective if they make an effort to let go of their need for things to be "right" and "best" (according to their own standards, of course) and practice the skills of getting into their children's worlds to discover what is important to them, always making sure the message of unconditional love gets through.

They can also learn to model and teach that mistakes are wonderful opportunities to learn, and listen to and accept their children's ideas for solving problems. Sometimes significance adults are so focused on the final goal that they completely miss the joy of the process.

Mr. Lyndol's priority is significance. He used to tell his children about all his wonderful accom-plishments, as well as what he expected from them. He believed this would inspire and motivate them to follow in his footsteps, and he invested much of his self-worth in the expectation that they would surpass him.

This dad's significance personality was actually counterproductive to the goal of helping his children achieve excellence. One of his children became a trouble-maker at his preschool. (If he couldn't be the best of the best and live up to his dad's expectations, he could at least be the best of the worst.) This child also had developed a significance priority, but was exercising it in opposition to his dad. His other child became a perfectionist who couldn't stand to lose, and he couldn't relax and enjoy his accomplishments even when he won because he was constantly afraid of the embarrassment and humiliation of failure.

Mr. Lyndol was motivated to emphasize the assets of his significance priority instead of his liabilities and to be the sort of father he'd always intended. He and his family worked to cultivate a sense of humor when discussing mistakes and began projects they could work on together. Sometimes they would even risk making mistakes together, just to reassure themselves that it was okay. He learned to use family meetings to improve communication with his children. They worked at enjoying and cooperating on the process and not just emphasizing the excellence of the finished product.

Mr. Lyndol stopped lecturing and invited discussions about differences of opinions. He and his children decided to work on a community service project, which they planned together. Mr. Lyndol discovered that he was better able to communicate with his children and felt encouraged by what he was learning from and with them. The children began to exhibit signs that they, too, were encouraged: they were enthusiastic and willingly cooperated both at home and at preschool.

Mr. Lyndol also volunteered as a coach for a children's soccer team. At first, he had wanted only children who had strong skills and who wanted to practice hard; he especially wanted children who wanted to win. Mr. Lyndol's new insights helped him to see that all of the children had potential if he would only encourage them. He began to work with these children, to hone their kicking and running and passing. He taught them that it was more important to do their best than to win a game—a lesson he was learning, too.

They won many games (and lost a few), but Mr. Lyndol found his greatest pleasure in the attitude his team displayed. They worked together and enjoyed the work. In sports, a significance priority proved to be an asset. Mr. Lyndol used his drive for excellence to help a group of children become highly motivated to do their best. He worked to discover ways to encourage and include each member of his team.

Lifestyle Priorities in Adult Relationships

WE HAVE DISCUSSED what happens when parents and teachers learn about priority styles and Positive Discipline parenting skills. An understanding of priority styles coupled with Positive Discipline parenting skills can also help couples live together with fewer conflicts. Remember the two couples we introduced in the beginning of this chapter? As Alfred Adler often said, "Opposites attract, but they have difficulty living together." Each is attracted to the other for possessing the assets he or she lacks. But sometimes what seemed cute and adorable at first becomes downright irritating after marriage. Take the case of Mr. and Mrs. Johnson.

David and Suzanne Johnson met on the ski slopes. There was an immediate attraction between the two, and a relationship quickly developed. Suzanne was attracted to David because he was relaxed, easygoing, and really comfortable to be around. Even when he skied, he seemed to glide easily down the mountain.

For his part, David was attracted to Suzanne because she was bright, attractive, articulate, creative—one of the most successful and talented women he had ever met. They had a lot in common. And they both loved to ski. Little did they realize how the ups and downs of the ski slope would become a metaphor for their relationship and for their parenting styles when their first child arrived.

An understanding of priority styles coupled with Positive Discipline parenting skills can also help couples live together with fewer conflicts.

David's priority was comfort, while Suzanne's priority was significance. We are often attracted to someone who seems to have what we believe we lack. David never stood in the way of Suzanne's many activities; in fact, he encouraged her accomplishments. After all, her ambition and drive made life easy for him. David's easy charm and relaxed manner were a perfect foil for Suzanne's lofty goals and excessive energy.

Then their first baby arrived. Before long (and with absolutely no knowledge of lifestyle priorities), he seemed to have an uncanny ability to cause Dad discomfort and to make Mom feel less than significant. He also had an ability to get Mom and Dad arguing about parenting skills and styles, too. Dad was too easy, Mom too hard. Or at least, that's what David and Suzanne had to say about each other.

When a kind soul eventually explained lifestyle priorities to them, things began to turn around for David and Suzanne. They attended a parenting class together and made an effort to parent their youngster as a team. They focused on appreciating the attractive aspects of their priorities (which had brought them together in the first place). They agreed that each of them would work on his or her own liabilities and that each would offer support and understanding rather than criticism. They were especially delighted to find that their new Positive Discipline parenting skills fit both their styles and helped them achieve what they most wanted to create: a happy family.

Growth happens when we learn to turn our liabilities into assets. As we gain insight and awareness, growth can be exciting and rewarding. Understanding our own priority and how it influences our relationships with our children can help us, with time and patience, learn to be the best parents—and the best people—we can be.

PART THREE

Discipline (Not Punishment) Designed to Empower and Teach Life Skills

Everyone is familiar with the old adage "spare the rod, spoil the child." Many people truly believe that if everyone raised their children by the "rod" the world would be a better place. But would it?

Understanding your child's unique temperament, development, and special characteristics will help you avoid many parenting (and teaching) struggles. Still, children (like their parents and teachers) are all too human and misbehavior is inevitable. What then? Does the rod—good old-fashioned punishment—work? If it doesn't, what does?

More and more parents are reporting that the more often and more severely they punish their children, the worse those children seem to behave. As you will learn in the chapters ahead, punishment only seems to "work" for the moment. When we explore what children are really feeling, thinking, and deciding when they are spanked, slapped, grounded, lectured, or shamed, we have to question the truth of our old beliefs.

Punishment creates discouraged children. And as you will see, discouraged children misbehave. The good news is that Positive Discipline tools and skills will help you decide on realistic limits, teach your children to choose their behavior wisely, and follow through with dignity when you must. The end result is children who feel encouraged, who have learned to weigh the results of their choices, who possess the skills to be successful and responsible, and who can trust that the adults in their lives mean what they say.

Of course, nothing works all the time for all children and all adults. But we're confident that as you learn more about Positive Discipline in chapters 11 through 15, you and your active, curious preschooler will be able to work together to help everyone do his best.

11

"I've Tried Everything . . . or Have I?"

Discipline Versus Punishment

EXPERTS ON HUMAN development tell us that at no time in the human life span do we have more physical energy than when we're three years old. And all too many parents of toddlers and preschoolers will swear that most of that inexhaustible supply of energy is used for "defying" adults. Listen to some frustrated, frazzled parents:

Q. *I have tried everything when it comes to discipline, but I am getting absolutely nowhere! I have a three-and-a-half-year-old daughter and a one-year-old son. My daughter is very demanding and very stubborn. Can anyone help me?*

Q. *What do I do if nothing works? I have tried time-out, taking away a toy or television, and spanking—and none of it works. My four-year-old is way out of control. What do I do?*

Q. *I have a class of fifteen four-year-olds. Two of them fight all the time, but I can't get them to play with anyone else. I put them in time-out, threaten to take away recess if they play together, and this morning I started yelling when one of them tore up the other's drawing. I don't know where to turn. These two won't listen to anything I say. I feel like a total failure!*

A. As we've already learned, when parents and teachers say they've tried "everything," they usually mean they've tried every punishment they can think of. They yell and lecture, they spank and slap hands, they take away toys and privileges, and they plop children in a punitive time-out to "think about what they did." If we're truly honest, most of us will admit that in our more desperate and vulnerable moments, we've tried these things (or thought long-ingly of them) too. And these adults are right: punishments don't work. They may *seem* effective at the moment, but they never seem to change behavior permanently. Punishments only seem to make a challenging situation worse, inviting both adults and children to plunge headfirst into one power struggle after another.

The reason punitive solutions don't work is that they are based on the premise that people will only improve or do better after they are made to feel worse—that children (and adults) can only learn if they experience pain, shame, or some sort of humiliation. Positive Discipline is based on a different premise: that children (and adults) do better when they feel better. For this rea-son, all Positive Discipline methods are nonpunitive. When children experi-ence a safe environment (instead of punishment), they are able to learn important life skills that will serve them throughout their lives. In truth, learn-ing to respond to situations with an eye to the big picture holds the key to an-swering these adults' desperate pleas for help.

Why Discipline Becomes the Big Issue

DISCIPLINE EMERGES AS *the* big issue during the preschool years. The tiny baby who cooed at us, wiggled her toes for entertainment, and thought the sun rose when we appeared in the room has disappeared. A small but pow-erful person around two feet tall with a determined set to her chin, who can voice demands and opinions (often loudly) and sprint in the opposite direc-tion from us (both literally and figuratively), marched into our lives sometime around the age of two, give or take a few months. And we'd better learn how to work with her, because she's going to be here for a while!

It is important to remember that young children come with a variety of temperaments. Some are cooperative and easygoing by nature, while others seem to thrive on tension and opposition. Temperaments and developmental timetables vary widely. How parents and teachers respond to a child's behavior has a great deal to do with the choices a child will make as she grows up.

Perhaps you mastered the art of distraction with your toddler, and until now it has served you well. It probably came as a real surprise to you, just as it did to Annie's mom, when things changed.

One day, while touring the marine life exhibit at the local aquarium, Annie wanted to stay longer watching the sea otters when her mom said it was time to leave. In the past, Mom had found that reminding her of the yummy picnic lunch the two of them would share would distract Annie from whatever had captured her fancy. All Mom had to do was remind Annie of the fresh strawberries she'd helped pack into her lunch box and Annie would become so busy asking if she could have all the strawberries that she would hardly notice as they left the aquarium. Alas, that day distraction did not work. When it was time to leave, Annie clutched a fence post as if she were manacled to it. The strawberries were scorned: Annie wanted to watch the otters and was fully prepared to make a battle of it. How could Mom get her to the car?

Another parent remembers the "good old days" with her daughter:

Q. *My three-year-old daughter used to be very sweet and do what she was told. But lately, when she doesn't get her way, she becomes terrible. She whines, cries, and hits, especially if she is given a time-out. I usually end up carrying her to the corner and holding her there for her time-out. I find myself yelling at her, and I know that is not effective either. Is there another method for discipline that would work for her? She does like rewards, but she expects them all the time. Any suggestions?*

A. No wonder this parent is frustrated; it must feel like she's fighting a losing battle. And for good reason—unfortunately, she is! Over and over we hear the frustration of parents who complain that the punitive methods they are using aren't working, but they don't know what else to do. It is almost as though they can't see beyond the possibilities of punishment. Isn't there

> Positive Discipline is based on a different premise: that children (and adults) do better when they feel better. For this reason, all Positive Discipline methods are nonpunitive. When children experience a safe environment (instead of punishment), they are able to learn important life skills that will serve them throughout their lives.

something that works, something that encourages cooperation, responsibility, and closeness? There is—if we're willing to look at parenting and teaching preschoolers as a long-range activity and set aside, for the moment, our insistence on punishing defiant little ones.

Three-year-olds are active, curious, often strong-willed little people with a tremendous amount of physical energy. Their normal development "programs" them to want initiative and independence. When adults issue commands, try to control the child's behavior, and react to wrong choices with punishment or yelling, they set up one power struggle after another. And once one enters a power struggle with a preschooler, the battle is already lost.

The Old Toolbox

MOST PARENTS BRING to the task of raising young children the same box of parenting tools they inherited from their own parents. Those tools typically include spanking, rewards or punishment, and possibly a little modern-day time-out (a code word usually meaning to go someplace and think about what you did—and to suffer). Let's not forget those old favorites: yelling, nagging, and threatening. All of these tools share the same underlying goal. That goal is to "make this child obey me!"

Many adults believe that children will "obey" if they suffer for "bad" behavior and get treats for "good" behavior. Punishments and rewards, this sort of thinking goes, help children choose so-called good behavior over bad. This thinking might work with dogs, who live their lives in adoration of or submission to their owners; but people, especially the kind of people we want our children to become, are different than dogs. And it's interesting to note that many highly respected professional dog trainers reject punishments and rewards in favor of more effective methods. If there's a better way for dogs, shouldn't there be a better way for our children?

Changing Perspective

IT IS INTERESTING to ask parents and teachers what qualities they want the children in their care to acquire. When they've considered the question thoughtfully, adults often come up with terms like "compassionate," "creative," "responsible," and "able to think for themselves." Doesn't it make sense that children will develop these traits when treated in ways that invite them to do so? Demanding obedience does not invite thinking. Requiring unquestioning compliance will not foster creativity. Responding to misbehavior with anger, threats, and violence fails to teach much of anything, other than a desire to fight back or avoid detection. It may come as something of a surprise to the parent of an opinionated young child that saying no may serve a useful purpose. How do we want our older children to respond when a peer suggests that they try the latest drug?

Take a moment to think about your child or the children in your care. Who do you want them to be as adults? What traits do you believe are important? Ask your partner or your coworkers, and write down your ideas. Then post the list where you will see it frequently. When a child challenges you (and he will), consider your list before you respond. Will a time-out, a spanking, or angry words create the qualities you believe are important?

Once we begin to identify the traits we most want to nurture in our children, a shift in thinking becomes possible. Ask yourself, "What is it that I really want for this child?" "What am I doing to encourage the growth of self-reliance, courage, or feelings of capability?" Then ask yourself one more question: "Is what I am doing *discouraging* the development of those same traits?" It may surprise you to realize how differently you can respond to challenging behavior when you've shifted your focus in this way.

What Do You Remember?

WE OFTEN ASK parents and caregivers what they recall from their own childhood and invite them to share moments that live in their memories. The room usually becomes quiet and smiles appear. Stories are shared. One person recalls evenings spent throwing a ball with Dad on the front lawn. Another remembers family outings for ice cream cones. Another tells about a favorite cake a grandmother made or a special dish an aunt fixed on holidays, or of climbing a particular tree in a familiar front yard.

Then we ask what memories their own children or the children in their centers might have when they become adults. The room becomes still. What will our children remember most?

Each day we spend with a young child in the early years becomes part of that child. We are making those memories. We are shaping the beliefs and attitudes that our children will carry into their adult lives, beliefs that guide every decision they will make. What a wonderful opportunity parents and caregivers have to share the lives of young children. It is also an awesome responsibility.

Do we want to spend these precious moments marching children into time-out corners? Wouldn't we rather help them learn life skills, teach them to solve problems and to handle frustration in healthy ways? Discipline, when viewed from the perspective of time, becomes not a burden but an incredible opportunity. Instead of trying to make children mind, we can choose to see discipline for what it truly is: the privilege of teaching and shaping young hearts and minds. We are the memory makers whose voices will resonate in our children's hearts for the rest of their lives. And we only get one opportunity: childhood happens only once.

When you feel you have "tried everything," take a moment to ask yourself some questions.

- What do I want this child to learn from this experience?
- What is he really learning from what I'm doing?
- How does this child's temperament affect the situation?
- How appropriate is this behavior for a child of this age? Does it reflect his developmental needs?
- What is this child's behavior telling me? Is he discouraged, and if so, what role has he taken on in our family or classroom: the attention seeker, the controller, or the weak one, or is he lashing out to hurt others?

What, Me Change?

THE FIRST NIGHT of any parenting class inevitably includes one or more parents saying they came to class to learn how to make their child behave. Frankly, none of us can make another person do anything. Think for a moment: can you truly control another person's thoughts, feelings, or behavior? We certainly expend a lot of energy trying, but the reality is that while we can act in ways that influence the behavior of those around us, the only person over whom we have true control is ourselves—and some of us struggle with that! Like it or not, it's true: the only person whose behavior we can control and therefore learn to change is our own. And the biggest change of all may be simply recognizing this important fact. It may help to know that the changes in attitude and actions suggested throughout this book will invite (not force) positive changes in your children.

Once we determine that our old toolbox does not produce the results we really want, we recognize the need to restock the box with some new tools. When we realize that the best tools are those that change *our* ideas and behavior, we are on the path to enjoyable, successful parenting (or teaching). One

- How is my behavior contributing to the situation? Is there anything I should consider changing?
- How might my child and I work together to solve this problem? (It often comes as a surprise to adults to realize how many good solutions even young children can think of—and children are usually more willing to cooperate when they've had a voice in solving the problem.)

These questions take us away from the frustrating (and usually impossible) goal of trying to control children (making them do what we want, when and how we want it). Instead, we can focus on teaching and creating situations where children can learn to weigh choices, exercise judgment, and learn from the results—all valuable life skills.

parent relates her early experiences with learning to use Positive Discipline parenting tools—and the changes she had to make in her thinking before she could be effective:

"When I was first learning these concepts, I often thought something wasn't working. I discovered that this happened because I had not understood the concept or was applying it incorrectly. For example, it is very important to be both kind and firm at the same time. I found that often I would be firm without being kind—which made it punitive. Other times I would be kind without being firm—which made it too permissive. Being kind and firm at the same time is not easy, but it is very effective."

When Your Child "Doesn't Listen"

"I don't know what to do with Tyler," his mom sighed wearily. "I tell him to turn off the television or pick up his toys, and he ignores me. He's four—that's plenty old enough to do what I ask—but he acts like he didn't even hear me. When we're at the store and I tell him to come along, he runs in the opposite direction. I have to yell to get him to obey me, and I hate yelling—especially when he starts yelling back. He just won't listen to me!"

One of the most common complaints parents have about young children is the mysterious hearing loss known as "my child won't listen." We hear this complaint over and over. There are all sorts of reasons why children don't respond to adults' instructions—few of which have anything to do with their hearing.

Three-year-old Brianna, for instance, is hitting her playmate and barely pauses when her teacher tells her to stop. Gregory's dad tells him it's time to leave the park and go home, then gets no response—until he raises his voice and grabs Gregory's elbow. The response then is not the peaceful compliance he had hoped for. Megan's mom tells her calmly and clearly before they enter the store that there will be no treats or toys today, and Megan nods her head when asked if she understands; but as they wait at the checkout stand, Megan howls loudly for candy while her mom says, "But I told you no candy today!"

Sound familiar? The problem usually isn't that our children don't listen, but that what we're requiring or asking of them runs counter to some more basic

Children don't listen because:

- Adults yell, lecture, or nag, which does not invite listening.

- Adults set up a power struggle that makes winning more important than cooperating.

- The child is "programmed" by her development to explore—and the adult doesn't want her to. The voice of a child's development is usually louder than the voice of the adult.

- The child cannot understand a request because it demands social skills or thinking skills that have not yet developed.

- Children don't have the same priorities as adults.

need. Brianna, for example, is very young and is still working on her social skills. She needs to be helped to "use her words" and, if she continues to hit, to be removed calmly to another place. Gregory is experimenting with his initiative and autonomy, which, unfortunately, don't match his dad's concept of what he should be doing. He can learn from simple choices and from kind, firm actions. Megan is simply too young to keep instructions in mind that were given an hour earlier—especially when they're contrary to what she wants now.

In each case, adults can no more make these children listen than they can make them obey. Understanding temperament and age-appropriate behavior will help; so will avoiding yelling, punishing, or nagging, which only invite power struggles.

Yelling will not achieve cooperation. Neither will threats. Bribes might work, but when we ask, "What might this child learn from the experience?" we get answers that we don't like. A child may learn to look at any task with a "what's in it for me" attitude. She may decide that she will only do things for which she receives rewards. Remember: Cooperation must be invited—not demanded.

It is almost always more effective to invite cooperation than to insist on obedience: "There are blocks on the floor. Would you like to pick them up with me or can you do it all by yourself?" Usually, children cooperate when they feel empowered to choose.

So What Is "Discipline"?

YOU MAY HAVE noticed as you've read this book that we don't advocate spanking, slapping, yelling, or any of the other methods that pass so often for discipline in our society. You may have wondered why. Most people do. After all, weren't most of us raised with good old-fashioned discipline? Don't we hear people saying that if kids today just got a bit more discipline we would have fewer problems? It's important to look first at exactly what discipline is. As it turns out, when people talk about discipline, they usually mean punishment. Yet the two concepts aren't the same at all.

Most of us have absorbed our ideas about discipline from our own parents, our society, and years of tradition. We approach discipline with one subtle, basic belief: children have to suffer (at least a little) or they won't learn anything.

"A good swat once in a while lets my kids know I mean business," a parent might say. Or "My children lose all their privileges when they mess up. That's what teaches them not to disobey me." Or "Punishing my kids teaches them to respect me." It is tempting to believe that we can control our children, especially when they're young and can easily be picked up, moved, or confined. But a wise parent (or teacher) realizes that not only is total control unwise, it's rarely even possible.

Relying on control and the power of punishment turns parents and teachers into police officers, full-time enforcers who set the rules then watch constantly for violations. But what happens when the police officer isn't around? And how many parents and teachers want life with their children to become a constant power struggle? The discipline methods recommended in this book are designed to win cooperation and to teach children self-control (as soon as they are developmentally ready). Positive Discipline methods are designed for long-range positive results. Even though punishment may stop the behavior at the moment, the long-range results are usually negative.

Research confirms that children who are hit are more likely to hit others. Hitting begets more hitting. Most parents do not intend to teach their children to be aggressive. In fact, often children are spanked for being aggressive. Do you see the contradiction here? An angry adult strikes a child while saying, "That will teach you not to hit your little sister!" Will it? A child probably decides many things as the result of being spanked, none of which include ceasing to hit his little sister. Consider these possible conclusions:

- "This adult is dangerous. I need to hide what I do so I don't get caught again. (I'll be 'good' but only while I am being watched.)"

- "Only adults can hit. When I grow up, I can hit too." (Not a hopeful thought for a parent's future unborn grandchildren, is it?)

- "Hitting is what people do when they get angry. When I get angry, I will hit others. (Just watch me on the preschool playground!)"

- "I must be a terrible person. I can't expect other people to like me. I deserve whatever ill-treatment comes my way." (What a surefire recipe for finding an abusive mate, an unfair work environment, or becoming resigned to endless school or career failure.)

Did you see "I am definitely going to quit hitting my little sister" listed above? Absolutely not—nor would you be likely to. If the goal is to teach the child to stop hitting, this method failed spectacularly. Even if there were no other reasons to abandon spanking, the bottom line is that it does not work to attain the long-range positive results we want—even though it may seem to stop the behavior at the moment.

> An angry adult strikes a child while saying, "That will teach you not to hit your little sister!" Will it? A child probably decides many things as the result of being spanked, none of which include ceasing to hit his little sister.

Q. *Is there any way a parent can let a child know that her behavior is unacceptable, and what do you suggest for enforcing that? I think that children do need to obey the rules their parents set up, otherwise the parents just wind up being the tallest and oldest people in the house, with no say at all. That's not helpful to the kids and is even less helpful to the parents having to deal with them.*

A. Your concern is a typical reaction of parents who believe that the only alternative to punishment is permissiveness. We do not advocate permissiveness for the simple reason that permissiveness is no more effective than punishment. All of our methods teach self-discipline, cooperation, responsibility, and other important life skills.

True discipline is not about punishment or control. The word itself comes from the Latin word *discere,* which means to teach or to learn. The Latin noun is *discipulus,* which means student and, by analogy to the verb, "one who learns and teaches." At its best, discipline is about guiding and teaching young people, helping them to make wise decisions about their behavior, and allowing them to gradually accept responsibility for their choices and actions—to choose (or not choose) a certain behavior because they understand its implications, not because the police are in the vicinity. And, in the true sense, discipline is also about being willing to learn from our children. They have so much to teach us.

BEWARE OF WHAT WORKS

Q. *I spank and paddle my children. I have done it since they were four, and I believe that I am respected for it. If they do something that puts them or another child in a potentially dangerous situation, they are spanked. If they willfully disobey or lie to me, they are spanked. I believe that as long as they live in my house they will be spanked. Time-out does not work; writing "I will obey my mother" does not work; but spanking does work. And even just a slap on the bottom will not work. It sounds absolutely crazy, but they have to be bare-bottom and receive a couple of hard slaps. Is this wrong? Also, is it better to spank immediately after the child does something wrong or (as my friend does) tally up the bad things and give one big spanking at the end of the week?*

A. Yes, spanking seems to work, if all you are concerned about is immediate results. It usually does stop misbehavior—for the moment. However, sometimes we must beware of what "works" for the moment if the long-range results are nega-

Many parents believe that punishment, especially spanking, is mandated by the Bible. The Bible does say, "He who spares the rod hates his son, but he who loves him is careful to discipline him" (Proverbs 13:24, New International Version). Many Biblical scholars believe that the word "rod" has a number of meanings. It was a symbol of authority, and shepherds used a rod to guide and direct their sheep—not to beat them. The Bible also says, "Your rod and your staff they comfort me" (Psalms 23:4). How many children truly feel comforted by a spanking?

The question of how we choose to discipline our children goes right to the heart of parenting. Most of us grew up accepting that punishment and spankings were normal, even necessary, parts of raising children. And often, at least in the short term, punishment *seems* to "work." But we need to beware of what seems to work for the moment and consider instead the long-range effects of punitive discipline.

tive. Do you really think your children respect you for spanking them, or do they fear you? What are you teaching children by your example? We think you are teaching them that big people get to hurt little people. You are teaching them that it is not safe to make a mistake; they are not in a supportive environment where they can learn from mistakes. The long-range results of this may be one of two extremes: children who are afraid to take risks, or children who rebelliously take risks without thinking of the results of their choices. (Fear of punishment does not teach them to think through the consequences of their choices but only to fear the punishment.)

If we were gamblers, we would bet that either you will have very rebellious teenagers or your children will become "approval junkies." You are providing the kind of environment that teaches children to lie or to be sneaky so they won't get caught and be punished. Most parents would prefer not to spank if they knew what else to do to teach children self-discipline, responsibility, cooperation, and problem-solving skills.

What Your Children Are Really Learning

AS WE'VE DISCOVERED, children are constantly making decisions about life, how they feel, and how they will behave. Often the decisions they make after being punished are not those their parents intended.

A segment of the ABC television news show *20/20* took a close look at spanking, including studies of Murray Straus of the Family Research Laboratory at the University of New Hampshire. For this show, four families whose children are regularly spanked allowed the television cameras to follow them around and record the parents' interactions with their misbehaving children. Most parents who later viewed that show, including parents who had spanked their own children, found it painful to watch. Many agreed that the spankings they viewed didn't teach but only punished a child for wrong choices or vented parental frustration and anger. There was no emphasis on problem solving or on preventing misbehavior in the future; the spankings alone were supposed to take care of that.

> The TV show *20/20* quoted research showing that spanking and similar punishments produce children who are discouraged, have lower self-esteem, are more likely to seek out abusive relationships later in life, and consider hitting an acceptable way to solve problems—results that these parents, who certainly loved their children, obviously didn't intend.

Yet these parents kept on having to spank their children regularly. There appeared to be no lasting changes in undesirable behavior. Perhaps more important, the show quoted research showing that spanking and similar punishments produce children who are discouraged, have lower self-esteem, are more likely to seek out abusive relationships later in life, and consider hitting an acceptable way to solve problems—results that these parents, who certainly loved their children, obviously didn't intend.

Punitive forms of discipline often teach children unintended lessons: to misbehave when the enforcer isn't around, to get even if possible, or to focus on the "mean old parent" rather than on the behavior that got them into trouble in the first place. Spanking, in particular, presents several hidden problems. It becomes less and less effective over time, and it eventually becomes physically impossible. It commonly creates feelings of guilt and regret in parents.

Alternatives to Spanking

AT OUR PARENTING lectures we ask, "How many of you would prefer not to spank if you had other tools and skills to help your children learn self-discipline, responsibility, cooperation, and problem-solving skills?" Every hand in the audience is raised enthusiastically

It is possible to provide discipline in homes, preschools, and child care centers that teaches, guides, and encourages without spanking, yelling, or taking away privileges. It is possible not to punish yet still produce children who are responsible, well-behaved, and respectful (at least most of the time). Nonpunitive methods are suggested in every chapter of this book. Effective, consistent discipline takes a good deal of thought and preparation, but the benefits for your children and in your lives together will be well worth it.

12

Decide What *You* Will Do

A S YOU'VE PROBABLY recognized by this point, most of the questions parents of preschoolers ask have to do with their children's behavior—and what adults can do to manage it. The answer is simple—and one that parents don't particularly like. We cannot "control" children's behavior in the direct way we sometimes think we can. We can try telling children how high to jump and when to come down, but usually we will not be successful. What parents and caregivers can do is decide what *they* will do. Children's behavior will change in response to our actions.

Decide what you will do, do it, and the behavior of those around you will be affected. This is one of many tools for parenting success. Instead of nagging, yelling, and marching a child into a punitive time-out for not picking up his toys, decide what you will do. Explain to him that you will pack away any toys left on the floor at dinnertime and put them in the attic for three days. Then tell him that when you return the toys, you are confident that he will do a better job of putting them away on his next try. Now, he may still choose not to pick up the toys. The difference is that you don't need to wait around battling him about it. You just do what you said you would (you follow through). There are some important conclusions a child might form in response to a parent's or teacher's actions:

- "This adult means what she says."

- "My choices influence what happens to me."

- "There is responsibility attached to privilege, and if I want to enjoy the privilege, I'll have to accept the responsibility."

Taking control of your own behavior—rather than meting out either punishment or consequences—looks like this:

- Decide what you will do.

- Respectfully explain what you will do in *advance*.

- Follow through by doing what you said you would do, while remaining both kind and firm.

Most adults use punishment as a knee-jerk reaction. Children's behavior often pushes adult buttons that invite strong emotions of anger ("How could you do such a thing?"), revenge ("I won't let you get away with that!"), and fear ("Does your behavior mean you are a bad child or that I am a bad parent?"). Any time we are feeling anger, the need for revenge, or fear, we stop thinking rationally. We do not stop to think about the long-range effects on our children of what we are doing. We do not think about what they are thinking, feeling, and deciding about themselves and about what they are learning for the future. When we understand the long-range effects of what we do, we will take time to plan ahead.

The Beauty of Planning Ahead

AN OVERLOOKED PART of discipline is prevention, good old thinking ahead to the problems and situations that might occur. For instance, if you're about to take an airplane trip with a squirmy, active four-year-old, you can choose either to have a prolonged power struggle (with a curious captive audience) or to prepare by packing a bag with snacks, story tapes, puzzles, and several small, new toys to keep your little traveler occupied and interested. You can even plan your trip for a time of day when your child is normally quiet or even sleepy rather than a time when he's likely to be full of energy.

Let's take a look at the familiar scene of many parent-child battles: the shopping trip. We've all seen it—the fussy, whining child and the anxious,

> An overlooked part of discipline is prevention, good old thinking ahead to the problems and situations that might occur.

PREVENTING PROBLEMS AT THE STORE: STEPS FOR PLANNING AHEAD

- Look for danger signals before you go.

- Explore the rules and boundaries before entering the store.

- Anticipate problems.

- Make shopping a time to laugh and learn.

irritated parent. If discipline is really about teaching, you may ask, how can a parent take a child along and prevent problems before they begin? There are several things to consider.

Look for Danger Signals Before You Go

Did your child skip a nap or a meal? Is she already tired and cranky? Are you? It is usually wisest to postpone errands and trips until both of you are rested and relatively cheerful. Don't plan to do a list of errands at the end of a tiring day—you and your child will probably regret it!

Explore the Rules and Boundaries Before Entering the Store

If your child is old enough to understand, explore with her what sort of behavior is acceptable in the store. If a child isn't old enough to explore possibilities, she isn't old enough to understand your lectures. Ask your child, "How do we act in the store so we show respect for everyone? (You may need to offer clues in your exploration questions for very young children.) Are we supposed to run or walk? You may even want to play a game of "Let's Pretend" so your child has an opportunity to practice the skills of respectful behavior.

Be sure you explore together *in advance* about whining or begging for treats. And remember to encourage your child's cooperation by noticing when she behaves respectfully. Be specific: "I appreciate your help when you put groceries in the basket." "Thank you for walking quietly and respectfully in the store." "You did a great job of pushing the cart through the store. You went slowly and were able to watch for the other shoppers."

Anticipate Problems

Most young children are fascinated by shopping for about five minutes. What will you do when the novelty wears off? It may help to bring a small bag of "things to do," especially if the bag can be tied to the handle of a shopping cart or stroller. Markers and paper for a child's own shopping list may provide some amusement; a favorite stuffed toy may help your child feel more secure. It may also be wise to bring along a snack, such as cut-up fruit or a bag of cereal.

Make Shopping a Time to Laugh and Learn

See how creative you can be in keeping your child occupied as you shop. You may want to give him a stack of coupons and let him match the coupons to the items in your cart. Play "I Spy" and see who can find a fruit that begins with *B* or a vegetable that is yellow. See if you can find all of the letters in the alphabet on signs and advertisements. Invite your child to plan a funny meal from items in your cart.

If your child is old enough, allow him to shop with you from a "list" with pictures of the items you need, perhaps even carrying his own basket. Show your child how to help you select the shiniest apples or to thump the watermelons (gently, of course). You can even begin to teach comparison shopping by seeing which price is lowest. Giving a child a job to do is an excellent way to help him feel needed and learn respectful, cooperative behavior.

Give your child an opportunity to make some of the choices. Even a very young child can choose between two cereals (preselected by mom or dad), two flavors of ice cream, or striped or plain socks. It may all sound like a great deal of work—but it's undoubtedly easier than coping with a screaming youngster at the checkout stand! Even more important, you are teaching your child cooperation and life skills—and providing opportunities for building healthy self-esteem.

"My Kid Still Misbehaves—Now What?"

EVEN WITH THE best preparation and training, it's unrealistic to expect perfect behavior. Sooner or later (usually sooner) it happens—a temper tantrum, a child running toward a forbidden object, a toy thrown in anger. How can a parent or teacher stop unacceptable behavior without resorting to punishment?

First of all, take the time to think carefully about the result rules, limits, and discipline should accomplish in your child's life. Keeping a few things in mind may help you avoid unnecessary conflict.

Keep Expectations Reasonable

Nicholas sits fascinated, watching the fish pass back and forth in the aquarium window. Nicholas enjoys quiet play and possesses a remarkable ability to stay focused. Misty, his four-year-old cousin, prefers much more active play. Looking at fish bores her. She would much rather reach in to catch one. Misty's aunt would be wise to plan more active outings when Misty visits Nicholas. If she tried to take the cousins to an art exhibit or museum, chances are Misty would be hustled outside for a reprimand before the end of the first half hour.

When adults take into account the temperament (see chapter 7), abilities, and needs of children, there are far fewer problems. Deciding that a child "must just learn to deal with certain situations" promises skirmishes, frustration, and disappointment for both the child and the adults accompanying her.

It is true that sometimes adults must involve children in situations not well matched to their abilities. When these occasions occur, look for ways to provide a child with a higher chance of successfully managing her behavior. If Misty must sit quietly on a long car trip, it would help to bring along a coloring book, a puzzle game, or a bag of beads to string into a necklace. Be sure that she has eaten recently, used the bathroom, and does not need a nap. When we make the effort to support a child's needs, her behavior succeeds.

Choose Your Battles

Everything in family life can become a battle, if we let it. Take time to decide on the things that are important to you, and explore the issues about which you can afford to be flexible. Every family will be different. Some parents value church attendance, while it's not important to others. Messy rooms push some parents' buttons, while others couldn't care less. Be sure you save your energy for the things that really matter. When you've decided what matters most, communicate your expectations clearly and reinforce them with lots of training and appropriate action.

Think Before You Speak

Most parents have had the uncomfortable experience of making a rule or a promise in the heat of anger (such as telling a child you will throw away all of his toys if he doesn't pick them up immediately) and realizing later that they couldn't follow through. Remember to say what you mean and mean what you say. Don't tell your five-year-old that if she's not in the car "this minute" you'll leave for Grandma's house without her. She knows as well as you do that Grandma lives in the next state, and you're not about to drive away and leave her standing in the driveway. (Imagine, too, her terror if she believes you truly will leave without her.)

If we constantly tell children things we don't mean or make promises we're not willing to live up to, we teach them that they only need to listen to some of what we say, and we run the risk of damaging their trust. Be sure you've thought about the possible consequences of your words; if you're not sure you mean them, don't say them.

One preschool teacher learned this lesson the hard way when she found herself warning a child, "If you don't come down from that tree right now, I'm going to come up and get you." Guess what? She did. But she was much more careful of what she said from then on!

Remember That Children Do What "Works"

Children are intelligent little people, and if a certain behavior (or misbehavior) gets the desired response, they will almost certainly repeat it. For instance, if your child throws a tantrum at the grocery store checkout and walks away with candy or a pack of gum, what do you suppose you'll see the next time you arrive at the check-out stand? If a desire to "talk," a few tears, and big blue eyes allow your child to delay bedtime, can you expect to see these behaviors every night? Try to avoid inadvertently reinforcing the wrong sorts of behavior.

Work Toward Consistency

No one is consistent all of the time. But as much as possible, try to make sure that your goals, your rules, and your approach stay the same from one day to the next. Children find frequent changes confusing and may resort to constantly testing the limits just to find out what they are. Making your rules few, firm, and fair will help you to be reasonably consistent and will let your children know what to expect, which may eliminate a great deal of misbehavior.

Focus on the Belief Behind the Behavior

Human behavior (adults' and children's) never happens in a vacuum; we behave as we do for a reason, whether we understand it consciously or not. Take time before you react to something your child has said or done to decipher the code hidden in her actions (see chapter 19). Consider your child's feelings and reflect them (see chapter 3). If you can figure out why a child is misbehaving, you're a giant step ahead, not only in stopping the behavior this time but in preventing it in the future. And isn't that what discipline is all about?

Learn to See Mistakes—Including Your Own— As Opportunities to Learn

Remember all those things we've just talked about? Most parents manage to forget them and get hooked into reacting to exasperating behavior. And that's okay. You can't be perfect either, so you will have many opportunities to demonstrate to your children that mistakes are wonderful opportunities to learn. Take the time to cool down, and then acknowledge your mistake to your children, apologize (children are so forgiving), and work on solutions with your children. Things often turn out better than if the mistake had never been made in the first place!

Patience and Repetition

ADULTS WOULD NEVER expect a child to learn math, reading, science, or any academic subject without repeated exposure. Why then, do we expect children to learn appropriate behavior after one (or even one hundred) exposures to our guidance? How many children have heard an adult scream, "I've told you a hundred times . . ." as though the child were inadequate. Could it be that the adult's teaching methods are inadequate? When parents and caregivers decide what they will do and when the methods they choose are nonpunitive, lots of kind and firm repetition may be necessary.

Going Too Far

> Take the time to cool down, and then acknowledge your mistake to your children, apologize (children are so forgiving), and work on solutions with your children.

IT'S A SUBJECT no one wants to look at. It's ugly, and it's frightening, and it happens far too often in our homes and our communities. We're talking about child abuse and neglect. "I would never hurt my child," you may be saying. "Why talk about abuse in a book on Positive Discipline?" Few parents intend to injure their children. Yet every year thousands of children are beaten, burned, molested, neglected, even killed—and the vast majority of those children are under the age of five.

Child abuse in all its forms—emotional, sexual, verbal, physical—is a complex subject with many contributing factors. Parents are often under financial or emotional stress, possess too few coping skills, or have unrealistic expectations of their children, and when parents rely on spanking or other forms of physical punishment, it's dangerously easy to injure a small child, to shake an infant, to break a little bone.

All parents (and caregivers) feel frustrated and occasionally overwhelmed. Some adults never experienced loving, effective parenting themselves and literally don't know what to do. It is important to get help if you feel you need it. Take a parenting class to learn better skills or get counseling to work through your own emotional problems. Take care of yourself. Learn to recognize your own "triggers" and deal with anger and frustration before they reach the boiling point. Talk to friends, a pastor, a teacher, or a counselor.

What should you do if you see someone else hurting or threatening a child? Most of us feel reluctant to get involved, yet we could save the life or mental health of a child by doing so. There are things you can do that won't make the situation worse or direct the parent's hostility toward you.

Distracting the parent's attention from the child without challenging or shaming is one effective way to intervene. There are a number of ways to do this:

- Sympathize with the parent. Say something kind, like "I remember when my children were that age—they can be a real handful." Or, "Isn't it amazing how children think they can get their way by screaming?"

- Offer to help. If you know the parent, offer to watch the child for a while so the parent can take a break, get a drink of water, or calm down. Say, "You seem to be having a tough time. Is there anything I can do to help?"

- Find something positive to say about the child. Try, "Your little girl is beautiful" or "What wonderful curls he has."

Take action if necessary. If you feel the child's safety is in danger, speak to a store manager or other responsible person, or call your local Children's Protective Services. Such calls are kept confidential and anonymous in most states and may offer a family an opportunity to get help and make changes they otherwise might not have had. If you know the struggling parent well enough, you may want to give him or her a copy of this book or offer to go along to a parenting class. You may, in a very real way, be saving the life of a child, and because abusive patterns tend to repeat themselves through successive generations, you may change the lives of children you will never meet for the better.

Unfortunately, abuse and neglect sometimes happen in child care settings. If you are uncomfortable with a caregiver or question your child's safety, find other care. Trust your instincts and inner wisdom; if you can substantiate mistreatment, inform the authorities.

Our Actions Matter

IN A WORLD where people so often feel powerless, it is important that we and our children learn that we do decide our own actions, that we can take action thoughtfully, and that we can learn to accept responsibility for what we have chosen to do. All of us are entitled to dignity and respect. Make the best choices you can as a parent or caregiver; observe the results you get. What you do will make a difference—for a lifetime.

13

Positive Discipline Parenting Tools

THROUGHOUT THIS BOOK are many examples of Positive Discipline tools at work. These tools are as essential to parents as tape measure, needles, and pins are to a quilter. These tools are the choices we adults have at our disposal, things we can decide to do—all of which are more effective than wringing our hands and waiting helplessly for a child's behavior to change.

It is important to note that just as a quilter can't be successful with just one tool, neither can parents. Many tools are needed. Different children will respond to different methods at different times—even when their behavior seems to be identical! Parents and caregivers who know their children well and who understand temperament and development will know which tools will be most effective. Let's take a closer look at some of these tools in action.

Time-Out: Punitive or Positive?

Jean had absolutely had it. Four-year-old Paul would not stop teasing his eighteen-month-old sister, and the incessant fussing and crying had frayed Jean's nerves. "That's it, Paul," she finally exploded, "you're in time-out."

Jean dragged her kicking son to his room and closed the door. "I'm setting the egg timer for four minutes," she said firmly, following the rule she had always heard. Paul answered his mother by kicking the door and throwing a toy—and by opening the door as soon as his mom was out of sight.

POSITIVE DICSIPLINE PARENTING (AND TEACHING) TOOLS

- Positive time-out

- Selective attention: ignoring the behavior, not the child; resisting manipulation

- Acceptance: holding without becoming hooked

- Consequences and solutions

- Follow-through

- Kindness and firmness

- Humor and laughter

Jean heard the door open behind her and sighed, "I must be doing something wrong."

Jean certainly is not the only parent to find time-out a challenge.

Q. *What do I do if my three-year-old won't sit when I put him in time-out? He kicks, screams, and gets up. I get angry and spank him (not hard, of course) just to let him know that I mean business. Even this doesn't work; he still resists. Then I put him in his room until he and I have a chance to calm down. That works, but I don't feel like it's good parenting. Help!*

A. Many frustrated parents are learning that punishment, even when it's as nonviolent as time-out, simply does not work. So many children respond just as your son does—they resist and rebel. You are engaged in a typical power struggle. You are trying to make him understand that you mean business, but he is letting you know that so does he. The only way you can win is to make him the loser. Try "positive" time-out for a win/win experience.

Believe it or not, time-out need not be a punishing confinement or a battle of wills between parent (or teacher) and child. Positive time-out, effectively used, is an opportunity for children to feel better. And when children feel better, they behave better. (Thinking of it as a cool-off rather than a time-out may help.)

The "time-out corner" at Willy's preschool is a special place. All of the children had worked together to set it up, and it boasts an old-fashioned claw-footed bathtub filled with soft pillows, several teddy bears, and a stack of inviting books.

Willy was busily engaged in tripping the unsuspecting children who passed his spot on the floor. This amusing game came to a sudden end, however, when he tried to trip the teacher.

"Willy," the teacher said, "I thought we talked about tripping. Someone could fall and get hurt."

Willy looked a bit sheepish—they had discussed this habit of his several times recently—but his only response was a sullen silence.

The teacher smiled. "Perhaps you'd feel better if you visited the time-out corner. Go curl up and look at the books for a little while, and you can come back and play with us when you feel better and can change your behavior."

Willy spent almost ten minutes curled up in the old tub, looking at books and watching his classmates play. When he returned to the group, the teacher asked, "Feeling better, kiddo? No more tripping?"

Willy nodded and offered a tentative smile. "Come and join us, then," the teacher offered, and Willy moved to join the group.

Some parents and teachers believe that making a time-out corner inviting and pleasant rewards children for misbehavior. However, wise adults realize that all people have moments when they just can't seem to get along. A few moments in positive time-out (when it's not shaming or punishing) provides a cooling-off period, and children know they're welcome to return when they can get along and behave properly. If you still have doubts, ask yourself whether you'd rather be Willy's teacher or Paul's mother!

We invite you to see for yourself. Help your children set up a cozy corner in their rooms for positive time-out. You may want to include favorite stuffed toys, books, music, or coloring books and markers. Then, when you sense that your child needs a moment to cool off, suggest a time-out. Tell your child that he can return when he feels better and is able to follow the rules. Notice that the end result is to "return when he is able to change his behavior." It might be even more helpful to ask your child, "Would you find it helpful to go to your positive time-out area for a while?" A child who chooses time-out feels empowered by his own choice and his understanding that a quiet time will help him feel better and do better.

You may also offer to go with your child to a positive time-out, where your own modeling and behavior can teach your child to soothe himself. This can be particularly helpful with a younger preschooler who may resist separation from you. Remember, the goal is to teach a child how to feel better so that he can do better.

Punitive time-out is "past-oriented." It may make children suffer for what they have done, but parents and teachers might be surprised if they checked out the decisions (conscious or unconscious) that children are making for the future. Positive time-out is "future-oriented" and encourages children to make positive decisions about self-control and responsibility—training that will benefit both of you as your child grows.

Modeling Positive Time-Out

WHEN TEMPERS FLARE, who needs time-out the most? Perhaps the wrong person is being sent to cool off! Consider what might happen if instead of demanding that three-year-old Isabelle march into her room for a time-out Dad took a deep breath, then announced that he needed some time alone to cool off—and then marched into his own room. Not only does Dad get himself back under control, but he has just taught Isabelle how to handle her anger effectively. We model life skills with every step we take. Dad is not letting Isabelle "get away" with misbehavior, failing to control her, or being wimpy. He chooses to control his own behavior, thereby guiding Isabelle in how to control hers. Whatever the issue, it will be better handled when everyone's temper has cooled.

Selective Attention: Ignoring the Behavior, Not the Child

Marcy is an expert at throwing temper tantrums; she considers it her specialty. She has learned that when she throws herself down on the floor, kicks her feet, and howls, she's pushing Mom and Dad's buttons in a very effective way. They come running to see what's wrong and she gets all sorts of attention.

Today, however, something is drastically wrong. She pitches her very best tantrum, but Mom, who is fixing dinner in the kitchen, only smiles. Marcy throws her doll for added effect, but after a quick glance to make sure Marcy is in no danger of hurting herself, Mom leaves the room. Marcy hears her go into her bathroom and begin washing her face.

Marcy steps up her tantrum, screaming even louder and pounding on the carpet with her fists, but there is no response. After a while, Marcy begins to feel rather silly. She gets up and trots down the hall to see what Mom is up to.

If Marcy throws a tantrum in Mom's room, Mom can simply return to the kitchen. Eventually Marcy will get the message that her tantrum isn't working, and Mom will be able to deal with the situation in a calm, effective manner.

Ignoring misbehavior works well when the misbehavior is designed primarily to get our attention. Of course, you never want to leave your child in a situation where he or someone else could get hurt, but ignoring misbehavior,

POSITIVE TIME-OUT TO COOL OFF

Q. *I have a spirited four-year-old son. He is constantly challenging us, and when we send him to time-out, he undermines it by choosing to stay there forever—or he'll send himself to time-out. Is this usual or is he very skillful at manipulation? We never feel that he has gotten the message.*

A. It sounds as though your son already has the "message" of positive time-out. How wonderful that he can send himself to time-out and that he recognizes it as an opportunity to regain control of himself. Try thinking of time-out as a cool-off period.

Whenever your attempts at time-out carry the unspoken message that he should suffer, your son responds by showing you that he is in control. Follow his lead and use time-out as a positive way for him to regain his composure before rejoining the family with his behavior improved.

even if you remain in the room, can teach children with surprising speed that they can't manipulate you.

Acceptance: Holding Without Becoming Hooked

ANOTHER POSSIBILITY FOR dealing with tantrums is to hold the child (if she will allow it) without becoming hooked into the tantrum or trying to stop it. Holding a child or gently stroking her back lets her know that she can have her feelings as long as she needs them. This lets her know that you are there to provide support but cannot be manipulated. Some children have tantrums out of sheer frustration, and quiet support can be very comforting. Again, responding in this way is not rewarding misbehavior but acting on the belief behind the behavior (more about this in chapter 19). If a child can learn to deal with her feelings and make better choices about her behavior, that is true discipline at its best.

Consequences and Solutions

NATURAL CONSEQUENCES ARE things that happen without parental intervention. They are the everyday experiences of life. If you go out in the rain, you get wet. If you don't eat, you get hungry. If you make snowballs without gloves, your hands get very cold. If you throw your lunch on the floor, there's nothing for you to eat. Children can learn from these experiences *if* parents resist the urge to lecture and rescue.

Sometimes, however, natural consequences either don't exist or aren't acceptable. The natural consequence of playing in the street, for example, is a lesson we can't afford to have our children learn. In these instances, parents must intervene. Holding hands, teaching, and supervising are far more effective solutions than lectures or punishment.

Parents and teachers often get hung up in trying to deter-mine what the consequence should be for a certain action. We pre-fer to replace "consequences" with "solutions." Looking for solutions is almost always the best approach to problem behavior. Rather than focusing energy on blame or punishment, we can invite our children to work with us to solve the problem once and for all. The best solutions are those that children have a hand in designing and that focus on preventing problems in the future.

For instance, if a child draws on the wall with a marker, it is appropriate to have him help you wash the wall (and it may be a good reminder never to buy a young child permanent markers). You may then want to sit down with him and discuss what will happen if he chooses to draw on the wall again. You may agree that drawing on the wall means that a child isn't ready for the privilege of owning markers and will have to give his up for a while. You may decide to hang butcher paper on certain areas of the wall where he can draw. It isn't helpful to say unnecessary, hurtful things like, "Maybe this will teach you to obey me" as you take the markers. Such comments only shame and humiliate and will not encourage your child to do better. Be sure you provide for a time to try again when the child is ready.

> Looking for solutions is almost always the best approach to problem behavior. Rather than focusing energy on blame or punishment, we can invite our children to work with us to solve the problem once and for all.

Focusing on solutions invites cooperation, addresses the problem directly, and includes plans for preventing its recurrence. Take time to be sure that your child understands what has happened and why you feel the way you do, and decide together how to prevent repetition of the problem behavior. Remember, effective discipline is teaching for the future.

Follow-Through

FOLLOW-THROUGH MEANS that parents and teachers decide what they are going to do and then follow through with kind and firm action instead of punishments and lectures. As pyschiatrist Rudolf Dreikurs has said, follow-through means you "shut your mouth and act." Follow-through with young children is relatively simple: you do what you have said you would. The fewer words spoken, the better; many parents talk too much, and children learn they can safely ignore about half of what they hear. Let's compare the following two scenarios, the first without follow-through and the second with follow-through.

Five-year-old Alex is having a wonderful time with his Legos in the middle of the living room floor. His mother pokes her head into the room and says cheerfully, "It's bedtime, honey. Pick up your Legos and put on your pajamas."

TEACHING VERSUS RESCUING

Q. My son, who is about to turn four, has had a train set for a year now, and several pieces of track have gotten broken due to rough usage. I have told him that he needs to be more careful with them, because we have to throw them away when they break and he will run out of track. I gave him fair warning, but I don't think he really "gets" it. Future tense is not one of his strong points. What will happen when he really doesn't have enough track left to set up his train? I think he is going to have a total meltdown when I tell him that I am not going to buy any more.

How do you suggest that I handle this? Is he just too young for logical consequences, since he is not able to foresee them, or is "finding out the hard way" the whole point? Or am I looking at the wrong logical consequence? Perhaps I should take the trains away for a specified amount of time when I find a broken piece?

A. The term "logical consequences" usually refers to a plan of action the adult imposes for some sort of misbehavior. It is usually just another word for punishment. The focus most often stays on what the adult is going to make the child do, how the child will be made to suffer, or how the adult will prove he or she is in charge.

Alex appears to have developed a hearing problem; he ignores his mother and continues building his tower. Now Mom's voice gets a bit tense. "Did you hear me, Alex? I said it's time for bed. Put away the Legos now."

Still Alex doesn't move. Now Mom's voice sounds like an elastic band that is stretched to the breaking point. "If you don't pick up those toys and get ready for bed this instant, you're going to get a spanking. I'm counting to three . . ."

The situation you describe is not a logical consequence but a natural one. Your son breaks the tracks and then there is not enough track for next time. You need do nothing, except refrain from swooping in to the rescue with new tracks and express empathy for his disappointment.

What a great opportunity for your child to learn about taking care of his toys. Remember that it is not always possible (or wise) to avoid children's wrath. Your son might throw a tantrum. When he calms down, give him a chance to right the situation. Discuss a way for him to earn money to purchase new tracks. When a child truly is involved in doing something meaningful toward restoring the item, it is both effective and loving for a parent to help by matching or supplementing what a child can earn.

You may also decide what you will do: If more track is broken, you may decide your son is not yet old enough to care for his train properly. If so, explain your decision in advance. Offer him another chance after a short time.

Solution-based parenting focuses on teaching life skills. It is not rescuing. We rescue when we seek to protect our children from experiencing the results of their own behavior. Solutions do not require winners and losers. Solution-based parenting is win/win. You win because you take charge of your behavior, removing the train set (or simply showing empathy without rescuing). Your son wins because he will get another chance to take care of his train set before damaging it beyond repair.

Alex keeps playing, but when Mom moves toward him he is galvanized into action. He scrambles to pick up his Legos, but Mom delivers the spanking anyway and drags him off to his room, where she tells him, "It serves you right. You can just go without your story now. Maybe next time you'll obey me."

Alex gets into bed and screams for fifteen minutes. Mom returns to the kitchen, wishing fervently she were anywhere but home.

It's bedtime. Five-year-old Heather is sitting on the floor playing with her Legos. Her mother cheerfully says, "It's bedtime, honey. Time to put away your toys and get ready for bed."

Heather keeps building her tower. After giving her daughter a minute or two to comply, Mom walks over to Heather and gently but firmly takes her hand. Heather tries to pull her hand away. "Come on, Mom," she says, "just let me finish this wall."

Mom smiles, but doesn't say a word. She gently pulls Heather up from the floor. When Heather begins to whine, Mom says, "Do you want to pick out your bedtime story, or shall I do it?"

Heather's voice is sulky as she replies, "I want to."

Mom says, "Fine. Call me when you've brushed your teeth and put on your jammies and I'll come read as much as I can before 8:00. You'd better hustle if you want to read the whole book!"

By this time Heather has figured out that Mom means what she says. She still isn't entirely happy, but she gets ready as quickly as she can; she really does love reading with Mom.

After the story is finished, Mom tells Heather, "You didn't pick up your Legos tonight. You can do it tomorrow before kindergarten or I'll do it and put them on the high shelf."

Heather and her mom have already agreed that toys go on the high shelf when Heather doesn't pick them up. Heather must show that she's ready to have them back by picking up her things for two days.

Follow-through usually involves deciding what you will do. For example, a parent may decide to escort a child to the car for a while if a child is misbehaving. Dotty loved using follow-through because she always had a good novel with her. When her children misbehaved in the grocery store, she would kindly and firmly take them by the hand and walk to the car. Then she would sit in the car and calmly read her novel until they wound themselves down and said, "Okay, we'll behave."

She had discussed what would happen in advance with her children so they knew what she would do—and what they would need to do—before they could leave the car and continue their shopping. And Dotty was smart enough to shop for frozen foods last, because she might have to leave the cart, full of groceries, with the manager while they sat in the car.

When the children misbehaved while they were driving, Dotty would pull over to the side of the road and whip out her novel to read until the children said, "Okay, we'll stop fighting."

As with all Positive Discipline methods, follow-through is effective only when the parent is kind *and* firm. When parents decide to go sit in the car for a while, they can say to their children, "Let me know when you are ready to go back and behave respectfully in the store." This is more effective if you have role-played the difference between respectful and disrespectful grocery store behavior. Parents may feel that they are the ones who suffer from sitting in the car, but fussing, fighting children and angry stares in public places are no fun either. When your children learn that you will follow through with kind, firm action, such behavior usually diminishes. After all, it isn't nearly as much fun to annoy Mom when she just settles down to enjoy a good book!

Kind, firm follow-through makes it possible for children to learn from their own behavior and choices—and for parents to teach.

Four-year-old Tammie had learned some pretty exciting profanity at her preschool. The first time Tammie tried the "F" word on her mother, Barbara over-reacted.

"Tammie!" Barbara said strongly. "Don't you ever *let me hear you talk like that again!"*

Tammie was delighted that she could create such excitement. The next day she tried out some new words for her mother to hear, but this time Barbara was prepared.

She said, "I don't appreciate listening to that kind of language. It's very disrespectful. So I'm going to my room to read for a while. Let me know when you're ready to speak respectfully."

Tammie wasn't quite as delighted to find herself without an audience. Soon she was knocking on her mother's door saying, "I'm ready to talk good now, Mommy."

Later than evening, as she tucked her daughter into bed, Barbara took a moment to explain things to Tammie.

"Honey," she said, "most people don't like hearing those words you used earlier. If you choose to use them in the future you can either go to your room where others can't hear you or I will go to my room for a while. It's up to you."

Tammie snuggled closer to her mom, and Barbara asked her, "What could you do or say when you hear other people using disrespectful language?"

Tammie, inspired by her mother's example, decided that she could leave just like her mother did.

"Could you give them a chance to change their behavior, like I did with you?" Barbara asked.

Tammie said, "I could play with them again when they stop."

A few days later, Tammie heard one of her friends at preschool using one of the "bad" words. She said, "That isn't respectful. I'm going to play with someone else until you're ready to stop saying those words."

We can teach children so much through example and by exploring with "what" and "how" questions. Barbara also demonstrated that adults, too, can learn from mistakes and improve their behavior later. Parents and teachers can ask themselves several questions when responding to a situation.

1. Is the response respectful to the child, adult, and the needs of the situation?

2. Does it allow for differences in temperament?

3. Is it encouraging children to gain confidence and healthy self-esteem?

4. Does it teach life skills for now and for the future?

When you can answer "yes" to these questions, you'll know you're using Positive Discipline skills and effectively shaping your actions to your child's unique self.

As children grow older, it is most effective to involve them in discussing the problem and brainstorming solutions. As we'll see in chapter 15, preschool classes can set rules and find solutions in class meetings and teachers can follow through with firmness and kindness. Solutions don't always (or even usually) need to include consequences or follow-through. It is amazing how creative children can be when they are invited to use their considerable wisdom to solve problems—and how cooperative they can be when they feel listened to and taken seriously.

It is helpful to remember, however, that children simply don't have the same priorities adults do; they're usually perfectly content to have toys everywhere and bedtime whenever they like it. If you haven't discussed a problem or set a rule, it isn't fair to blame a child when he or she doesn't live up to your expectations. And honest mistakes should always be handled differently than willful misbehavior.

Remember that the way you interact with your children will be teaching them about mutual respect, dignity, and responsibility—gifts that will benefit them the rest of their lives.

Kindness and Firmness

Inga needed to stop at the mall to get some kitchen towels. Next door to the linen store is a giant toy store. Inga worried that five-year-old Jenny would demand a trip to the toy store and they would end up struggling with each other when Jenny insisted on a toy purchase. Inga decided to plan ahead and offer a limited choice.

Inga explained to Jenny that they could not buy anything at the toy store today.

> It is amazing how creative children can be when they are invited to use their considerable wisdom to solve problems—and how cooperative they can be when they feel listened to and taken seriously.

Inga offered Jenny a limited choice. They could look at the toys through the window or they could go inside, where Jenny could look at one type of toy.

Inga outlined what she would do. If Jenny began to insist that Inga buy her a toy or refused to leave after looking at the chosen toy or window display, they would leave the mall. If Jenny refused to walk with Inga, Inga would carry her to the car.

Follow-through requires kindness and firmness at the same time. Jenny chose to look at the toys in the building-blocks section of the store, and they went inside.

When Inga said they needed to leave, Jenny grabbed a box of blocks and shouted at her mother that she wanted them. Without a word, Inga calmly pointed to the shelf and Jenny reluctantly replaced the blocks. If Jenny had refused, Inga could have offered to hold her hand as they left the store or carry her—kindly and firmly, without further discussion.

Being kind and firm requires that the adult be calm—not always an easy task when confronted with an unhappy, defiant child. Children do, however, crave loving and effective discipline and are reassured by adults who say what they mean and act on it. Isn't it good to know that you can provide firm guidance without that scrunched-up, grumpy face and loud voice—and that children will respond to you when you can be kind and firm at the same time?

Humor and Laughter

CONTRARY TO POPULAR belief, it isn't permissive or sloppy parenting to have fun along the way. Sometimes the ability to laugh together or to find a creative and funny solution to a problem works better than all the other techniques put together. Humor can be a weapon if it's used to tease or humiliate children, but humor that allows parents, teachers, and children to laugh and learn together will help create an atmosphere of warmth and openness.

Beth was watering the petunias when she heard it: the sound she had grown to dread. Three-year-old Nathan had an unfortunate tendency to whine, and Beth was at her wit's end. She had tried talking, explaining, and ignoring, but nothing seemed to have any effect on Nathan, who continued to whine whenever he wanted something.

Beth turned, hose in hand, as her small son came toward her, and what happened next was probably more desperation than inspiration. As Nathan told her in his high-pitched voice that he wanted some juice, Beth turned off the water with a funny look on her face.

"Nathan," she said to the little boy, who was looking up at her with a perplexed expression, "something is wrong with Mommy's ears. When you whine, I can't hear you at all!"

Beth started toward the front door, with Nathan right behind her. Again Nathan whined for juice, but this time Beth only shook her head and tapped her ear, looking around as if a mosquito were buzzing near her head.

Nathan tried again, but again Beth only shook her head. By the time they reached the kitchen and Nathan opened his mouth to ask for juice, Beth heard something different. The little boy took a deep breath and said in a low, serious voice, "Mommy, can I have some juice?" When Beth turned to look at him, he added, "Please?" for good measure.

Beth laughed and scooped Nathan up for a hug before heading to the refrigerator. "I can hear you perfectly when you ask so nicely," she said.

From that time on, all Beth had to do when Nathan began to whine was tap her ear and shake her head. Nathan would draw an exasperated breath and begin again in a nicer tone of voice.

Not everything can become a game, of course, nor should it. But rules become less difficult to follow when children know that a spontaneous tickling match or pillow battle might erupt at any moment. Taking time to enjoy children and to laugh together works where discipline is concerned, too, and can make life far more pleasant for everyone.

Long-Range Parenting

YOUR OWN KNOWLEDGE of your children's strengths and needs will help you guide and teach them. Remember the list of qualities you wanted your children to possess as adults? Each conversation, every crisis, every act of discipline should foster those qualities in them, and in order to do that, you have to know your child.

The best part of discipline is something you may never have thought of as discipline before. It's the time you spend together talking and playing and learning. Babies, toddlers, and preschoolers are learning every minute of every day; we can either consider those learning experiences a challenge, or we can join with our children in exploring their world, helping them to learn about life and their own capabilities by sharing experiences with them. Warmth and trust, closeness and understanding are tools of discipline, too; with enough of these gentle tools, you may need the other sort far less often.

14

Courage
From "I Blew It Again" to
"I'll Try Again"

THE DICTIONARY TELLS us that "courage" is the ability to disregard fear; a synonym is "bravery." Although we rarely look at it this way, raising and teaching young children requires a tremendous amount of bravery. Remember what it felt like the first time you held a tiny newborn? Tiny fingers so perfectly formed; a fragile head attached to a body unable even to support its weight; veins visible through impossibly soft skin. What an awe-inspiring moment—and what a terrifying one. Here is a creature unbelievably tiny and delicate, completely dependent upon you for its survival.

Parenting and caregiving are daily acts of courage. The responsibility of raising, guiding, and nurturing a tiny child gives most adults more than a moment's pause. It doesn't seem to lessen as the child grows, either. Let three or four years pass: Now see the same child on one side of a room, stomping her feet, refusing to put on her coat, or daring you to stop her from throwing her blocks; position a weary adult with sleep-clogged eyes, a work schedule to meet, and two days' worth of unwashed dishes spilling out of the sink on the other side of the room, and you have a true picture of courage.

From time to time, though, we all lose our courage; the fear and the weariness take over and we become *dis*couraged. Our supply of courage gets drained away by fatigue, emotional and physical demands, and our child's failure to fit his needs conveniently with our own. It takes a brave heart to remain kind, act firmly, and behave with compassion—especially when we must also wrestle with doubts about our ability to manage work expectations, maintain healthy relationships with the other people in our lives, and cope with health, money, and safety issues. Then, all too often, we crawl into bed at night and find our sleep haunted by anxieties about being a "good" parent or caregiver. We and the children in our care need to move from discouragement to encouragement.

> No astronaut stepping into outer space can rival the courage adults display in the daily act of raising or caring for young children.

To feel encouraged is to be filled with courage and hope. And it takes courage to be willing to learn, to risk new ideas and ways of responding. Whenever we risk changing our own behavior, we step into the unknown. No astronaut stepping into outer space can rival the courage adults display in the daily act of raising or caring for young children.

"I Blew It—Again!"

Nancy, a preschool teacher, attended a training workshop where she learned about the mistaken goals of misbehavior (see chapters 19, 20, and 21). She was eager to apply her new knowledge in her classroom. Imagine her dismay when the very next morning she found herself chasing a resistant four-year-old around the table in the art room. As she chased after the child, she strove desperately to find a different way to deal with this situation. She kept repeating to herself, "Give the child choices! Give her choices! Give her choices!" But she couldn't seem to think of any!

In another part of town, Mary Collins eyed the stack of parenting books on the shelf beside her. She lay on her bed listening to her three-year-old sobbing on the other side of the bedroom door. She felt overwhelmed and overcome with despair and wondered if she was a complete failure as a mom. She tried to stay calm whenever her son misbehaved, but this afternoon, when she found the toilet overflowing from the wads of toilet paper he had been flushing, she had completely lost it. She yelled at him, spanked him, and then stormed into her own room. "I thought I would never do that to my kids," she thought miserably.

Nancy and Mary want to change the way they behave. They try to do so but find themselves acting in the old ways they so want to avoid. Are they hopeless failures? Of course not! They blew it, no doubt about that. But learning to change our behavior is all about "blowing it." The process of learning involves making mistakes. Next time, Nancy and Mary might do something more effective, beginning with adjusting their own attitudes. It is amazing how much a situation changes as soon as we see it with humor. Nancy might try spinning like a top instead of chasing the resistant child. That might make him stop running and stare in wonder. She then might wink at the child and say, "I'll bet you have some ideas about how to help me right now."

Mary might remember that an overflowing toilet will make a very interesting story for her child's "book of remembrance." She then might see the problem as an opportunity to teach her son the importance of cleaning up messes. There are many possibilities that are easy to see—in hindsight. It takes courage to get up and try again after we fall.

When a child falls and cuts his lip while still mastering the art of walking on wobbly legs, does he give up? He may sit and ponder the situation for a while, but inevitably he dusts himself off and goes at it again. That is the essence of courage. Just because Nancy can't think of alternatives in the heat of the moment, does that mean they don't exist or that she won't ever come up with any? Over time she will get better at learning to apply the new ideas she has learned. What about Mary? Mary may have acted in ways she abhors, but with courage she can face her son and apologize for losing it, and together they can try again.

The Process of Change

CHANGE RARELY HAPPENS overnight. It is a process; one that sometimes takes longer than we might like. Courage and determination, coupled with awareness and understanding, will carry us through. The first step in this process is to notice the behavior we want to change.

Anisha Pahwi was determined to quit nagging her daughter by always telling her to "hurry up!" One morning she looked at the clock and saw that it was nearly time to leave for work. She stomped to her daughter Suba's room and rapped on the door, calling out for her to hurry up. No sooner had she spoken than she clamped her hand over her mouth. "Oh no, not again! I blew it!"

But this is great! Not because she said the very thing she wanted to avoid but because she *noticed* that she said it. The very fact that Anisha noticed her actions represents the first step toward changing them. Just when we are tempted to feel discouraged, we need to congratulate ourselves for taking this first step. That is how we get the courage to keep trying. Next time, Anisha might try saying, "What ideas do you have to speed things up so we won't be late?" It is so encouraging—for adults and children— to see mistakes as opportunities to learn.

Jennifer wanted to learn how to involve her son Jeb at mealtime instead of feeling annoyed with his constant attempts to distract her while she prepared dinner. She was pretty sure that Jeb's behavior fit the pattern of the mistaken goal of undue attention (chapter 20). Armed with her new understanding, she felt confident and ready for a fresh start. That evening, as she worked at the kitchen counter, she made a space next to her on the pastry cloth and set out some biscuit dough for Jeb to shape.

The project began with great promise. Jeb was an eager helper. Unfortunately, he too was involved in the change process. Jeb's part of the change process is called "change back." He knew what his mother's old style looked like. It was familiar. When she acted differently, Jeb tried to get her to change back to her old, familiar responses, even though they weren't all that much fun for either of them.

So within a few minutes, Jeb was complaining that the dough was sticking to his hands. Jennifer helped him clean his hands. Then he began to fuss that he wanted a different set of cutters, insisting he needed the one his mother was using. She coaxed him to use the ones he had, but he was soon whining that he was thirsty.

At this point, Jennifer lost patience and told Jeb to wash his hands and go into the playroom until dinner was ready. She said she would take care of the biscuits herself. Jeb wandered down the hall, looking and feeling discouraged. As Jennifer furiously rolled out the remaining biscuits, she watched Jeb retreat; then she stopped working, realizing she had blown it. She shook her head and gave a weary sigh. Then she decided to start all over.

Jennifer followed Jeb to his room and apologized, and she asked him if he would like to try again. Jeb was eager to rejoin his mother in the kitchen, even though he brought a hangdog expression with him. It didn't take him long to pick up his pat-

terns of whining and complaining. This time, Jennifer refused to be hooked. She simply said, "I'm sure you can figure out a way to solve that problem" and "What do you need to do about that?" Soon Jeb realized that his mom was not going to give him special service. He also began to feel good about solving the problems himself.

We hope that the words in this book become like a little voice whispering to Jennifer and Jeb, Nancy, Mary, Anisha, and all the other people out there whose shoulders slump in discouragement. "Way to go!" we whisper, "you've taken the first step! Good job!" All of us are discouraged occasionally, because all of us make mistakes. When we can learn to recognize and celebrate even our smallest steps toward success, we are halfway home.

Preliminary Phase: Awareness That Change Is Needed

Change begins with awareness, when we discover a behavior we wish to change and a new one with which to replace it.

THE PROCESS OF CHANGE

Change is a process. It happens over time and involves a number of stages that we can learn to recognize and celebrate along the way. Understanding these phases can remind us that we are normal, encourage self-forgiveness, and give us the courage to learn from our mistakes.

- Preliminary Phase: Awareness that change is needed

- Phase One: Change after the fact

- Phase Two: Change and change back

- Phase Three: Change during the act

- Phase Four: Change before the act

- Phase Five: "Autopilot"

You hate taking your daughter to the store because you know what always happens. You tell her she can choose a treat but she throws a tantrum when she insists upon a two-pound bag of candy, which you refuse to buy. When you offer her the box of animal crackers you had in mind, she shoves them away. You have become aware of the concept of limited choices.

Phase One: Change After the Fact

We begin to notice when we do the "same old thing." You are at the toy store checkout stand; your daughter is screaming because she wants a limited-edition fairy tale book that costs $60 and you will not buy it. You thought you had given a limited choice by telling her she could pick out a book for her treat. You meant that she could have an inexpensive paperback book. You realize the choice you gave wasn't very limited. Oops!

Phase Two: Change and Change Back

Eventually, we choose to change our behavior. Those around us become uncomfortable and try to get us to change back to the old, more familiar behavior.

You are ordering dinner at the local diner. You did a good job of giving a limited choice, telling your daughter that she could select anything from the children's menu. She is just not used to having you set clear limits with which you are prepared to follow through. She demands a more expensive adult menu item. You repeat her choices and ignore her complaints. Either she quits fussing or you calmly leave the restaurant with her. Her "change back" behavior does not work.

Phase Three: Change During the Act

We notice we are repeating the old behavior while we're actually doing it.

You get out of the car and tell your daughter that she can pick out a book for a treat. Whoa! You catch yourself. You add that the book can cost no more than $5. That was a close call!

Phase Four: Change Before the Act

We catch ourselves just before we act in the old way and change to the new behavior.

As you unbuckle your daughter's seat belt in the mall parking lot, she asks if she may have a treat. "Sure," you say. Then you stop and think. You remember to offer a limited choice. You smile and say, "You may have $2 to spend on a toy." She knows you mean it and complies willingly.

Phase Five: "Autopilot"

We act in the new way without even thinking about doing so. It has become automatic.

You read the menu choices and tell your daughter she may have milk or juice. She readily selects milk, and no one gets indigestion. Effective, limited choices have become a part of your natural style. Your child accepts the "new" you. The change process is complete.

Remember, it is usually easier—on us and on those around us—to work on changes one at a time. Choose simple things; practice patience. As the old saying tells us, "The longest journey begins with a single step."

Encouragement

IF THERE'S ONE message parents and their children need to get firmly in mind early in the parenting process, it's this: if we can be human with each other, give each other room to learn and grow, trust one another to continue loving, and laugh together occasionally, we can survive just about anything. Allowing both children and parents the room to make mistakes and own up to them is one of the best ways to build a relationship based on trust, warmth, and closeness—and it begins in the earliest days of childhood.

We all make mistakes. The change process helps us understand the role mistakes can play, why we meet resistance, and that such steps are normal and not signs of failure. When we accept ourselves, even during the times we feel disappointed with our own behavior, we model courage to our children. We make mistakes, learn from them, and move on. When a child sees courage in action, she too feels encouraged.

Children need courage, too. They face new tasks, frustration with their own lack of skills, and constant demands on their behavior. Encourage what children *can* do instead of focusing on all the things they can't do. This means noticing small successes. Change is as challenging for children as it is for adults. Maybe your child did not manage to stay quiet for the full ten minutes of your phone call, but be sure to let him know you appreciate the five minutes he played quietly while you talked to your friend. Encourage him with your faith in him: "I bet the next time I am on the phone you will play quietly with your toys even longer."

Vague Praise Is Not Encouraging

ALL OF US need encouragement, and warm words and appreciation are effective ways to offer it. Remember, though, that vague "attaboys" aren't always the best way to encourage young children. Be sure to keep your encouragement specific. For instance, if a three-year-old at the child care center brings you his latest drawing and you tell him, "Oh, it's the most gorgeous picture I've ever seen—I'm going to frame it and hang it on the wall," you may not be helping him as much as you think. You may have taught him that the most important thing he can do is to please people, which can be a dangerous creed to live by. Telling that same child, "I see you really like red and yellow. Can you tell me about these shapes?" opens the door for talking and learning together.

Celebrate the Positive

AS WITH SO many other aspects of life around young children, our attitude is a key. Do we even notice the small successes and efforts to cooperate? Or is our attention focused on the blots and boo-boos that are an inevitable part of a preschooler's day?

Observe yourself closely sometime soon. What do you notice? Do you walk into the room after a child has put away the crayons and art supplies and notice the two pens he missed? Or do you congratulate him on taking such good care of the art equipment and thank him for putting things away? If there are tasks that need doing, ask if he sees anything else that needs to be put away. When he notices the pens, smile warmly as he adds them to the box on the shelf. This way, he feels competent twice, once for his first attempt and again for noticing the items left out and taking care of them too.

Attitude Counts

WHAT IS YOUR attitude toward young children? Do you see them as darling dolls to be dressed and fussed over? Do you regard them as dangerous circus animals who require vigilant supervision? Or do you look at a small child and marvel at the amazing skills, talents, and abilities gathered in such a small package? The attitude with which we approach young children has a powerful influence on the way they see themselves and the world around them (and on their behavior). Our attitude can be characterized in three ways. We can see children as:

- Recipients
- Objects
- Assets

> The attitude with which we approach young children has a powerful influence on the way they see themselves and the world around them (and on their behavior).

Children As Recipients

We treat children as recipients when we do too much for them, rescue them, and overprotect them. Children learn to see themselves as recipients when adults fail to recognize their inborn competence and capability.

When Howard entered preschool at age three, he brought his lunch with him, packed in a bright new container. At lunchtime, he sat passively in front of the unopened lunch box. A teacher noticed and offered to help him open it. Howard continued to sit and wait. The teacher opened his lunch box and went off to help another child. A few moments later, the teacher glanced at Howard and stared in surprise.

Howard was sitting quietly, making no attempt to eat his lunch. His teacher came over again, this time to offer help with opening containers, pouring juice, and unwrapping his food. Still Howard did not eat.

That evening, the teacher approached Howard's mother, worriedly explaining about lunchtime. His mother looked down nervously and admitted that Howard never had fed himself. She explained that Howard's grandma lived with the family and still fed Howard all of his meals. Howard's role in his family is that of a recipient. He has not learned that he can do things on his own.

Children As Objects

We treat children as objects when we lecture, demand, and try to control their feelings and behavior.

Martha attended a preschool run by a very energetic woman. This woman's energy did not extend to cleaning up children's messes. She told the children what to do, when to do it, and how to do it. When the children washed their hands at lunchtime, she stood guard over the sink, telling them when they had enough soap, when their hands were sufficiently rinsed, and when they were adequately dried. She did not have time to clean up the messes that might result from young children doing things for themselves.

Is it any surprise that the children in Martha's class did not learn many new skills? They were objects to be directed and were not viewed as capable people able to learn skills.

Children As Assets

We treat children as assets when we involve them and treat them as capable people who deserve dignity and respect. An asset is something or someone we value. Children do not decide one day that they are valuable and significant; adults must have faith and patience (and teach the skills) that enable children to believe in their own competence.

At mealtime, Josh's parents can find ways for him to help out rather than ways to keep him from getting underfoot. Josh can count out the silverware, plates, and napkins as his dad stirs the stew bubbling on the stove. When it is clean-up time at the preschool, Josh and his classmates sort paper into the recycling bins, gather mats into a pile, and clear their cups after snack time. Grandma appreciates Josh's helping hands when he holds the yarn she is winding into a ball. Even very young children can be encouraged to contribute, viewed as capable, and genuinely appreciated for their efforts.

Children can do far more things than most adults realize. It takes training and patience and probably will mean cleaning up a mess or two, but seeing children as assets (and helping children see themselves this way) makes the task worthwhile.

Loving the Child You Have

MOST PARENTS HAVE dreams for their children. We want them to be healthy and happy, but more than that, we want them to fulfill all the potential we believe we see in them. We may cherish visions of our child as a star athlete or musician, a Nobel prize–winning scientist, or even (yes, it's true) president of the United States.

Michael had dreamed of the day his son would be born. He proudly carried his newborn into a room decorated with pennants and some of Dad's own trophies, and he placed a tiny, blue football in the infant's crib. As little Kevin grew, he was signed up for every sport. His dad was never too busy to toss the football or to take some batting practice. Kevin played tee-ball with the other five-year-olds and soccer with the youngsters' league. He had a miniature basketball hoop and a perfectly oiled baseball glove. His dad never missed a practice or a game.

There was only one problem: Kevin hated sports. He did his best, but he had little natural ability and he loathed competition. Alone in his room, he dreamed of being an actor or a comedian, of standing on a stage before smiling, applauding people. He lined up his stuffed animals and told his favorite stories and jokes, hearing in his mind the enthusiastic response. He regaled his neighborhood buddies with tall tales.

As Michael talked eagerly to his son about the "majors," Kevin only sighed. Shattering his dad's dreams would take more courage than he possessed; he was afraid of losing his father's love and approval. So he played on, growing just a little more discouraged with every game, feeling disappointed that he would never be the son his father really wanted.

> One of the most beautiful ways of expressing love for a child is learning to love *that* child—not the child you wish you had.

Does Michael love his son? Undoubtedly. But one of the most beautiful ways of expressing love for a child is learning to love *that* child—not the child you wish you had. All parents have dreams for their children, and dreaming is not a bad thing. If we are to encourage our children, though, and build their sense of self-esteem and belonging, we must avoid "buts" and take time to teach.

"I Love You, But . . ."

We've all heard it before: the compliment that simply sets up the criticism. "You did a good job, but . . ." "Thanks for picking up your toys, but . . ." "I'm glad you dressed yourself today, but . . ." All too often, parents can't resist following a compliment with a helpful suggestion for doing even better. What we fail to realize is that whatever comes after the "but" is what sticks in the mind; what came before the "but" is minimized or even lost entirely.

Sometimes, too, children develop the "compliment flinch." They've learned that whenever Mom or Dad says something nice, it means something not-so-nice is sure to follow. When that happens, whatever power our encouragement and appreciation might have had is gone.

If what you truly want is to encourage your children and build their sense of worth and belonging, separate your suggestions for improvement from your encouragement. Let your smiles, thanks, and appreciation stand alone; find a quiet moment another time to give that helpful hint or suggestion. Most important of all, be sure you've provided your children with the skills and knowledge they need to do their best.

HOW TO TEACH A YOUNG CHILD

Teaching a young child has four basic steps:

1. Let him watch you. As your little one watches you set the table, feed the dog, or make a bed, explain in simple terms what you are doing and why.
2. You do it with his help. Next time there's an opportunity, encourage your child to help you do the task. Remind him of the things you told him before, and let him know you welcome his help.
3. He does it with your help. Now it's time for your child to try his hand at the task, with your occasional help—and lots of encouragement.

Take Time to Teach

It was a busy Sunday morning, and Anita Casper was in a rush. Church started in just an hour; breakfast still needed to be cleaned up, and the beds needed to be made. Keith was dressing the baby, but both Anita and her four-year-old daughter, Lindy, still had to get dressed. Suddenly Anita decided that it was time Lindy helped out a little. After all, she was four years old.

As Anita combed Lindy's hair, she asked, "Would you help me out, sweetie? While I get dressed and do the dishes, would you make your bed?"

Lindy looked up into her mother's harried face and smiled. "Okay, Mommy," she said. "I can do it."

Sheets and blankets are big, and four-year-old arms are short. Lindy wrestled valiantly with the covers, tucking and smoothing as best she could, but as she set her favorite teddy bear next to her pillow, she knew it didn't look quite like it did when Mommy made it. But she felt pleased; after all, it was her first time.

Anita didn't have a chance to check on her daughter's handiwork until after church and lunch. She took one look at the bunched covers and tangled sheets, sighed, and set about straightening things up. When she'd repaired Lindy's work, she went on to the next chore without a second thought.

She might have thought again if she'd seen Lindy's face a little later. The little girl stood looking at her tidy, perfectly made bed and felt her spirits sink.

---

4. You watch him. By now, your child should feel confident enough to do the task on his own, with encouragement and loving support from you. Remember to keep your standards realistic; expecting perfection can cause both of you to become discouraged. Offer encouragement and appreciation for your child's efforts. If you make "helping Mom and Dad" a pleasant adventure now, it will take much of the hassle out of chores during the years ahead!

The same four-step process works in preschool classrooms, too. Keep demonstrations simple, and encourage children's efforts. There is no "wrong" way to do a task—only first steps in the process.

She'd done her very best, but obviously it hadn't been good enough: Mom had to fix it. The next time Anita asks her daughter to make the bed, she may receive a different, less willing response. After all, why try when you know you can't succeed?

The Magic of Teaching

Teaching children can take many forms and is one of the most genuinely encouraging things we can do. Surprisingly enough, it doesn't have to be unpleasant. Most young children have an inborn desire to imitate their parents and to do "grown-up" things—a desire parents sometimes unwittingly squelch. It's amazing how often we tell an enthusiastic three-year-old, "No, honey, you're too little," and then find ourselves wondering why she won't help out when she's seven or eight.

Taking the time to teach gives children the skills and abilities to succeed (an essential part of developing self-esteem), and it can also provide us with precious moments of closeness and even fun with our young children.

Unconditional Love: "No Matter What!"

SOME DAYS WE feel just plain snarly, gnarly, and low—and so do our children. Wouldn't it be interesting if we could hear our children's thoughts?

They might wonder, "Who will love me if I am mean, grumpy, and can't even pour milk without a spill?" "Who will love me when I am tired, cranky, and in trouble for hitting my little brother?" "Who will love me if I can't even make it to the potty in time?"

What answer do children hear? They might hear (in our words and in our actions) "I love you only when you meet my expectations." Or they might hear "I love you no matter what! I will love you always!" The second answer is the voice of unconditional love.

The arms we seek when we feel low and unlovely, the people who offer hugs when we mess up, the safe harbor where the water is always calm and warm—that is unconditional love. Children need to know that they are loved "just because" and that there are no strings attached. They need to know we love and accept them when they are "good" and when they are not so good, that we will always be in their corner with a welcoming smile, that there will always be a soothing hand to smooth life's troubled brow. In short, our children crave the same sort of reassurance, acceptance, and affection that we long for ourselves.

Matt came home one day with a note from his preschool teacher saying he had had a "pretty rough day" and "found it exceptionally difficult to share this morning." His mom knew they would need to figure out what had happened, but first she knew Matt needed some time to compose himself. He stomped off to his room without even saying hello to her. She gave him about half an hour, then she joined him and asked if he could use a hug. Sure enough, Matt came into her arms and within a short while was sobbing out a story of how mean the other kids had been to him. Matt's mom knows that he probably had contributed to the morning's problems, but for now she just lets him pour out his hurt without any comments, reprimands, or advice.

> Children need to know that they are loved "just because" and that there are no strings attached. They need to know we love and accept them when they are "good" and when they are not so good, that we will always be in their corner with a welcoming smile, that there will always be a soothing hand to smooth life's troubled brow.

Children need a place where it is safe to be less than perfect. They need to feel worthwhile even when they are difficult to be with. When a child throws a tantrum, soils his pants, or breaks a treasured vase, he needs to know that the adults in his life will continue to have faith in him and that they will not heap shame, blame, or criticism upon his already bowed head. The message adults need to give a young child is that making mistakes does not mean he will never master a new skill.

Manuel was dressed in a new shirt and pants, proudly sporting his first bow tie. Manuel was to be the ring bearer in his cousin's wedding, and he was duly aware of the gravity of the occasion. At three and a half, Manuel had mastered drinking out of a cup long ago. Yet today of all days, in all the excitement, he missed his mouth and tumbled half a glass of milk onto his glorious bow tie. His eyes brimmed over with tears.

Seeing his distress, his auntie quickly helped him blot up the milk and suggested they get some water to clean off his bow tie. She gave Manuel a big hug, saying, "I am sure you are feeling pretty excited today, like the rest of us. Don't worry about it. We all have accidents sometimes. I spilled my orange juice when I was pouring it this morning." Manuel smiled and shared a giggle with his aunt. It felt good to know that others make mistakes too.

Labels and Other Self-Fulfilling Prophecies

IMAGINE A CHILD with a paper bag over her head. Painted on the bag are several words: "noisy," "messy," and "picky eater." Wouldn't it be difficult to look at that child and notice how quietly she works on a puzzle or how carefully she carries her juice to the table, especially when she spilled it while setting it down, or how eagerly she ate the sample of salmon the class prepared together? Once we apply labels to a child, it is like placing a large bag over her head. We can no longer see other possibilities because we have become blinded by the labels that hide her true identity from us.

> Once we apply labels to a child, it is like placing a large bag over her head. We can no longer see other possibilities because we have become blinded by the labels that hide her true identity from us.

It seemed that Rick and Carol were forever telling their five-year-old daughter, Lizzie, to be careful. Lizzie, they often told their friends and relatives, was "accident-prone." Each day, as Carol sent Lizzie out to play, she called after her, "Be careful, baby. You know you get hurt so easily." Over and over again, she sighed as she cleaned off the latest scrape or bump and kissed away Lizzie's tears.

"I should buy stock in a bandage company," Rick joked as Lizzie played nearby. "We go through a case a week!"

It was after a parenting class one night that Carol and Rick sat down together and decided that something had to change.

"We need to do something different," Carol said. "Maybe if we don't make such a big deal out of things, Lizzie will stop having so many accidents."

"I don't see how that could help," Rick said, "but it's worth a try."

So the next time Lizzie appeared with a scrape, Carol said warmly, "Why, honey, that's not like you!" And after she'd calmly comforted her daughter, she gave her a hug and sent her off to play again.

Slowly but surely, Rick and Carol began to tell Lizzie by words and actions that she wasn't doomed to injuries, that she could do lots of things and take good care of herself. Unbelievable as it seemed, the day dawned when Rick and Carol realized that it had been several weeks since Lizzie had hurt herself.

Children often see themselves through our eyes. When we tell them they're lazy or rude, they may respond with an emphatic "Am not!" but deep inside it is hard not to believe that the powerful adults are right. When we refer to a young child as "a little monster" or "the beast" or "a discipline problem" (even when we tell ourselves that we're "only kidding"), we shouldn't be surprised when children see themselves that way—and act accordingly.

The concept works in reverse, too. By naming the qualities we appreciate and value in young children, we can reinforce them. Preschool teachers, for instance, can make a practice of taking time each day to simply observe.

One day Miss Ellen stepped back and watched the children in the housekeeping corner, draped in colorful scarves and vests, twirling merrily. In another corner, Melissa was busy serving up pretend pizza, while David soothed the baby doll. Ellen found a time to comment on what a caring and loving "father" David was to his baby and told Melissa what a thoughtful host she was and what a careful job she did of dividing up the pizza.

Comments like these give names to the qualities we value and encourage, and they help children not only learn but practice them.

A Matter of Time

MANY PARENTS COMPLAIN that they have to do everything for their children, that they must nag and remind them to get things done, or that their children are lazy. Using the power of encouragement and appreciation, looking for the positive, and taking the time to teach appropriate skills can harness children's natural energy and desire to "help" and produce competent young people.

Undoubtedly, encouraging children takes time and effort, and teaching children is time-consuming. But letting children know what's expected, the best way to do things, and how to succeed in life is an investment of time that will more than pay you back as your children grow.

Yes, teaching and encouraging our active young children takes an immense amount of time and energy. And yes, it usually is easier to just do it ourselves. But when we pick up the toys, put on the coat, or wipe up the spilled juice in the name of efficiency, we miss valuable opportunities to teach and encourage skills and beliefs that give our children a sense of self-esteem and self-confidence, attitudes they will carry with them for a lifetime.

Teaching and parenting preschoolers is a time-consuming business. But healthy, confident children who've learned they are capable of learning grow up to be healthy, confident, enterprising adults. Isn't that worth the effort?

Roots and Wings

YOUR CHILDREN WILL have their own dreams. Take time to explore your children's hopes and dreams with them; use these opportunities to learn about each other. A wise person once said that good parents give their children two things: one is roots and the other is wings. Loving your children as they are will give them roots; encouraging your children to believe in themselves, to develop life skills, and to dream will give them the wings to take risks, to try new things, and to live fully.

Will there be rough times along the way? Of course! Parents and children alike will make their share of mistakes. Both will get lots of practice in learning to change. But remember what we've been saying all along: mistakes are wonderful opportunities to learn!

15

Class Meetings for Preschoolers

It is class meeting time at the ABC Preschool. As the youngsters settle into a circle, Mr. Scott, the teacher, consults the agenda.

"It sounds like we've had a problem on the playground with people throwing wood chips at one another. Does anyone have something to say about this problem, or can someone offer a suggestion of how we might solve it?"

Five-year-old Girard raises his hand. "Whoever throws wood chips could take a time-out!" Four-year-old Natalie waves her hand, and when called upon, offers, "We could not have wood chips anymore and have grass instead."

The teacher looks toward three-year-old Cristina, whose little hand has been patiently held aloft, and calls on her. "Guess what?" Cristina says with a bright smile.

"What, Cristina?" Mr. Scott asks.

"I had bananas in my cereal today."

"Mmmm, that must have tasted good." Mr. Scott smiles and thanks Cristina for her comment, then asks for more suggestions about the wood chip problem. Although Cristina was clearly not thinking about wood chips, she was still a valued member of the group. When children are old enough to participate actively in group or circle time activities (usually around the age of two and a half), they are ready for class meetings.

What Is a Class Meeting?

CLASS MEETINGS ARE far more than group problem-solving sessions. In a class meeting, children gather on a regular basis to help each other, encourage each other, learn communication skills, and develop their judgment and wisdom. By far the most powerful effect of class meetings, though, whatever the age of the child, is to create a sense of belonging. Because the need for belonging lies at the heart of all mistaken goal behavior (see chapters 19, 20, and 21), it makes sense that addressing this need will have the greatest long-range effect on the behavior of children in the group.

Class meetings provide many opportunities to learn and strengthen skills. They aid in the acquisition of social skills and promote language development.

> Class meetings provide many opportunities to learn and strengthen skills. They aid in the acquisition of social skills and promote language development.

The meetings foster a sense of both group and individual responsibility and empower young children with positive attitudes about their own capabilities and significance—attitudes that not only help shape their behavior but also build their self-esteem.

"I can see the value of class meetings for elementary school children," you may be saying, "but aren't preschoolers a bit young?" Even the youngest members of your preschool group can begin to cultivate the attitudes nurtured by the class meeting process. In this chapter we will take a look at ways you can begin class meetings for the preschool set. For a broader discussion of class meetings, see *Positive Discipline in the Classroom* by Jane Nelsen and Lynn Lott (Prima Publishing, 1997).

How Young Is Too Young?

PRESCHOOL TEACHERS MAY be wondering how valuable class meetings can be for young children. Three-year-olds like Cristina will certainly have different contributions to make than will older children. Still, there is real value in including the little ones, the greatest being that their sense of belonging to the group is established.

Children ranging from two and a half to five years old can work together in a productive and encouraging class meeting. The younger children can learn from their older role models, and the older children can learn to consider and include the needs of the younger ones.

Even if your entire class consists of two- or three-year-olds, you can still enjoy class meetings together. The teacher becomes the role model when older

THE FOUR ELEMENTS OF CLASS MEETINGS FOR PRESCHOOLERS

- To give compliments and appreciation

- To empower children to help each other

- To solve problems that affect the group

- To plan future activities

children are not present; he may need to generate most of the suggestions and help the children learn to make choices. Even toddlers can get into the act, although the main purpose of meetings for them may simply be planning an outing or fun activity together rather than solving problems. Taking into consideration the social and language skills of the children you work with will help you know how much you can expect to accomplish.

Young children learn the elements of class meetings by jumping right in and participating. For example, the concept of "helping others" can be taught by finding someone to help. (Young children often need to experience something before they can put a name to it.)

It may be helpful to list the four elements of class meetings on a chart, perhaps in bright colors, and to follow them in order. Even for children who can't read, seeing that there is a plan can help focus their attention.

Compliments and Appreciation

COMPLIMENTS ARE CLEARLY affected by the age of the children offering them. Four- and five-year-olds may say things like "I compliment Jane for being my friend" or "I compliment Eddie because he played dress-up with me." You may even hear an occasional "She pushed me off the swing!" (Well, they don't have it completely perfected yet!)

Two- and three-year-olds don't always understand the concept of compliments. They are more likely to say "I love my mommy," "I have a teddy bear at home," or "I get to go to McDonald's for dinner." These little ones usually say whatever is on their minds, but teachers can smile and thank them for their comments. The feeling of having contributed is no less because the "compliment" was a bit off target.

Teachers can ask some helpful questions to guide children in learning how to give compliments. "What is something that you like about the school?" for instance, or "Is there someone who helped you feel good today?" They can also model giving compliments. "I want to compliment all of you on the delicious cake you made yesterday. And I loved how all of the tables were washed and cleaned up after we finished mixing the batter." "Mary, I want to compliment you on letting us help you with the problem you were having about not liking your lunch. I appreciated the ideas that I heard because I can use some of them too."

"Kid of the Week"

A special preschool variation on compliments is what has been dubbed "Kid of the Week" at one child care center.

Each week there is a special "Kid of the Week" circle time, and every child in the class will be selected at least once during each year. The teacher brings a large sheet of paper and an assortment of colored pens to the circle. At the top of the page she writes the child's name.

Let's say that today Maureen is Kid of the Week. The teacher has written "I like Maureen because . . ." at the top of the paper. Just to get everybody in the mood, everyone sings the following words to the tune of "Camptown Races" while Maureen grins with pleasure.

> *We like Maureen, yes we do*
> *Doodah! Doodah!*
> *We like Maureen, yes we do*
> *Oh, yes we do.*
> *Gonna like her all day,*
> *Gonna like her all year,*
> *Thank her for the things she does*
> *We like her because . . .*

Then each of the children take turns saying what it is they like or appreciate about Maureen while the teacher writes their comments on the sheet of paper. Maureen's classmates have this to say about her: "I like her because she's my friend." "She plays with me." "She has a sparkle in her eye." (Wow!) "She jumps like Tigger." Toward the end, two-and-a-half-year-old David says, "She is like a mommy." What a beautiful and heartfelt tribute.

If the children seem to be a bit stuck about what to say (or if they resort to comments like "I like her shoes"), the teacher can offer some guidance by asking questions. "Who wants to say that Maureen can come to his or her birthday party?" "Who remembers a game you played in the dress-up area with Maureen this week?" The teacher can also add comments to show appreciation for the child and to model the skill of complimenting others.

If some of the children still have trouble thinking of something to say (or are just a bit shy), the teacher can ask, "Who would like to have his name written on the paper as one of Maureen's friends?" Even the youngest child can make this contribution. When all who want a turn have finished, the teacher rolls up the paper and ties it with a bright ribbon. Another child is chosen to present the scroll to Maureen, and the circle finishes with another song, perhaps a variation on "For He's (or She's) a Jolly Good Fellow."

Not a bad way to start a child's day, is it? For the rest of the week, Maureen is the teacher's special helper. She is invited to dismiss the others from circle, help set out lunch boxes, and ring the bell at the end of playtime. The scroll goes home with Maureen's parents that night. Many families report that for months the scroll remains showcased on their refrigerator doors. Children frequently request that the scroll be read to them each day. Can you feel the tremendous value of this paper? It represents a warm outpouring of love and caring for Maureen from her peers.

Helping Each Other

NEXT UP AT the class meeting is "helping each other." This time in your class meeting is an opportunity for children to ask for help with something that is a problem for them.

It is Tuesday morning at the Hill Harbor Child Care Center. The class of three-and four-year-olds is just beginning their class meeting with their teacher, Mr. Silk. He asks if anyone needs help from the group today.

Matthias raises his hand and announces, "I can't wake up in the morning." Many of the other children agree that it's hard for them, too. Mr. Silk asks if anyone has a suggestion for Matthias. The children offer all sorts of helpful ideas: "Go to bed earlier." "Get up anyway." "Come to school in pajamas."

Mr. Silk turns to Matthias. "Do you think any of these ideas will help you, or should the group think of some more?" Matthias pauses to consider, then says he is going to "get up anyway."

Next, Julian raises his hand and says he needs help because "my mom doesn't have enough money." After sympathizing with Julian, other children volunteer that they have that problem, too. Julian's friends are eager to help. Some of the children offer to bring in money. Bobby suggests that Julian could do some jobs to get money. Katie says, "My mom will help." Devon recommends, "Your mom can get a job that makes more money."

It is unlikely that Julian's mom will have more money as a result of this discussion. But Julian was genuinely concerned about money and his concern was treated respectfully. He has also learned that his classmates care about his needs, and that some of them share similar worries. "Helping each other" can become a very powerful part of class meetings.

Parents may be invited to place items on the agenda too and to visit and join in the class meeting. Seeing firsthand the experience their child is enjoying may encourage them to try similar meetings at home.

"Put It on the Agenda!"

An agenda is a list of topics and tasks simply written on a piece of paper or a corner of the chalkboard that everyone can reach. Children and adults list things they wish to discuss at the next meeting. Effective class meetings follow an agenda. In addition to providing a list of things to discuss, an agenda can serve as a cool-off device as well.

When Jon comes stomping over in a rage to tell the teacher that "Ben just killed a beetle," the teacher can share his concern and suggest that "How insects should be treated" would make a very good topic for their class meeting. She asks Jon if he would like to put it on the agenda. He readily agrees and together they write "bugs" on the agenda. The teacher sounds out the word "bugs" with Jon and he writes his name next to it. If Jon is very young, the teacher may write down "bug" and Jon's name. Or she may encourage Jon to draw a picture of a bug and either trace over his own name or make his own mark. Involving Jon in some way is respectful and creates a sense of responsibility and influence.

When it's time for problem solving, the teacher will look at the agenda and ask Jon to explain the problem of bugs to the others. Because Jon felt listened to when he was angry and placed his item on the agenda, he can now discuss the problem calmly.

Jon's teacher will watch to see that the group focuses on the treatment of insects—not on who killed the beetle or how he should be punished. Class meetings are for solving problems together and for nurturing concern for others and respect; they aren't intended to serve as judge and jury. Teachers love class meetings because they don't have to solve every problem and they can delay solutions until everyone can be involved.

> Class meetings are for solving problems together and for nurturing concern for others and respect; they aren't intended to serve as judge and jury. Teachers love class meetings because they don't have to solve every problem and they can delay solutions until everyone can be involved.

Solving Problems

IT MAY COME as a surprise, but even young children can be remarkably creative when it comes to solving problems. One afternoon, the following note appeared near the sign-out sheet at the Mountain View Preschool: "We are having a small bake sale this Thursday afternoon. We are learning to be responsible by replacing a ripped-up library book. We will bake cookies at school and sell them for twenty-five cents each. The children would also like to earn twenty-five cents at home by doing a special job. The bake sale idea came out of our class meeting discussion about a damaged book. We also discussed and demonstrated how to carry books and how to turn pages at the edge."

Over the course of the next week, the children prepared several batches of cookies during class time, learning new skills (and having a great time) in the process. On Thursday, the sale took place and was so successful that even after subtracting the cost of the cookie ingredients, the children had raised enough to replace the damaged book and to purchase a new one. They spent time at the next class meeting discussing what type of new book they wanted for their classroom.

Imagine if the teacher had scolded the children and taken away their book-corner privileges. The opportunity to learn and practice these vital life skills would have been missed.

Class meetings can also provide valuable opportunities to learn social skills.

One morning at meeting time, Candace, who is four, said that another child had called her friend Eric a bad name. The teacher asked Eric if this was a problem he would like the group to address. (It is important that children learn to be responsible for their own needs.)

When Eric had told his story, the teacher asked whether anyone else had ever been called names. "How does it make you feel?" she asked. Others in the group had had the same experience, and a lively discussion followed. The children agreed that it hurt to be called names. They then came up with a list of possible solutions, which the teacher wrote down for them on the board.

"Maybe the name-calling person could control himself." "Walk away." "Say, 'Don't say that!'" "Get a teacher to help." "Tell them you don't like it." "Ask them to take a cool-off time-out." "Say, 'Stop!'" "All walk away and discuss it somewhere else."

The suggestions may have sounded similar, but all were honored and written down. Eric and his classmates could now talk about the possible results of each choice (with some gentle help from their teacher) and decide ways they might respond to name-calling in the future. Remember, preschoolers are still refining their social skills; suggestions like "call him a worse name" or "punch his lights out" would provide opportunities to learn about more acceptable responses.

Planning Future Activities

WHEN YOUNG CHILDREN are asked about fun activities they might do as a group, not all of the suggestions will be practical: "We could all go to Disneyland." "I suggest we go to the beach." (Never mind the snow outside.) "We can go on an airplane trip. My daddy will take us with him."

Once children start offering improbable suggestions, they tend to "get on a roll," so it is helpful for the teacher to guide them by offering some practical, fun ideas for activities and outings.

There are dozens of ideas. Trips to the police station, fire station, zoo, and park may be possible field trips, depending on your program. Remember that a field trip can be a wonderful opportunity to invite the children to solve problems in advance. Ask them what problems they had on their last field trip or what they think some good rules for the group would be. If the children can't think of anything, the teacher can make suggestions, such as discussing expectations about crossing streets, pushing and shoving, running around, or not listening quietly and respectfully when the fire chief talks. The children can then brainstorm solutions. Children are far more willing to follow rules when they've had a part in making them!

More immediate activities can also be planned. Classroom treats such as ice cream or popcorn are fun and easy to provide. If an expenditure of money is involved, the children can work out plans to raise the needed funds. They can earn money at home through special tasks or do so at school as a group. One bunch of enterprising youngsters decided to sell baked potatoes at the end of the day to tired and hungry parents. The aroma as parents entered the school was wonderful, and needless to say, this fund-raiser was a rousing success.

The group may set a goal, such as throwing a pizza party when all of the shelves and toys have been washed. The teacher can provide buckets and sponges, and the children can pitch in. One program has an occasional floor scrubbing day during which the furniture is cleared away and there are buckets and scrub brushes for all. The children love the water play, training, and social interest, all rolled up into one activity. Remember that involv-ing children in planning an activity, whether in art or cooking or play, will make that activity more successful. When children are invited to feel capable and creative, they almost always respond with enthusiasm.

Special Tips for Effective Class Meetings

KEEPING A FEW ideas in mind will ensure the success of your class meetings. The following sections discuss them.

Be Aware of Timing

Class meetings for preschoolers may require that you be flexible. Depending on your children's mood, abilities, and attention span, you may need to keep meetings short or focus on only one element each time. Your meetings don't need to be long to cultivate belonging and encouragement. Many preschools find that one meeting each week is ample. Others like to have a short meeting every day. Trial and error will help you find just the right balance.

Use Special Signals

Young children love special signals, such as the same song being sung each day to signal cleanup time. A ringing bell could mean that everyone should freeze and listen to an announcement from the teacher.

It works well to develop a special signal to open and close class meetings. In one class, they all sit on the floor in a circle and place their arms together with the elbows bent. To begin the meeting they slowly move their arms apart, like opening a book, and announce, "Class meeting is open!" At the end of the meeting, they reverse the process while saying, "Class meeting is closed!"

Include Voting (When Appropriate)

In preschool, children can vote when the choice involves everyone, such as whether to have a popcorn party, a pizza party, or to make homemade ice cream. At this early age, children can learn that people think and want different things, and they can learn to give and take. It is not appropriate to allow children to vote on a "solution" for another person. The person with the problem should be allowed to choose the solution she thinks will be most helpful for her.

Take Notes

Keeping track of what happens in a meeting can be helpful, especially when your class needs to remember just what it was they decided! Because most preschoolers can't write, an adult probably will need to take the minutes. Preschoolers can take turns running the meeting when they have learned the process. They love to call the meeting to order, call on people who have their

TIPS FOR EFFECTIVE CLASS MEETINGS

- Be aware of timing.

- Use special signals.

- Include voting (when appropriate).

- Take notes.

- Use a "talking stick."

names on the agenda (sometimes with a little prompting from the teacher), ask for suggestions to solve problems, and close the meeting.

At the beginning of each meeting, you can review the previous meeting's notes and see how your plans and decisions are working out. If a problem persists, give it precedence over new agenda items. Evaluate what did not work about the solution that was tried. Look over the other suggestions that were not used and come up with new ideas as well.

Use a "Talking Stick"

A decorated stick, a magic wand, or a koosh ball can be passed around the circle. Whoever holds the object has permission to speak.

A physical symbol can help young children learn to listen respectfully and speak in turn, and may encourage shyer children to contribute to the group discussion.

Family Meetings with Preschoolers

IF YOU HAVE older children, you may have already discovered the many benefits of having family meetings. If your children are all preschoolers, the concept may be new; you may even question the value of having family meetings with young children. You may wonder, "What can my preschooler possibly learn? Will she be able to sit still? How can a little child solve problems?"

Very little effort is required to adapt the material presented at the beginning of this chapter on class meetings to family meetings, and the benefits and blessings are well worth the time and energy you spend. Family meetings teach children that they are valuable, capable members of the family, and you may be amazed at your preschooler's resourcefulness and creativity. Preschoolers can offer compliments, help solve problems, plan family fun, and learn to express their needs and get help in positive (and surprisingly enjoyable) ways. Regular family meetings will help you and your children build a sense of mutual respect, trust, understanding, and love—and that can lay the foundation for the many years that lie ahead.

Here are a few ideas to keep in mind when beginning family meetings with preschoolers:

- *Be realistic.* You can have worthwhile, entertaining family meetings with children as young as three years old, but remember that the younger the child, the shorter the attention span is likely to be. Keep your meetings short and to the point; that way, no one will get tired of them.

- *Make family meetings a priority.* Our busy lives have a tendency to get in the way of even our best intentions. If you want your family meetings to work, set a regular time to get together, and stick to it. Don't allow telephone calls, chores, or other distractions to get in the way. Making the time you spend as a family a priority will help you build a sense of unity and will let your young children know that you value them and the time you spend together.

- *Begin each meeting with compliments and appreciations.* This can feel awkward at first, especially if you have siblings who are more comfortable putting each other down, but looking for and commenting on the positive will encourage everyone and will get your meeting off to a friendly start.

- *Post an agenda board in a handy place and help your preschoolers use it.* Even young children can "write" their problems and concerns on an agenda board or make a mark to indicate they have something to talk about. Taking these concerns seriously (and being careful not to squelch your little one's sometimes unrealistic ideas) will show your children that you value them. The mere act of writing down a problem can be the first step to finding a peaceful, effective solution.

- *Leave time for fun.* Make sure part of your meeting is devoted to just enjoying each other, perhaps by playing a game, watching a video together, planning a family activity, sharing a special dessert, or reading a favorite story. Some families like to alternate "business" meetings with family meetings that are just for fun.

However you decide to do them, family meetings are one of the best habits you and your children can get into and will help you stay tuned in throughout the increasingly busy years ahead. For more information on family meetings with children of all ages, refer to *Positive Discipline* by Jane Nelsen (Ballantine, 1996). You will also find the information in this chapter on preschool class meetings helpful in planning and holding your family meetings.

A Learning Opportunity

CLASS MEETINGS ARE astonishingly productive, teaching many life skills while helping children develop a strong sense of belonging. Adults sometimes underestimate the ability of young children to be creative and responsible, and class meetings allow this learning opportunity for everyone. You may discover that the youngsters in your care not only learn self-esteem and cooperation but have a marvelous time as well!

As we have learned, parents can begin family meetings using the same format when their first child is about three years old. If your child is participating in class meetings at preschool, you will be amazed at how quickly he applies his new abilities at home. Class meetings are a wonderful way for children and adults to experience just how much fun learning can be.

> Class meetings are astonishingly productive, teaching many life skills while helping children develop a strong sense of belonging.

PART FOUR

"You Can't Make 'Em Do It"

Exchanging Power Struggles for Respectful Cooperation

There is a familiar children's fable about a wager between the North Wind and the Sun. A man was walking along the beach one day wearing a heavy woolen overcoat. The North Wind boasted to the Sun that he could make the man remove his overcoat. The Sun agreed to the bet, and the North Wind began to blow. He blew steadily along the beach and the man buttoned up his coat. The North Wind blew harder and it turned icy cold, but the man only held his coat about him more tightly. After a great deal of blustering and wild blowing, the North Wind surrendered.

Now the Sun took her turn. She shone brightly on the man, letting her warm rays caress him. Soon the man undid his coat. The Sun shone more brightly and the warmth increased. The man eventually removed his coat and the Sun won the wager.

This story is a lovely example of the power of gentle persuasion, and it is a great deal like parenting young children. When we offer gentleness and understanding, warmth and trust, firmness and kindness, our children open up to us. The more severe and punishing we are, the more our children "button up" and resist us. Yet many adults insist on blowing like the North Wind, especially in the three areas of their children's lives where they actually have little or no control. Can you guess what these battlegrounds are?

Meet the terrible trio: sleeping, eating, and toileting (think "S*E*T"). There are very few parents who don't have war stories to share!

For instance, Joey's mother storms into his child care center and demands that the teacher make sure he eats all of his lunch today. Or Grandma purses her lips and tells her son that it's a disgrace her granddaughter is still wearing diapers. Or a bleary-eyed single mom asks her parenting class if anyone knows how to get her daughter to go to bed. These are battlegrounds where no amount of force, threats, or manipulation will succeed, for these areas are the child's ultimate responsibility and are within his control.

Of course, that doesn't mean you should just give up or let children do as they please. Parents and caregivers need to learn the methods of steady, gentle persuasion available to them in these challenging areas. In chapter 16 we will cover sleeping. Chapters 17 and 18 will be devoted to eating and toileting.

16

"Doesn't She *Ever* Get Tired?"

Solutions for Bedtime Battles

*I*t is nap time at the preschool, and all of the children are asleep—except *Margaret. The teacher has read a story and offered back rubs, but Margaret is still squirming. The teacher has even stroked Margaret's eyelids gently, but in spite of her best efforts, Margaret is still awake.*

Mary is a different story. Mary's mother worries that Mary sleeps too long at nap time, which makes it difficult to get her to bed at night. The teacher promises to keep Mary awake longer or to wake her up earlier, but despite her best efforts, Mary is usually the first to fall asleep and the last to wake up.

The bottom line is that you can't make a child sleep, and you can't control when he will wake up. Sometimes we feel so in need of time to ourselves that we try to establish a bedtime or nap time that just doesn't coincide with our child's needs. During the preschool years, most children give up taking a long, regular nap—if they ever did! Parents sometimes find themselves without those peaceful afternoon hours during which they could get something accomplished or rest a bit themselves. It becomes very tempting to try to coerce a child into continuing to take naps—and unfortunately, making him fall asleep (whether at night or during nap time) is simply beyond adult control.

Most parents have experienced the frustration of a child who is happily wide awake long past bedtime, tumbles out of bed at awkward moments, or refuses to wake even when Mom and Dad have urgent business to attend to. Is there anything parents can do to help children settle into a sleep cycle that works for everyone?

Routines: Everyday Magic

CHILDREN IN THE preschool years thrive on routines. They like their lives to be clear and predictable, and they enjoy the security of comfortable repetition (which is, incidentally, one of the easiest ways for young children to learn). A familiar routine in the morning, at mealtimes, and at bedtime can eliminate the need children often feel to test their boundaries. Clear expectations and predictable activities can smooth the rough spots out of a youngster's day (and that of his parents and teachers).

> Children in the preschool years thrive on routines.

As children grow older and begin school, using routines can eliminate many of the hassles surrounding chores or homework, especially when the child is old enough to help create the routine during a family or class meeting (usually around the age of three; see chapter 15). The routine can then become the "boss." A teacher or parent has only to ask, "What is our routine?" and everyone knows what should happen next. Routines will vary from family to family, from preschool to preschool, but they are useful ways to take the struggle out of the terrible trio of sleeping, eating, and toileting. There are some basic guidelines that are helpful when planning any type of routine.

Bedtime Routine Possibilities

WE HAVE DISCUSSED the importance of having a predictable, familiar routine to take the struggle out of bedtime. How do you find a bedtime routine that works for your family? The following ideas may help you build a routine for your child that helps him (and you) enjoy sweet dreams.

Playtime

A family playtime may be a good way to begin your nighttime routine. One family enjoys playing table games, while another likes a rousing game of tag or

STOP THE STRUGGLE

Q. *I am a single mom with a four-year-old boy. Every night I have a horrid time trying to get him to bed. I try to get him to bed by 8:30, but it is usually 10:30 or later before he goes to sleep. Every night it is the same thing: Will you rub my back?" "Will you rock me?" "Can I have a glass of water (and another, or a different glass, or juice instead)?" The list goes on and on. I usually cave in out of total frustration, just to get some peace.*

A. The solution for much of our daily hassling over events such as bedtime, morning preparations, or mealtimes is creating and following *routines*. Routines often take on a life of their own. Parents no longer need to play the role of super-cop, children know what is expected, and everyone is more likely to get some rest!

a pillow fight. It may be best to place more active games toward the beginning of your routine. The idea is to move steadily toward quiet, calming activities.

Bath Time

A soak in the tub can be wonderfully soothing—and it can be a time for closeness and play, too. There are many wonderful bath toys available (although your kitchen measuring cups and spoons will probably do quite nicely), and the sound and feel of warm water helps relax most children. An evening bath time should probably follow your active games and begin the "settling down" part of your routine.

Tooth Brushing

Did you know that brushing teeth can be fun? Some families put toothpaste on each other's brushes and all scrub happily away together, not only teaching good oral hygiene but having some good, clean fun as well.

Story Time

Telling or reading stories is a familiar part of bedtime, for good reason. Young children love to hear stories; in fact, some never tire of hearing the same story over and over—and woe to the lazy parent who tries to leave a paragraph out! (How many parents have scurried to hide a particularly familiar book before their little one can request it yet again?) A child's earliest "reading" experience may consist of reciting a book to you, even turning the pages at the right spot. Children's poetry and simple rhymes are wonderful, too, and actually help your child learn language. As your child grows older (or if she often has difficulty falling asleep), you may want to let her look through books as she lies quietly in bed.

A variation on this theme is to play a story tape and let your child follow along in the accompanying book. Or you might tape yourself reading or telling a favorite story; then, if your child has more than one home or if you must be away for a while, he can hear your reassuring voice even when you can't be with him.

Do beware of manipulation: Some children beg for "just one more story," and then, "just one more, pleeeeeease." This can be prevented by agreeing to one or two stories when creating your bedtime routine. Then when the begging starts, ask, "What does our routine chart say?" Another possibility is to give your child a hug and say, "Nice try" (with a warm smile) as you leave the room or move on to the next part of your routine. Children know when you mean it and they know when you don't. Being kind and firm at the same time will let them know that you mean what you say.

Special Activities

Since children often feel cozy and willing to talk just before they fall asleep, bedtime can be one of the best parts of your day together—if you let it be. You may want to pray together or sing a special song. One dad carries his small son around his room to say good night to each stuffed animal and picture. A tape of soothing lullabies or soft music can create a relaxing atmosphere.

Some parents enjoy asking their children to share the happiest and saddest moments of their day and then letting their children ask them the same questions. (Because children's grasp of time is a little fuzzy, you may hear about

CREATING A BEDTIME ROUTINE

- *Create the routine together.* Invite your children to help you make a list of things that need to be done to get ready for bed. Together, identify tasks such as quiet play time, taking a bath, putting on pajamas, brushing teeth, story time, prayers, and hugs and kisses. Keep the list short; it should have no more than six or seven tasks on it.

- *Make a routine chart (with estimated start and end times for children four and older).* Provide a large poster board and colored marking pens. Children enjoy drawing pictures to illustrate the list. Or they may enjoy cutting out magazine pictures, such as a toothpaste ad, a child in pajamas, a bath, and so on. Paste the pictures in appropriate spots on the chart, decorate with glitter or stickers (you might as well have fun with this project, and fun often invites children's cooperation), and post the chart in a strategic location.

things that happened this afternoon, last week, or even last month!) You may be amazed at how much you and your children learn about each other. Such moments go far beyond helping a child sleep; they are filled with shared love, trust, and closeness.

Hugs and Kisses

There are families where hugging, kissing, and saying "I love you" happens daily. In other families, these things rarely happen. Not surprisingly, researchers have discovered that a daily ration of hugs encourages emotional health, and if you haven't been dispensing regular hugs and kisses, you might consider giving it a try. Bedtime is the perfect time for hugs, kisses, and gentle reassurances of love.

Rick and Tracy McIntyre love to sit on the edge of three-year-old Cissy's bed and say, "If we were to line up all of the three-year-old girls in the world, guess which one we'd pick? We would say, "We want that one!" Rick and Tracy would both

- *Let the routine chart be the boss.* When bedtime rolls around, use the chart to determine what should happen. Ask your child, "What is next on our routine chart?" Keep coming back to the chart, checking with your child at first and later simply letting him do it. Hint: Do not try to establish more than one routine at a time. Get one in place and working smoothly before tackling the next one.

Once a routine is established, do your best to stick to it. Children won't follow routines if adults don't help.

It isn't necessary to be rigid, but do try to follow the routine respectfully. If your child makes suggestions that would improve cooperation and success, add them to the chart. Remember, a routine chart isn't a rewards chart; it's a way for children and adults to learn what comes next and to work together without argument.

point at Cissy, who would giggle happily and launch herself into her parents' arms for a hug. The glow from your child's face during moments like these can illuminate the entire room!

Practice Your Routine

REMEMBER, IT ISN'T necessary (or even wise) to do everything on our list as part of your bedtime routine—you might all be up until midnight! Nor will a bedtime routine guarantee that your child will never have difficulty falling asleep. If a child says he "can't sleep," tell him it's okay. He just needs to lie quietly in bed and look through a book or think quiet thoughts.

Keep in mind that falling asleep is your child's job. You can only provide him with the opportunity. The hardest part of your job may be to ignore (with kindness and firmness) demands for more drinks and stories after you have completed a loving bedtime routine.

MURDER BY TOOTHBRUSH

Many families engage in battles over tooth brushing. Some dentists urge parents to brush their children's teeth for them until they are well past preschool age. If you find yourself sitting on a squirming child, forcing a toothbrush between clenched jaws, or trying to figure out how to hog-tie a three-year-old, please pause for a moment.

Exactly what outcome are you trying to prevent? Look into the eyes of your captured child. Take a deep breath. Which is more damaging? Cavities or crushed self-esteem? To eliminate both try to limit sweets, provide healthy treats, and buy an electric toothbrush; this makes more sense than dutifully turning your bathroom into a torture chamber or battlefield.

Lest the dental community misunderstand, we are not saying it is not important for children to brush their teeth. We are saying that you are more likely to help your children develop this important habit by involving them in the process than by creating a power struggle that might invite them to decide they would prefer to lose all their teeth than to lose the battle.

A bedtime routine may make it possible for you and your young child to enjoy sharing a special part of the day together rather than rehearsing for World War III. The possibilities are endless. Pick out some ideas that appeal to you—or use your own creativity to find a routine that works for you and your child. Whatever you decide on, practice it often enough that it becomes a familiar, predictable part of your day—and a peaceful way to help and encourage your child to fall asleep.

Preschool Routines for Naptime

FOLLOW A SIMILAR procedure to create naptime routines in the preschool or child care setting. Include soft music, muted lighting, or gentle back rubs.

Involve children by allowing them to help set out nap things, take off and line up shoes, and use the potty before and after lying down to rest. Calm caregivers invite children to enjoy a restful atmosphere.

The Importance of Comfort

EVEN THOUGH WE stress the importance of getting children involved, there are many things adults can do on their own to help children sleep cozily. We can make sure children are comfortable in pajamas that fit, in beds or cribs that are secure, and with the appropriate number of blankets.

We can remember to consider our child's temperament. Is the sleeping area warm or cool enough? Does this child need absolute quiet or a steady hum of activity? A night light or complete darkness?

If your child spends time in more than one household, special smells and textures can make bedtime much less stressful. A pillow or blankie that travels with your child from home to home or a special cuddly toy at the child care center are very important. Children have been known to curl up with their jackets tucked under their heads, drawing comfort from the familiar feel and smell.

An evening snack containing calcium, such as milk or yogurt, may help your child relax enough to sleep. Some people believe that sugar stimulates children. Although research is inconclusive, avoiding sugary food late in the evening or before naps may prove helpful. (Be sure to read labels; you may be surprised at the sugar content of some so-called healthy foods.) Use trial and error to discover what works best for your child.

How many times have you heard that plaintive cry, "Mommy, I'm thirsty"? It may be helpful to agree with your child on how many drinks of water she will get (and put the allotted number on your routine chart). When children are allowed to negotiate the number of requests they can make, they seldom use their full quota. Whatever your agreement, follow through with kind and firm action.

Like adults, children have different needs regarding light and dark, noise and quiet. Some children enjoy solitude, while others need people close by; some children prefer total darkness, while the steady glow of a night-light comforts others. There is no right or wrong; finding out what works best for your child will take patience and a bit of trial and error.

Control Your Own Behavior

PERHAPS IT IS time for a reminder that the only behavior you can control is your own. The magic that occurs is that children usually change their behavior in response to you.

Q. *We have a three-year-old daughter who has been having a very difficult time going to bed at night. We give her a bath with her baby sister, read her two stories, and say prayers as her bedtime routine. We also get her a glass of water.*

As soon as it's time for us to leave, she starts acting up. We tell her that if she keeps yelling or crying that we'll have to close her door because she's going to wake up her sister. She doesn't care about this and will call us stupid, stick her tongue out at us, and so on. When we close her door, she goes absolutely crazy—banging on the walls and doors, messing up her blinds, dumping her toy box, or yelling by her window, "Somebody help me—I need my mommy and daddy."

We wait for three minutes (one minute of time-out for each year of her age) and then open the door and ask her if she's finished being mad and ready to get back in her bed and behave. She'll say no and go through it again for another three minutes.

We give her one more chance and then tell her that we'll have to close her door for the remainder of the night. The other night we had to stand by her door until 1:30 A.M. with her going crazy for four hours! She sleeps for nine hours and takes a nap, but we can't do that. We're exhausted. Help!

A. It sounds like no one is getting much rest except your daughter. If she is still up at 1:30 A.M., does she sleep in until 10:30 A.M.? (We'll bet you don't get to!) Four things will help to close the curtains on this nighttime drama: help her feel sleepy; respect her needs—and yours; quit battling and work towards cooperation; and use kind and firm follow-through.

Help Her Feel Sleepy

It seems that your daughter is able to marshal all her physical and emotional reserves for bedtime. She just isn't all that sleepy after her sleep-in and long nap.

Try making active play part of your bedtime routine. Consider taking a trip to the park, engaging in some rough and tumble play or even signing up for evening swim classes. Allow her to feel tired. Once she is tired, you will have nature on your side. You might also consider giving up naps so that she is ready for an earlier bedtime.

Respect Her Needs—and Yours

Your daughter is feeling "dethroned" by her baby sister. Babies and toddlers take up lots of adult time and energy. What is left over for the older child? Your three-year-old has discovered an effective way to get her parents' attention. You can replace this negative attention with positive attention at other times of the day.

Carve out time to enjoy a moment with her alone. Be sure to point out to her that this is a time for just the two of you, that you are glad to have time alone with her, and that you enjoy having an older child with whom you can do special things. Such time can be as simple as a trip to the grocery store or library or a walk around the block. When her need to feel included, noticed, and special is met in this way, she will have less reason to seek attention through bedtime battles.

You have needs, too. Your children will be more likely to respect you if you demonstrate that you respect yourself. Give yourself time to unwind, relax, and focus on the evening together. A late-afternoon shower, a cup of tea, or a short exercise routine might make a real difference in your energy level. Remember that meeting your needs means you are better able to respond to the needs of other family members.

Quit Battling and Work Toward Cooperation

Where does your daughter get her amazing tenacity? Two parents who are willing to wait at her door for hours must have some genetic connection to the howler on the other side. It is time to start building cooperation, and the only people in this power struggle you can control are yourselves. In other words, you may not be able to control your daughter's sleep habits, but you can decide what you will do. Here are some suggestions:

- Ask for her help. (You might be surprised at how well this works.)

- Explain that you do not like to hold her door closed at bedtime. Ask her if she has any ideas about ways you could stop doing that.

- Work out a routine together.

- Decide what you will do instead of what you will try to make her do. Let her know your plan. Some possibilities are to go to bed yourself, read a book, and keep your own door closed rather than stand guard over her door.

- Seek solutions that work for all of you.

Use Kind and Firm Follow-Through

It may be comforting to know that you are not alone in your bedtime hassles. If you have tried all of the above and your child is still getting out of bed, simply put her back in bed. This is effective when you remember the following:

- Don't say a word. Actions speak louder than words—and they are much harder to argue with.

- Be sure your actions are both kind and firm. This means you eliminate even the nonverbal lectures (anger). One mother gave her a child a kiss on the cheek every time she put her back in bed—but that was all.

- Be consistent. If you put your child back in bed five times and then give in, you have taught her that she only has to be more persistent than you are. The mother mentioned above shared that on the first night they tried this new plan, her daughter was put back to bed twenty-four times. The second night, it was twelve times. The third night, it took only twice before the daughter knew her mother meant what she "didn't" say. By the fourth night, her daughter was happily following the bedtime routine—to the letter.

- Be sure you are spending special time with your child at other times during the day. This is especially important if you have a new baby in your home.

What About Naps?

YOUNG CHILDREN MAY resist sleep, not because they don't need it but because they don't want to miss out on anything as they explore their exciting world. All children do not need the same amount of sleep. Quiet time may work better for some children than nap time. Some are through with napping by two or two and a half years old. Others need naps until they start kindergarten (or, like one of the authors of this book, forever).

Whether it is a nap time or quiet time, follow these guidelines:

- Don't tell your child she is tired. Admit that you are tired and need some quiet time.

- Get your child involved in planning for his nap time or quiet time. Allow your child to choose a special nap time stuffed animal, a different bed, or a different blanket than what he uses for bedtime.

- Teach your child to use a simple cassette player. Let her choose from a collection of nap-time music and start the cassette player herself.

- Give her a limited choice: "Do you want to start your nap (or quiet) time at 1:00 or at 1:15?"

One mother we know lets her child choose a special Disney sleeping bag that can be used only at nap time. During family meetings, her three-year-old daughter chooses the room she wants to take a nap in. To avoid manipulation (stalling by choosing different rooms), she agreed that whichever room she chose would be the one she would use for the whole week. She then sets a kitchen timer (so she won't miss out on too much, and so she'll be sleepy at bedtime) for one hour. Mom has promised that if the "ding" doesn't wake her up, Mom will.

> Don't tell your child she is tired. Admit that you are tired and need some quiet time.

Taking naps in different beds can work for nap time, but bedtime routines require the consistency of the same bed. This raises the question of whose bed a child will sleep in.

Whose Bed?

THERE ARE MANY people who believe in the family bed. Our purpose is not to argue with that philosophy. Our point is that many parents have small children in their bed not by choice but by default—and they are begging for help about how to solve this problem. They may have enjoyed snuggling with their little one for a while, but now they want their privacy back.

Parents need to decide what they truly want and be ready to follow through with kind and firm action. The reality is that like all habits, breaking this one can be painful for everyone. Children read our unspoken messages quite well. If a child senses you are ambivalent about where he should sleep, he will recognize your doubts. When you are sure of your decision for him to sleep in his own bed, he will sense that as well.

Marissa and her husband want their bed back. Jonathan had slept with them until he turned two. For the past six months, Jonathan has had his own bed. He starts each night out in his bed. The problem is that he comes into his parents' bed in the middle of the night. It often isn't until the next morning that his parents discover him in bed with them. How do they break this cycle if they aren't awake when it happens?

Jonathan's parents are afraid he will walk in on them one night during a more intimate moment. They'd also simply like to have the opportunity for such moments to occur a bit more often. It is hard to feel sexy with a preschooler under the covers!

This issue is a bit more complex than it may seem. Since Jonathan shared his parents' bed for quite a while, it isn't surprising that now he wants to continue. Being with his parents at night probably has many meanings for Jonathan. He gets attention, security, and lots of cuddles. On the other hand, being alone in his bed feels lonely and a bit scary at times. Jonathan's feelings may be logical, or they may provide an excuse for him to continue seeking undue attention—a habit his parents have unwittingly reinforced. He may be missing an opportunity to learn "self-soothing," an important life skill.

> Parents need to decide what they truly want and be ready to follow through with kind and firm action.

Now the real question is what his parents want to do—and what they are willing to do to change their son's habit.

Jonathan's parents must decide what they want, as must all parents. Opting for the family bed has some long-range implications. The biggest one is: What will happen when you decide you want your child out of your bed? What if you are a single parent who has decided to remarry? Is your child going to be willing to share you?

If you have decided that it is time for your child to sleep in his own bed, reinforce that by lovingly carrying him into his bed. Your resolve will allow you to train yourself to notice his arrival during the night. Reassure him that you trust he will get back to sleep in his bed. Give him a nice snuggle, then head back to your own bed. Repeat this as often as necessary. (Note the words "often" and "necessary." Do lots of deep breathing, because this plan requires patience.) It can also be helpful to choose your child's room as the spot for a story or game during the day (without lectures or warnings about where he should be sleeping). If he perceives his room as a cozy and pleasant place to be, you may meet with less resistance at night.

Be prepared to have a few nights of interrupted sleep (or tedious repeat trips to his room at bedtime) while he becomes accustomed to your new expectations. He will learn to stay in his own bed, though he may check it out to see if you really mean it by testing for several nights. Within a surprisingly short time you may be ready to unpack that new lace nightie.

Coddled or Capable?

LEARNING TO SLEEP alone will not create lifelong trauma for your child; it is usually more traumatic for parents than for children! Your attitude is the key. If you feel confident that you are doing the right thing by teaching your child that he is capable of getting to sleep on his own, he will feel the energy of your confidence. On the other hand, if you feel guilty, angry or ambivalent, that energy will be communicated and will invite manipulation, helplessness, or power struggles.

Kindness and firmness at the same time are the keys to effective parenting. Giving in to a child's continuous demands is not loving behavior. Children do not feel safe when adults fail to establish clear boundaries. Allowing a child to learn to fall asleep on her own is a lifetime gift.

Sleeping is a natural and much-needed bodily function. Where do the power struggles come from? When children are small, many parents have power struggles over getting them to stay in bed. When their children are teenagers, many parents have power struggles over getting them to get out of bed in the morning.

The suggestions in this chapter can help parents use bedtime as an opportunity for teaching their children important life skills instead of manipulation and power struggles. Children can learn thinking skills, problem-solving skills, self-control, and trust—that when parents say it they mean it. They can also learn to trust themselves and to believe "I am capable." Bedtime truly can be heaven instead of hell. Sweet dreams!

17

"Open Wide . . . *Please?*"

Preschoolers and Eating

IMAGINE FOR A moment that you're sitting down to dinner with some friends instead of your family. Suppose you've invited Mary, her husband James, and your neighbor Sam over for a meal. As you pass around your favorite lasagna and a bowl of broccoli, the conversation goes something like this:

You: "I'm so glad you're all here for dinner. I'll pass around the lasagna."

James: "Just a small serving for me, please. I'm not very hungry tonight."

You: "Oh, nonsense! A big man like you needs lots to eat. Here—I'll give you a proper serving. Sam, have some broccoli."

Sam: "No, thanks. I'm not much of a broccoli eater."

You: "Sam, broccoli is good for you. You have to try a little bit or there will be no dessert for you! Now, Mary, I expect to see your plate all clean; there are still some yummy veggies there."

How do you think James, Mary, and Sam would feel? Would this be a successful dinner party? Does this sound a little bit like the conversation around your own dinner table?

All too often, the dinner table becomes a battleground for parents of young children. Parents worry about what their children eat—or refuse to eat. Have they had enough? Did they get enough vitamin C? Too much sugar? Enough calcium and protein?

Eating under surveillance is not relaxing, and children don't enjoy it any more than adults do. Listen to your own mealtime comments and ask yourself, "Would I say this to an adult guest?" Children treated with respect learn to treat others the same way. Just because they are small people doesn't mean they aren't entitled to opinions about food. It may help to remember, though, that those opinions often change as they grow and mature.

Picky Eaters

Kim Chong fretted constantly about what a picky eater her son Jimmy was. Jimmy rejected most foods and seemed to like only the things that Kim considered "junk food." She worried about his health, charting the nutrients and vitamins he received each day. But no matter how much she fussed, Jimmy ate what he pleased. Oddly enough, he seemed healthy.

When he reached his teen years, Jimmy suddenly developed an appetite and began to eat everything his startled mother put in front of him. Although Kim's years of fussing had very little effect, Jimmy eventually developed his own healthy eating habits.

Q. *I have a daughter who just turned five. She is a very picky eater, and I cannot remember the last time she ate the same thing we ate during a meal. Breakfast is usually okay: she will eat waffles or oatmeal or French toast. Lunch and dinner are struggles. She does taste everything I make, but she insists she doesn't like anything.*

I read someplace that if children won't eat what you make for dinner, give them a "no-cook" alternative, such as a peanut butter sandwich or a bowl of cereal. I have been doing that, but now, that is all she will eat. I don't feel right about her consistently eating peanut butter sandwiches for dinner. What should I do?

A. Many university early childhood programs have conducted studies to see what foods toddlers would eat when all kinds of foods were placed on the lunch table. The children were allowed to eat whatever they wanted. The results were always similar. Sometimes children would eat dessert first. Sometimes they would eat broccoli first. The main finding of this program was that the children did not fuss. When children were left to follow their own "instincts," they chose a balanced diet over time.

> Children treated with respect learn to treat others the same way. Just because they are small people doesn't mean they aren't entitled to opinions about food.

HELP FOR PICKY EATERS

- Avoid becoming a short-order cook. Teach children how to make their own peanut butter sandwiches.
- Offer choices. When children complain about a food, say, "You can eat what is on the table or fix your own sandwich. What is your choice?"
- Invite solutions. If a child complains about the food served, ask, "What do you need to do about that?" This invites children to use their thinking skills and problem-solving skills. It invites them to use their power in positive ways, instead of in power struggles, and to feel capable.
- Invite children to help plan menus during family meetings. They are more cooperative when they have been included. Get them involved in creating the shopping list.
- Share tasks. Let children help with shopping. Many grocery stores now have small carts that can be pushed around by preschoolers. Let children

Is your child getting too much undue attention for not eating? Does she get sugar at any time? (Sugar can really mess up the body's natural craving for good foods). Are you fixing simple foods that children usually enjoy? Some children are more suspicious than picky. If they can identify individual foods, they are more willing to eat them than when they are blended together into a casserole. Try some of the suggestions in the box above.

What, Not When

STUDIES HAVE SHOWN that young children will usually eat a healthy diet over time; that is, they may not eat what their parents think is healthy in any one day or even in a week, but over the course of time their bodies tell them what is needed. Arguing over the vegetables accomplishes little except raising everybody's blood pressure and making mealtime an unpleasant ordeal.

find certain items on the shopping list to put in their carts. When they want something that isn't on the list, kindly and firmly say, "That isn't on our list."

- Let children help with cooking. During the family meeting, let them decide which nights they want to help cook. Again, they are more likely to eat what they help cook and to be more cooperative when it is not their turn if they have been involved in the planning process.
- Respond without rescuing. Simply avoid the sparks (bids for undue attention) that become bonfires when you feed them. Use reflective listening ("I guess you don't like that") and avoid engaging in discussions beyond reflective listening. And allow your children to handle the problem ("You don't have to eat it. I'm sure you can make it until our next meal.")
- Ease your own anxiety about nutrition. Give your child a good multiple vitamin. Then—relax.

Martha Black was convinced that her son needed a warm bowl of oatmeal to start his day off properly. When three-year-old Lex refused to eat his oatmeal one morning, his mother decided she'd better teach him how important it was to eat the right foods. Martha got out some plastic wrap and covered the bowl of oatmeal. When Lex came in for lunch, Mrs. Black microwaved the oatmeal. After half an hour, it had turned as cold (and as hard) as stone. Lex glared at it but refused to taste it, so Martha resolutely covered it up again. Can you imagine how appetizing that oatmeal looked at dinner after another trip to the microwave? Lex would willingly have starved before letting a spoonful pass his lips. What, do you suppose, has Lex learned about oatmeal? And what has his mother learned about Lex?

Sometimes we marvel at how children survive on the diets they eat. However, most children, given healthy alternatives, seem to survive and even thrive. Remember: Children typically change their eating habits in time—and do so much more quickly when parents don't fuss.

There is an important truth about food, eating, and young children. You provide the food; the children do the eating—or not, as the case may be. It is interesting to note that children raised during the Depression didn't experience eating problems. Since food was scarce, members of the family were delighted if someone didn't want their share. Coaxing someone to eat was not considered. In this atmosphere, children were allowed to follow their own instincts about eating or not eating—and usually chose to eat as much as they could.

It is important to offer children a wide selection of nutritious food. (Special menus only reinforce finicky eating.) Be sure that at least one food on the table is considered edible by your child, then serve whatever else you wish. Even toddlers can learn to dish up their own food (with training) and often get so caught up in the activity that they forget to say no. An important part of training is to teach them to take small helpings, because they can always take more if they want it. It is not helpful to make them eat everything on their plate when they make a mistake and take too much. It is helpful to help them explore, through "what" and "how" questions, what happens when they take too much and how they can solve the problem.

There are a number of things parents can keep in mind to encourage healthy eating habits in their children and to make mealtimes together pleasant for the entire family.

Timing

Young children see no reason to get hungry on anyone's schedule but their own. Infants nurse on demand, toddlers want food when they're hungry, and preschoolers often just can't make it from one meal to the next without something in between. These are normal variations; the key is to be certain that the choices available to your children are healthy ones. If your children aren't eating full meals, their snacks should provide them with the nutrients they need. A pile of carrot sticks or even a baked potato, for instance, is much better than French fries and a soda—especially when followed by a dinner skirmish over the peas.

A child who doesn't eat his entire lunch at the child care center can snack out of his lunch box on the way home. *When* children eat is not as important as *what* they eat. Lunch food is just as nutritious eaten at 5:00 as it would have been at noon.

Simplicity

Your church group may have raved about your prawns in Cajun sauce, but your preschooler may be totally unimpressed. Children are often suspicious of unfamiliar foods or unusual mixtures. A cheese sandwich with lettuce and tomato may be spurned, while a piece of cheese, some tomato slices, and a few crackers will be consumed quite happily. If your little one looks askance at the pasta and vegetable salad, try serving the ingredients to him separately. You certainly don't need to provide a separate menu, nor should you, but being aware of your child's natural preferences will help you find ways to encourage cooperation and experimentation.

Choices

Allowing children to develop their own eating habits requires mutual trust. Children will eat foods their bodies need, and if you provide a variety of healthy and appetizing foods, they will be more likely to choose foods that are nourishing. Remember, though, that even adults need a splurge now and then; thousands of children have been raised on occasional doses of fast food, pizza, and hot dogs without suffering permanent damage. The key, as always, is balance. Providing a regular diet of nutritious foods will help you feel better about the Easter jelly beans, chocolate Santas, and Halloween tummy-aches that seem to be an inevitable part of childhood. However, if you have jelly beans, potato chips, cookies, cupcakes, and soft drinks around the house all the time, you are inviting poor eating habits and food battles.

> When children eat is not as important as *what* they eat. Lunch food is just as nutritious eaten at 5:00 as it would have been at noon.

Avoid becoming the Food Police! Families committed to special diets often defeat themselves by creating a vigilante atmosphere around food. If you want your child to avoid foods with sugar, do not become frantic when a stray cookie passes his lips. Your overreaction is more likely to invite food-related problems, now and later.

Choose Your Battles

IT MAY BE absolutely imperative to you that your four-year-old eat her lima beans. Or you may feel comfortable watching your child eat a steady diet of salami slices, raisins, and crackers. But be aware that if you insist, your child may feel compelled to resist—and it's doubtful that staring at a plate of cold lima beans after everyone else has left the table ever persuaded a child to love veggies.

Some parents gloat about making their children sit at the table until they finish their dinner—and claim it works. If you talk to the children, you get a different story. They either figured out how to feed most of the food to the dog or hide it in their napkin (weren't the parents suspicious when their children offered to clean up the table?). Or they developed eating problems as adults. Someone will always lose in battles over food, short-range or long-range.

Mealtime Routines

YES, ROUTINES WORK for eating, too. Mealtimes in our busy families often become hectic, rushed, and stressful occasions that no one truly enjoys. Parents arrive home tired after a long day's work; children are often both hungry and cranky. The milk of human kindness does not make it to the dinner table. Comfortable routines can make mealtimes proceed far more smoothly. The elements are simple: here are some suggestions that may help you create routines for your own family.

Take Time to Relax

If dinnertime is often rushed in your home, try beginning the process differently. For instance, Tom Shelton always packs an extra-large lunch for his four-year-old daughter, Katie. During the drive home after work and preschool, Katie opens her lunch box and enjoys whatever is left over from lunch. When they arrive home, Katie is not urgently hungry and her dad doesn't feel pressured to serve dinner immediately. Instead, they usually manage time for a cuddle and story before Dad tackles the dinner preparations.

Taking time to wind down at the end of the day is almost always worth the investment. You may want to spend a few minutes curled up on the sofa with your child, reconnecting and sharing moments from your day. A warm bath or shower might refresh you for the evening ahead, or you may want to take time for a walk or a quick game together. Slices of fruit or a bag of crackers may satisfy the hunger pangs long enough for the entire family to catch its breath. "But I don't have time," you may be saying. "I simply have too much to do!" Regardless of how busy your lives may be, taking time to relax and reenter your family's world will eliminate the hassles that often consume even more time.

Prepare the Meal Together

Nothing wins over a finicky eater better than helping plan and prepare the meal. And most parents fail to recognize the wonderful little helpers they have right there beside them. Get a big apron, pull up a stool to the sink, and invite your child to slosh and tear the lettuce for tonight's salad. A two-year-old can use a brush to scrub vegetables, and at three, your child can place silverware and napkins on the table.

Giving your children a way to contribute encourages the growth of their sense of initiative and helps teach life skills. It also invites children to see themselves as contributing members of the family or community, building their sense of belonging in the process.

Create Moments That Draw You Together

Lunch at the Roundtree Child Care Center is a special time. The children join hands around the table, and each day one child is invited to share something she feels grateful for. After the other children have listened respectfully, they take turns squeezing the hand of the person on their right. When the "squeeze" has gone all around the circle, the children begin their meal.

Aaron Linski is from a traditional Jewish family. Before each meal in the Linski household, he recites special Hebrew prayers. In the Jones family, each person stands at his or her place at the table, and when all have gathered, they sing a grace together.

There are innumerable ways that families can add special beginning rituals to their meals, moments that create a sense of identity and closeness, warmth and love. Some of these rituals are religious; some are not. In our busy families, meals are often eaten on the run—everyone has somewhere to go, and the moments of communication and togetherness can be lost if we're not careful. Rituals can be wonderful ways to preserve the sense of family and teach our children to value it.

Set Guidelines for Finishing Up

Should children be expected to sit quietly until everyone has finished eating? Or should they be allowed to leave the table to play quietly? There is no "right" answer, but it may be wise to decide the matter beforehand rather than arguing over the cold mashed potatoes.

Even young children can be involved in some aspect of cleaning up after a meal. If your child can walk well on his own, he probably can clear away his plate, scrape away uneaten food, or load his utensils into the dishwasher.

To avoid power struggles over medications, food allergies, and special diets:

- Avoid lectures. Instead, engage children in self-exploration by asking "what," "why," and "how" questions: "What happens when you don't take your medication (or when you eat this food)?" "How do you feel when that happens?" "What do you learn when this happens?" "How can you use what you learn in the future?" "What ideas do you have to solve this problem?" (This will not be effective if children sense even a hint of a lecture instead of true curiosity about their thinking and abilities to learn and solve problems.)

- Involve children in creating a medication routine. Decide "together" on a time of day that works best for both of you. Work "together" on creating a

Allergies, Medications, and Special Diets

MANY A BATTLE is being fought to "make" children take their medications or to "make" them avoid foods that create serious problems. It is amazing what children are willing to suffer to avoid being controlled. We emphasize over and over how important it is to engage children in the thinking process and the problem-solving process so they develop thinking skills and problem-solving skills—and so they feel empowered and capable.

Overweight Children

MANY OF THE ideas suggested to avoid power struggles over medications and food allergies are also effective for overweight children. Though few very young children are overweight, the seeds for this problem are planted very early on. There are genetic causes as well. When overweight is genetic, it is

reminder chart and on reminder methods. (Perhaps an alarm watch that goes off at the same time every day, or a special juice concoction that includes the medication and that your child helps mix just before breakfast.)

- Take your child to the library to explore food allergies—and exactly what happens to the body. (Be sure your goal is education, not fear.)

- Decide what you will do. This could mean that you are willing to take responsibility to kindly remind your child every day at medication time, or that you will stay out of it because you have faith in your child to handle the problem or to learn from mistakes. (If the problem is life-threatening, choose the former, and do it without lectures or the display of over-concern.)

very important to help children feel accepted just as they are—and to work with them (if they want help) on how to manage their challenge in life.

Overweight can create a vicious cycle when children also feel low self-esteem. Low self-esteem may invite overeating to "fill the emptiness." Children will do better when they feel better. Offer lots of unconditional love and encouragement by stating that you have faith in them to deal with the challenge of overweight—if they want to. Offer your support, not your control.

Of course, modeling is very important. Don't expect children to do something you have not done. Take care of your own overweight issues (you might even work together on this). Together you can prepare healthy meals and avoid putting junk food on the shopping list.

Bon Appétit!

REMEMBER THAT ALLOWING children to be involved, encouraging mutual trust and respect, and having realistic expectations will take much of the struggle out of eating and may make mealtimes together an event the entire family looks forward to. No matter how tempting the foods on our tables, children must to choose to eat them. Remember: You can't make 'em do it!

18

Preschoolers and Potties

An Ongoing Battle?

WAIT JUST ONE moment!" you may be thinking. "Surely preschoolers have mastered toilet training. Aren't kids supposed to be trained by the age of three?" Well, not necessarily. Bathroom habits and hygiene remain issues of concern for young children and their parents well beyond the age of three— or even four. Few topics arouse such strong emotions as "potty training."

The Petersons took a great deal of pride in the fact that their first child was using the toilet at the age of eighteen months. They were so pleased, in fact, that Paula Peterson thought about writing a book about toilet training to help other, less fortunate families. Before she could get around to it, however, her second child was born. Much to the Petersons' surprise, this child wanted nothing to do with his parents' prize-winning toilet-training techniques. In fact, despite being placed on the potty for long periods of time, this child was almost four before the "training" worked.

So much for genius. The reality is that children will use the toilet when they are ready to do so. You can cheer, beg, and threaten, but hang on to your diapers. Each child has his or her own unique schedule—and absolute control. There are six important factors that can help parents set the stage for this important developmental milestone: physical readiness, ease of wakefulness, understanding your child's perspective, logic versus power struggles, cooperation, and detachment. We will explore each of these six factors in greater detail in this chapter.

Physical Readiness

MANY CHILDREN BECOME potty-trained before they reach the preschool years. This fact adds to the frustration of parents whose preschoolers have not yet reached this important step in the socialization process. The delay could be due to power struggles between adults and children (which children always win), or it could be because children are not yet physically ready to perceive and respond to the signals sent by their bodies. Potty training power struggles will be discussed later in this chapter. First, it is important to understand that other factors may be involved, such as physical readiness.

Physical factors can influence a child's ability to use the toilet. He must have a bladder large enough to allow him to wait for increasingly long periods of time before urinating, especially for overnight control. Some children simply don't develop bladder control as soon as others.

The Phillips were very familiar with the level of bladder control of their three children. This knowledge helped them know how quickly they needed to stop the car when their children requested a bathroom stop on long trips. In response to seven-year-old Kenny's request, Mom would remind Dad, "We can keep driving for about twenty minutes." When three-year-old Lori would ask for a bathroom, Mom would say, "Well, we have about ten minutes to find a good stopping place." However,

IMPORTANT FACTORS AND ATTITUDES TO END TOILET BATTLES

- Physical readiness
- Ease of wakefulness
- Understanding your child's perspective
- Logic versus power struggles
- Inviting cooperation
- Detach, relax, and enjoy

when five-year-old Jacob said, "I have to go." Mom would say, "Pull over immediately. If we can't find a bush, Jacob will just have to settle for the side of the road." Jacob had very little bladder control.

Ease of Wakefulness

ANOTHER IMPORTANT FACTOR in toilet training is ease of wakefulness. Many children who remain bed wetters, even past their preschool years, have difficulty waking up. Even sheets with alarms that go off when urination begins do not wake these children. When parents try getting their heavy sleepers up in the night to take them to the toilet, they are like limp rags who cannot stand or sit. They simply cannot wake up. Lighter sleepers may fuss and complain when awakened for a night trip to the toilet, but boys can still stand up, though seemingly half asleep, and girls can sit on the toilet without falling off. Some children cannot wake enough to do either.

All children should always be treated with dignity and respect, but it is especially discouraging to use punishment with children who don't have the physical capacity to do what is expected of them. An understanding of readiness may inspire more patience.

Understanding Your Child's Perspective

IMAGINE FOR A moment that you are a very small child. You know that Mom and Dad are eager for you to learn to use the potty, to be a "big boy" and wear "big boy pants." Suddenly, you feel that strange tingly feeling that is beginning to mean you have to "go." So you head toward the bathroom, becoming aware as you trot down the hall that there may not be a lot of time.

Somehow you know you have to get your pants down, but the buckles on your overalls are stiff and your fingers are so small. Then you glance at the toilet, which looks huge from your point of view. Maybe, you think, a little assistance is called for. But by the time you alert Mom, Dad, or the teacher, it's too late. No wonder children often decide that it's easier just to stay in diapers!

Understanding the occasionally overwhelming nature of the task can help parents set the stage for their child's success. Remember, toilet training is

THE IMPORTANCE OF PATIENCE

Sometimes the passage of time is all that is required for children to master the toilet. Listen to the frustrated question of one parent—and the difference six months made:

Q. *We are at the end of our rope. We have been trying to toilet-train our three-and-a-half-year-old for over a year, but he still won't stay dry. He wets his pants several times a day. Do you have some advice?*

Just a few months later, this same parent wrote again:

It is amazing how time works wonders. My son is now four and is fully toilet-trained. Thank you for encouraging me to be patient.

vitally important to diaper-weary adults—but rarely does it matter that much to a child. As with eating and sleeping, creating a "toilet-friendly" environment with easy-off clothing and kind training is a parent's job; deciding when (and where) to "go" is a child's!

Logic Versus Power Struggles

THE ABOVE FANTASY of a child being overwhelmed by the whole toileting process illustrates a logical point of view. Problems regarding potty training are more often based on illogical power struggles. The more determined parents become to have urination and defecation take place in the toilet, the more determined many preschoolers become to have it take place somewhere else—usually in their pants.

Remember, your child is still developing a sense of autonomy. A child's "me do it" attitude may begin in the second year of life, but it does not end when he becomes a preschooler. When parents try taking control of a child's bodily functions, they often meet with resistance. It could be that the child is deciding (at a subconscious level), "It is more important to walk around in urine-soaked pants than to give up my sense of power."

In other words, when parents insist on winning power struggles, the only option for the child is to become the loser. Most children will fight diligently to avoid the "loser" position, thus forcing that role onto their parents. So the power struggles continue. Since parents are the "mature" ones, it is up to them to end the power struggles and find ways to invite cooperation. The following question illustrates a typical power struggle that begins elsewhere but ends up as a "toilet" issue. The answer includes many suggestions for ending the power struggle and encouraging cooperation.

Q. *I'm at my wit's end. I have a four-year-old boy who, after a play date with an older cousin, learned the joys of peeing off a bridge. Now he is peeing everywhere: the carpet, trash can, off the porch, and so on. It seems to be an act of rebellion, often happening after I tell him to do something he doesn't want to do (like get dressed). He has always been my little rebel; this just seems to be his latest expression of rebellion.*

It doesn't help that at first we thought it was the cat, banished the cat to the garage, and then caught my son in the act. Now when I find a spot, he tries to blame the cat. We've tried time-out (which only precipitates a tantrum) and taking away privileges (TV, computer time, or dessert). I have to admit I spanked him in frustration when I caught him in the act last time. I've tried talking to him about this problem but I get nowhere. I'm at a loss. Help!

A. What a great opportunity for you to make some changes that could redirect these power struggles into useful power. Four-year-olds are ready to use their personal power in ways that contribute to the family. When parents use controlling methods and punishment, children resort to destructive power instead. Our crystal ball suggests that when you say, "I've tried talking with him . . ." what you really mean is, "We've sat down and I talked, and talked, and talked, and lectured, and lectured, and lectured." Maybe our crystal ball is wrong, but "talking" often means "telling"—over and over again.

The first suggestion is to stop "telling" and start asking "what" and "how" questions. You might ask, "What happened? What were you trying to accomplish? How do you feel about what happened? How does this create a problem for you or for others? What ideas do you have to solve this problem?"

It is essential that these questions be asked in a friendly tone of voice and with a sincere curiosity about your child's point of view instead of trying to get him to share your point of view. You also should be feeling calm, which may mean waiting a while. Inviting discussion (rather than lecturing) will help your child develop thinking skills, awareness of the consequences of his choices, and problem-solving skills. "Telling" invites your child to become defensive or even more rebellious.

Another possibility is to get him involved by teaching him to use his power to problem-solve in all the areas of his life, not just where toilet habits are involved. This can take many forms:

- *Ask him what he needs to do in a given situation.* If it is morning and time to get dressed, ask what he needs to do when he finishes eating.

- *Let him help you create morning and bedtime routines by creating picture charts.* Then ask, "What is next on our routine chart?" You might be surprised by how well this invites cooperation instead of rebellion.

- *Stop using any form of punishment.* Punishment feeds the rebellion fire until it becomes all-consuming. Even time-out can be nurturing and encouraging instead of punitive (see chapter 13). Your child will feel "positive power" if he chooses the time-out. He will feel rebellious if you "make" him go.

- *Start having regular family meetings so your child will learn respect and problem-solving skills.* If your son has many opportunities to use his power in useful ways, he is less likely to be rebellious.

- *Teach him to clean up any mess he makes.* With a kind and firm tone of voice say, "You'll need to clean that up. Would you like my help, or do you want to do it by yourself?" If he resists, say, "Would a hug help you feel better? I know you will want to take care of this problem when you feel better."

Many people think that holding a child on their lap rewards the misbehavior. It does not. Remember that a misbehaving child is a discouraged child. Children do better when they feel better. Punishment may work to stop the problem for the moment, but the long-range results are rebellion, revenge, or sneakiness.

All of the methods we suggest create positive long-range results. Ask yourself, "Do I want to make my child pay for what he did or help him learn to do better in the future?"

Inviting Cooperation

NOT SURPRISINGLY, POTTY training is just that: training. And there are many things parents can do to make it easier. The first involves your attitude. Knowing your child's temperament and abilities will help you keep your expectations reasonable. If you are relaxed and comfortable, your child is likely to feel the same way.

Pressure to "succeed" will only frustrate both of you. If accidents happen—and they will—be patient. If your child is wet, change her. If she is old enough, buy pull-up diapers so she can change herself (which often encourages a child to be more aware of her body's signals). Be sure, however, that you never humiliate or shame a child about toileting setbacks. Dry pants aren't worth damaged self-esteem.

It can help to train your child in the steps he must master along the road to successful use of the toilet. It's a good idea to provide clothing that is easily pulled down (and up); elastic waistbands are perfect. If the weather is warm, wearing underpants alone (or nothing at all) may simplify the process.

Be sure to teach your child the importance of washing his hands. Have a stool available so he can reach the sink, with soap and a towel for drying within easy reach. One preschool teaches children to sing this song (to the tune of "Skip to M'Lou") while they wash their hands (when repeated twice, the song lasts about 20 seconds, just the time it takes to kill *E. coli* bacteria):

Wash, wash, wash your hands,
Wash your hands together.
Scrub, scrub, scrub your hands,
'Til they're clean and sparkly.

Having regular toilet times may encourage youngsters to develop the habit of using the bathroom regularly. When leaving for an outing (even a short one), it is wise to invite a young child to use the toilet beforehand. (Most parents quickly learn where the restrooms at the neighborhood grocery store are located.)

One preschool teacher decided to take her class on a field trip to pick blueberries. They blithely sailed out of the preschool together and into a nearby field. Trouble soon arose, however; the teacher had forgotten to remind the children to use the toilet before leaving, and now the only option was a well-used outhouse. This teacher spent most of her field trip holding one child after another over the outhouse toilet, and she never forgot pre-outing reminders again!

Pull-ups and extra-strength diapers are now available for children two and a half, three, and even four and five years old. They have become a big factor in kids not using the potty because they never feel wet. You might consider using less effective diapers.

Detach, Relax, and Enjoy!

WHEN READINESS AND training have been taken into account, it is time to relax and trust that successful toileting will result in due time. Perhaps the best advice is simply this: Relax. Using the toilet on his own is a very significant thing for your child to do. When he's ready, he'll do it—and probably not a moment sooner, as illustrated in the following question and answer.

Q. *I have a son who needs to be potty-trained. He turned three two months ago. He does not like to use the potty. He does not show me signs when he has to go, but he will tell me when to change him. I feel so discouraged. Please, I need some advice!*

A. It does not take great intuition to hear your desperation. It is so hard to keep changing diapers as children grow older. All children are very individual in this area of development. Your son's delay in using the toilet is magnified by your own discouragement. He will succeed eventually, but it may take more patience than you knew you had.

Try to de-emphasize the whole issue. Meanwhile, when he needs to be changed, show him ways he may help out. He can help wash or wipe himself off, help empty the stool into the toilet bowl, and wash his own hands afterward. In the meantime, enjoy him and his other life successes. Express your confidence in him that he will manage using the potty successfully one day. He too needs encouragement.

You will be amazed at how quickly time passes when you detach from the potty training issue. Your detachment will eliminate power struggles and may actually speed up the process. Children are much more likely to become interested in potty training when allowed to do so according to their own timetable—and when there is nothing to rebel against.

A big part of detaching and relaxing is to know that a number of things can cause a temporary setback.

> You will be amazed at how quickly time passes when you detach from the potty training issue. Your detachment will eliminate power struggles and may actually speed up the process.

Setbacks: "Whoops!"

WHEN A CHILD is experiencing new things—a new preschool, a new house, or a new sibling—it's common for potty training to suffer a setback. A new environment or an especially exciting activity can cause a child not to pay attention to his body's signals; other major life events, such as death, divorce, illness, or travel, can interfere with toileting. All of these events represent major adjustments in a child's life, and toilet issues often take second place to coping with change.

Your attitude as a parent or caregiver will make all the difference in how your child handles accidents. Imagine how confused a child might feel when she not only loses control of her body but faces a parent's anger and disappointment as well.

Ann was four years old when she was asked to be flower girl in her aunt's wedding. She wore a lovely, long white gown made especially for her with a lacy veil and tiny pearl necklace. People smiled and nodded at her as she walked down the aisle scattering rose petals, and Ann glowed with the attention and excitement.

The reception was beautiful, and Ann was thrilled by the festivity around her. She had crawled under a table and was listening to the adults talking when she became aware of something she'd been ignoring all afternoon. Before she could get up, it happened: she had a bowel movement, soiling her lovely white dress.

When Ann's mother discovered her, she was horrified.

"I can't imagine what got into Ann," she told the assembled aunts and grandmothers. "She never does this anymore."

Turning to her crying daughter, she said coldly, "You should be ashamed of yourself." Ann was changed into her old play clothes and spent the rest of the day feeling disgraced.

When children have toileting accidents, the last thing they need is a disapproving audience. Ann's mother could have taken her quietly aside, helped her to change, and explained to her daughter that excitement can sometimes make us forget to do the things we should.

It may be wisdom to keep a change of clothing nearby when your child is learning to use the toilet. It is also immeasurably helpful to be patient and to offer your child unconditional love and acceptance. Once you have taken into account your child's personal time clock, provided him with appropriate clothing and accessible facilities, and taken time to train him in the skills he needs, it is time to relax, celebrate his successes, and sympathize with his disappointments.

Constipation

BOWEL CONTROL IS another issue where a parent's desire to speed training may cause complications. Some children will not release their stool, sometimes to the point of physical peril to themselves.

Quentin's grandma had a lot to say on the issue of toilet training, most of it to his mother. "My children were all trained by the time they were two," she said disapprovingly, glaring at four-year-old Quentin while his diapers were changed.

So Quentin's mom embarked on a full-scale assault. Quentin was placed on the toilet several times each day while his mom knelt nearby and urged him on. Quentin grew to hate the bathroom, and so did his mom. She would encourage, threaten, and scold; he responded by refusing to produce the desired result—

anywhere or anytime. Before long, Quentin lost even the ability to respond to his body's signals and could no longer tell when he needed to have a bowel movement.

One day at his regular check-up, his pediatrician gave Quentin and his mom the news: he had a severely impacted bowel, with stool backed up well into his intestines. Daily doses of mineral oil and enemas were prescribed to relieve the problem, and both mother and son shed many a tear until the problem—which need never have existed—was resolved.

It is never helpful to force toileting issues. If your child is resistant, first look for natural or environmental causes. Does your child eat sufficient fiber to produce soft, regular bowel movements? Switch to juices containing fiber, such as peach or apricot nectar. A spoonful of prune juice mixed in with other foods might help. Serve kiwi fruit daily, and your child's stools should improve quickly. Offer cereal such as raisin bran or other high-fiber choices. Serve fewer dairy products and apple juice, which tend to be constipating. But do be careful: don't set up a new power struggle trying to get him to eat these foods! We said "offer them," as in make them available—not "force feed them."

Is your child experiencing excessive stress? Major life changes affect all family members. One parent, concerned over her own father's terminal illness, did not make the connection between her struggle to face this crisis and the toileting problems her son experienced. Although he had been totally potty-trained, he began having daily accidents. When the family crisis resolved itself, his problems disappeared.

What about the expectations placed on a child? The Mackey family deferred all kinds of decisions to their three-year-old. "Where should we eat dinner?" they asked. "Should Mommy and Daddy go out tonight?" "Do you want to go to preschool this morning?" The list went on and on. This child experienced severe constipation, because she felt overwhelmed by all the decisions placed on her shoulders. Her parents worried that setting limits would restrict her too much. They went so far in the other direction that she experienced enormous distress.

Pushing a child to master too many tasks by signing him up for an endless string of classes may also create stress. Similarly, expecting perfection from your child invites anxiety. Betty insisted on an hour of writing drill every evening for her four-year-old daughter. Though some children may show interest in such skills early on, forcing them to do so takes an emotional toll. One of the areas where children display the results of such stress is in toileting problems.

Finally, control issues play a role in stool retention problems. Avoiding power struggles, empowering your child in positive ways, and encouraging cooperation are as effective in solving bowel problems as they are in other areas of family life.

Children with other problems, such as attention deficit disorder, have a high percentage of associated bowel control problems. These problems can be resolved with time, patience, and encouragement; simply knowing that your child is not the only one experiencing such difficulties may help you feel better able to cope with this troubling behavior.

Remember: You Just Can't Make 'Em!

AS WITH SLEEPING and eating, when it comes to toileting, we can't make 'em do it! Following the guidelines in this chapter should bring success to your young toilet trainee. Just look around any grade school, middle school, or high school classroom. Count the number of diapers. Zero. Whoopee! That must mean that even you won't be changing diapers forever.

There are many ways to get the message of love through to children. One of the most important is to offer your trust. Sleeping, eating, and toileting can be battlegrounds where parents and children oppose each other, or they can be opportunities for sharing respect, kindness, and encouragement. Healthy sleeping, eating, and toileting habits are gifts that will serve your children well. Although you can't make 'em do it, there is much you can do to set the stage for success.

PART FIVE

Understanding Your Child at a Deeper Level

Decoding the Belief
Behind the Behavior

Understanding your preschooler's development and temperament and filling your toolbox with Positive Discipline parenting tools will go a long way toward resolving conflicts with your young child. Isn't it good to know that there is even more you can do to raise responsible, respectful, resourceful children?

A young child's occasional misbehavior is not intended to drive his parents and teachers crazy. It *is* his most expressive means for letting you know what he feels, believes, and needs. There is always a message hidden in your child's behavior; when you can learn to "break the code," you are more than halfway there to dealing with his behavior successfully.

In chapter 19 we will take a look at the messages hidden in children's behavior. In chapters 20 and 21, we will discover the "mistaken goals" of their behavior, define what they look like at home and in a child care setting, and (most important) explain what parents and teachers can do to deal with the beliefs *behind* a child's behavior and to help him make better choices. You may find that you never look at your child's misbehavior in quite the same way again!

19

The Messages of Misbehavior

Reading the Code

W E H U G T H E M , laugh with them, buy them presents, brag about them, and celebrate them. At times, we're exasperated with their behavior. Sometimes we resort to yelling or spanking; sometimes threats are hurled in both directions. Parents and teachers may respond to a child's behavior in ways that leave both child and adult feeling discouraged and miserable.

How can adults possibly hurt people they love so much? How can such a tiny and vulnerable person trigger such strong responses from others? Part of the answer is that adults tend to respond to a child's behavior as though it were the whole problem. All too often, adults resort to punitive measures because they are the only tools with which they are equipped. Simply put, they just don't know what else to do.

This chapter is about learning to see and interpret behavior in a new way. We will look at behavior as a message or code that reveals a child's underlying beliefs about himself and about life. When children misbehave, they are communicating to us in code. When we look for the message behavior sends us—when we learn to decipher the code—we usually find that our responses change.

There is a parable that urges us to walk a mile in someone else's shoes before we condemn or criticize his actions. This parable can also apply to our children and their behavior. Another phrase for this is "getting into the child's world."

An amazing thing happens when we decipher the code in our children's behavior and change our own responses: the child's behavior changes, too.

What Is Misbehavior?

WHEN DOES A child's behavior become "misbehavior"? When we react without taking a moment to think about what might be going on from the child's perspective, we are likely to regard any atypical behaviors as misbehaviors. Put yourself in your child's place for a moment; make an effort to get into his world.

Four-year-old Randy was at home with his mom, recuperating from the chicken pox. Mom had had to take a few days off from work and needed to spend some time on the phone keeping up with business. One afternoon, after a particularly long phone call, she walked into Randy's room and found him absorbed in using the permanent marking pens. The imaginative little boy had looked at his chicken pox spots and been reminded of his dot-to-dot coloring book. Randy had removed his clothes and was busily drawing lines from one spot to the next with the marking pens. Now Randy was covered with brightly colored lines connecting his red spots.

Randy's mom was wise enough to realize that this was not misbehavior. He was not trying to get attention or make a mess; he was being wonderfully creative. His mom realized that Randy had discovered that his body looked like a large dot-to-dot drawing so he had simply connected the dots! What did his mom do? She let her sense of humor take over. She went and got the washable markers and finished connecting the dots with him.

It would have been easy for Mom to scold and humiliate Randy. The entire event could have disintegrated into tears and misery. Instead, Mom made room for one of childhood's treasured moments. When Randy is a dad himself, sitting with his children around Grandma's table telling "Remember when . . ." stories, Randy and his mom will both laugh as they remember Randy's dot-to-dot chicken pox! And as they laugh, they can re-create that moment of fun and love shared long ago, passing it on to a new generation.

When three-and-a-half-year-old Elsie's dad picked her up from preschool one evening, he immediately noticed that Elsie's hair was significantly shorter in the front than it had been that morning. "Did someone cut Elsie's hair today?" the perplexed father asked Elsie's teacher.

"No, she did that herself," the teacher replied. "Elsie has been practicing a lot with the safety scissors lately."

Was Elsie misbehaving? When Dad let himself get into Elsie's world, he realized that Elsie was actively exploring the wonders of using scissors. Today she had discovered that hair can be cut. Dad may not like his daughter's new hairstyle, and he will surely explain to Elsie that he would prefer that she not cut her own (or anyone else's) hair. He might also tell his intrepid daughter, "Let's find some things you can cut." This dad knows that Elsie's experiment was a learning experience. Hair grows back. Elsie made a mistake, and her dad helped her to learn from it.

Both of these children were behaving in ways that are developmentally normal—and quite creative. Yet many parents would have interpreted both situations as misbehavior.

So, how do we know when a behavior is misbehavior? Randy's behavior might have been misbehavior if he had wanted his mother to play with him rather than talk on the phone. His behavior then might have been intended to get attention or power as a mistaken way to feel belonging.

One of the primary human needs is the need to belong, to feel a sense of worth and significance. When a child believes he doesn't belong, he feels discouraged. Out of that discouragement he chooses what Rudolf Dreikurs, author of *Children: The Challenge* (Hawthorn/Dutton, 1964) called a "mistaken goal of misbehavior." (The four mistaken goals of misbehavior—undue attention, misguided power, revenge, and assumed inadequacy—will be discussed in more detail in chapter 20.) They are considered mistaken goals because the child mistakenly believes the behavior will help him regain a sense of belonging. It puts a new light on misbehavior when we can remember that a misbehaving child is simply a discouraged child who wants to belong and has a mistaken idea about how to achieve this goal.

Misbehavior or Coded Message?

THREE-YEAR-OLD MARY IS visiting her grandparents' house on Thanksgiving, with all the other aunts, cousins, and members of her family. When Mary is found tearing toilet paper to shreds, is she misbehaving? It would be understandable if her grandmother's first response were anger.

Getting into a child's world is a bit like looking through a kaleidoscope. Pretend that you are Mary's grandmother. What do you see when you look through the kaleidoscope? You may see piles of shredded paper everywhere, tinged by the red glow of your own anger. Now turn the kaleidoscope slightly and look again.

Look at Mary, who has just been chased away from the kitchen because she was "underfoot." Look at Mary, who just got told by her big sister Joan that she was too little to play Monopoly with Joan and her older cousins. Look at Mary, who wanted to show Grandpa how to do "Itsy Bitsy Spider" but was abandoned when he had to go help move the table into the dining room. What might Mary really be saying with her toilet paper? What might stop Mary from further acts of destruction? The kaleidoscope reveals a lonely little girl surrounded by a discouraging gray haze.

How do you suppose most adults would react to Mary's behavior? What would you do? Does understanding what Mary's world feels like just now influence your response?

Understanding Mary's world does not mean that deliberately making a mess is okay. But understanding some of what Mary is experiencing is likely to affect how we respond. Mary will still have to pick up all the tiny bits of paper. Armed with love and understanding, Grandma may be more likely to help Mary pick up the pieces and maybe to invite her to help roll out pie dough afterward.

> Misbehaving children are discouraged children, and encouragement is like rain to their parched souls. It is important to create opportunities to help children feel encouraged and valuable, to let them know they belong.

Misbehaving children are discouraged children, and encouragement is like rain to their parched souls. It is important to create opportunities to help children feel encouraged and valuable, to let them know they belong.

Let's turn the kaleidoscope together and take a look at the four coded messages of discouraged children.

Breaking the Code

IF WE CAN learn to read the code behind children's behavior in different situations, we can deal effectively with the message instead of just the behavior itself.

There are three specific clues that will help you break the code to identify the message behind the behavior. Let's examine how parents and caregivers can understand the message behind a child's misbehavior—and decide what to do about it.

Your Own Feelings in Response to the Behavior

How *you* feel in response to a child's misbehavior is the first important clue to understanding the mistaken goal. For instance, when the child's mistaken goal is undue attention, adults feel annoyed, irritated, worried, or guilty. When it's power a child is after, adults usually feel challenged, threatened, or defeated. When the child's mistaken goal is revenge, adults feel hurt, disappointed, disbelieving, or disgusted. When a child is so discouraged that he gives up completely (the mistaken goal of assumed inadequacy), adults also feel inadequate, despairing, hopeless, or helpless. When you look at the mistaken goal chart on page 264, you can usually find one set of feelings in the second column that best describes your feelings when faced with a misbehaving child. Note that you don't need to *do* anything about your feelings; simply notice and use them to help you understand your child.

Your Usual (Ineffective) Attempts to Stop the Behavior

Another clue is your usual response to your child's behavior. Adults often respond to the behavior of each mistaken goal in predictable ways. For instance, Dad and Ryan are constantly battling over something, whether it's time to brush teeth, what to wear, how much to eat, and how long Ryan can play at

TABLE 19.1 Mistaken Goals Chart

THE CHILD'S GOAL IS:	IF THE PARENT/ TEACHER FEELS:	AND TENDS TO REACT BY:	AND IF THE CHILD'S RESPONSE IS:
Undue attention (to keep others busy or to get special service)	Annoyed; irritated; worried; guilty	Reminding; coaxing; doing things for the child he could do for himself	Stops temporarily, but later resumes same or another disturbing behavior
Misguided power (to be boss)	Provoked; challenged; threatened; defeated	Fighting; giving in; thinking: "You can't get away with it" or "I'll make you"; wanting to be right	Intensifies behavior; defiant compliance; feels he's won when parent/ teacher is upset; passive power
Revenge (to get even)	Hurt, disappointed; disbelieving; disgusted	Retaliating; getting even; thinking: "How could you do this to me?"	Retaliates; intensifies; escalates the same behavior or chooses another weapon
Assumed inadequacy (to give up and be left alone)	Despair; hopeless; helpless; inadequate	Giving up; doing for; overhelping	Retreats further; passive; no improvement no response

THE BELIEF BEHIND THE CHILD'S BEHAVIOR IS:	HAT MESSAGES:	PARENT/TEACHER PROACTIVE AND EMPOWERING RESPONSES INCLUDE:
I count (belong) only when I'm being noticed or getting special service; I'm only important when I'm keeping you busy with me	"Notice me, involve me"	"I love you and _____." (Example: I care about you and will spend time with you later.); redirect by assigning a task so child can gain useful attention; avoid special service; plan special time; set up routines; use problem-solving; encourage; use family/class metings; touch without words; ignore; set up nonverbal signals
I belong only when I'm boss, in control, or proving no one can boss me; "You can't make me"	"Let me help; give me choices"	Redirect to positive power by asking for help; offer limited choices; don't fight and don't give in; withdraw from conflict; be firm and kind; act, don't talk; decide what you will do; let routines be the boss; leave and calm down; develop mutual respect; set a few reasonable limits; practice follow-through; encourage; use family/class meetings
I don't think I belong, so I'll disbelieving; hurt others as I feel hurt; I can't be liked or loved	"Help me, I'm hurting; acknowledge my feelings."	Acknowledge the hurt feelings; avoid feeling hurt; avoid punishment and retaliation; build trust; use reflective listening; share your feelings; make amends; show that you care; act, don't talk; encourage strengths; put kids in same boat; use family/class meetings
I can't belong because I'm not perfect. so I'll convince others not to expect anything of me; I am helpless and unable; it's no use trying because I won't do it right	"Show me small steps; celebrate my successes"	Break task down to small steps; stop all criticism; encourage any positive attempt; have faith in child's ability; focus on assets; don't give up; set up opportunities for success; teach skills/show how, but don't do for; enjoy the child; build on his interests; encourage, encourage, encourage; use family/class meetings

the computer. This constant struggle reveals an ongoing battle for power. Dad gives a command, Ryan resists, and Dad reacts by fighting with Ryan, thinking, "You can't get away with this; I'll make you do it." Some adults just give in. In either case, there is an ongoing power struggle with a winner, a loser, or a slight pause while each gathers strength and ammunition to continue the battle. The third column of the mistaken goal chart lists the common reactions of adults to each of the four mistaken goal's behaviors.

Your Child's Response to Your Ineffective Action

The third clue in deciphering a child's mistaken goal is how a child responds when the adult tries to stop the misbehavior with punitive or permissive methods (instead of Positive Discipline methods).

When the teacher at his child care center tells five-year-old Matthew to stop misbehaving, he usually responds by damaging his toys or knocking over other children's blocks. Sometimes he even yells, "I hate you!" Matthew's mistaken goal is revenge. When the goal is revenge and a parent or teacher tries to stop the misbehavior, children react by hurting others, damaging property, or retaliating in some other way, such as using insulting words. The fourth column of the mistaken goal chart lists a child's typical responses to ineffective intervention by adults for each mistaken goal behavior.

Q. *My husband and I don't know how to handle our daughter's latest behavior. Periodically, our daughter, who just turned three, will have nothing to do with her dad. She loves him dearly, but lately she balks at kissing him good-bye in the morning, resists his attempts to read bedtime stories, or refuses to let him take part in her evening bath or play times. I have explained to him that "this too shall pass"; however, it puts an additional burden on me, since I need a break. I am a stay-at-home mom, home alone with her all day long. I need my husband's help in the evening. What can we do?*

A. What happens when your daughter "ignores" her dad? Do you feel annoyed and irritated by her behavior? Do you try to coax her to "go to Daddy"? Do you give in and bathe her, read to her, and put her to bed yourself? If so, what she's doing is working.

Sometimes children who are home with one parent all day resent the loss of that parent's exclusive attention when the other parent returns home. The child may believe "I'm only special when Mom is taking care of me or when I'm monopolizing Mom's time." It invites attention when she refuses to kiss Dad (even when he's loved very much) and sees the hurt or frustrated expression on his face.

In a nutshell, don't overreact; remain kind and firm. If it's Dad's turn to do bath time, smile—and leave them to it. Once children learn they can manipulate adults by tears or whining, they'll keep right on doing it. When it no longer works, they will stop.

It may also help to "wean" her gradually from your time by doing tasks together with her dad before withdrawing. Most importantly, decide what you will do—then follow through with dignity. You're right: stay-at-home moms need time to nurture themselves, too! Reassure your husband that this is not a rejection of him but rather a way to sustain your undivided time and attention.

> Once children learn they can manipulate adults by tears or whining, they'll keep right on doing it. When it no longer works, they will stop.

Stick to the Spirit of the Principle

SOMETIMES IT IS hard to determine a child's mistaken goal. Don't be overly concerned about getting the "right" answer, and don't get hung up in the "paralysis of analysis." Observe carefully, and do the best you can. Remember, no one is perfect. Learn to see your mistakes as opportunities to learn and grow. After all, you are a scientist of sorts! Always remember that behavior never happens in a vacuum; there is a message behind the behavior, and the message involves some form of discouragement. No matter what the goal, it is always safe to use encouragement through unconditional love, hugs, patience, and letting children know you have faith in them.

Seeing the Possibilities

NO MATTER HOW hard we try, we can't force someone to change his behavior, at least not more than superficially. And when behavior is tied to deeply held beliefs, those beliefs will have to change before the behavior will. You may be able to make a child stop banging his spoon against his cup by removing the cup, but if that child believes he is important only when he is getting attention, he will surely be banging his leg against the chair within the next five minutes.

Stopping a symptom provides only temporary relief from the condition. When the child's deep need to feel belonging is satisfied, his mistaken method of reaching that goal is no longer necessary. There are a number of ways to invite a child to form a new belief, depending upon the goal. Alternatives for responding to the mistaken goals are shown on the mistaken goal chart in the sixth and seventh columns. You may find this a useful addition to the front of your refrigerator.

Satisfaction

MISBEHAVIOR TAKES A lot of energy from both children and adults. That energy can generate some pretty intense feelings. And being chased around the playground or carried kicking and screaming to bed might just seem better to a discouraged child than feeling unimportant, unnoticed, and powerless.

Getting into the child's world can help us understand the meaning of behavior. Remember, not all behavior, even when it's somewhat inappropriate, is misbehavior. Although it may seem like it from time to time, children really don't lie awake at night plotting ways to frustrate and annoy adults. Young children are still learning social skills, and they are natural explorers and scientists, looking for ways to investigate the world around them. Remember, too, to consider the influence of a child's developmental processes, temperament, and personality. It can be tremendously helpful during the preschool years to maintain this perspective—and to keep a good sense of humor handy!

In the next two chapters we will explore examples of each of the four mistaken goals. We will see what they look like at home in our families (chapter 20) and what they look like in the preschool setting (chapter 21). When you understand the meaning behind a child's misbehavior, you are well on your way to dealing with it in a loving and truly effective way.

20

Mistaken Goals
at Home

W<small>E'VE EXPLORED SOME</small> of the reasons children occasionally misbehave. To understand the code behind our children's actions and to work with them effectively, we need to learn to recognize mistaken goals in "real life." What do the goals of misbehavior look like in our homes and families? Get out your kaleidoscope and we'll take a look. (Refer to the Mistaken Goals Chart on page 264 as you learn.)

Undue Attention, or
"I'll Keep You Busy with Me!"

Mom, Catherine (age seven), and Ann (age five) are in the doctor's office because Catherine has a fever and cough. Mom gets Catherine settled in the waiting room and gently tucks her coat around her. She feels her forehead for fever and generally tries to help her feel as comfortable as possible. Mom then sits down and begins to look through a magazine. Ann comes over with a children's book she has found and asks her mom to read it to her. Mom says, "Not right now." She reminds Ann that she was up most of the night with Catherine, and now she just wants to sit quietly and look at a magazine.

Ann wanders away, but a few minutes later she begins to bounce up and down on the couch. "Stop," Mom calls out. "You need to sit quietly." Ann stops bouncing but within minutes is asking if she can sit on Mom's lap. Mom says, "No, of course not. You are much too big a girl for that!" Mom gets up and goes over to Catherine to check on her fever again.

Then they are called into the examining room. As the three of them are waiting for the doctor, Ann begins to complain of a stomachache. Mom looks at her anxiously and feels her forehead. When the doctor arrives to examine Catherine, Ann starts tugging on Mom's sleeve, saying she has to go to the bathroom. Mom sighs loudly, gets up, and takes Ann down the hall to the bathroom.

If we look through our kaleidoscope, we see that Ann has noticed Catherine getting a lot of attention. Ann may have decided that Mom loves Catherine more. At least, it certainly looks that way from her perspective!

How do you think Mom is feeling right now? Annoyed? Irritated? Guilty? She probably wishes she'd left Ann at home. How would Mom feel if she got into Ann's world? What might she do differently?

Ann's behavior is saying, "I want attention, too. I want to be noticed and to be a part of what is going on." Ann believes that she belongs or matters only when she is being noticed or when Mom is busy with her. The first of the four messages (or mistaken goals) is attention.

Identifying the Goal of Undue Attention

ANN'S MOTHER FELT irritated and guilty. These feelings are significant because they are the first clue to what is going on in this situation. When Mom and her daughters were at the doctor's office, what sorts of things were taking place? Mom asked Ann to sit quietly and stop bouncing on the sofa. Mom coaxed Ann out of sitting on her lap by reminding her that she is a "big" girl now. Finally she walked her down the hall to the bathroom, which Ann may have been able to do on her own. All of these were reactions to Ann's behavior. Children whose mistaken goal is undue attention successfully keep the adults in their lives busy with them most of the time. All children need their parents' attention, but they may not be seeking that attention in positive, encouraging ways.

What was Ann's response to her mother's actions? Ann stopped each behavior when her mother told her to, but each time she quickly discovered another. Looking at the feelings and reactions of Ann's mother and Ann's responses to her mother, we can see that all three clues lead to the mistaken goal of attention.

"Notice Me, Involve Me"

THE CHILD WHO sends a coded message by seeking undue attention believes that the only way he is able to count or belong is to keep others busy with him. He is willing to accept any attention, even negative attention, to achieve this goal. He wants to be noticed and to receive special service from those around him. Peer through your kaleidoscope: Picture this child wearing a large sunbonnet covered with feathers, fruit, flowers, or flying dinosaurs. There is a colorful banner on this hat. It says, "Notice Me. Involve Me."

Ann came to the conclusion that Mom loved her less than Catherine because Catherine was receiving most of Mom's attention. Not surprisingly, Ann's behavior reflects this belief. Attention becomes the measuring cup for love in Ann's world.

> The child who sends a coded message by seeking undue attention believes that the only way he is able to count or belong is to keep others busy with him.

"But wait a minute," parents often say when they learn their children's behavior is focused on getting attention. "We give our kids lots of attention. We spend all our free time with them; we read to them and play with them. How could they possibly need *more* attention?"

Actually, giving children excessive attention (even in the name of love) may be part of the problem. Children with special needs or children who simply are loved a great deal may receive huge amounts of adult attention. This is fine— as long as it continues. When something happens to deflect adult attention even momentarily (a telephone call, a doctor's appointment, a conversation with a friend), children perceive this as a loss and do whatever they can to regain the usual amount. In other words, it isn't necessarily true that children whose mistaken goal is undue attention aren't receiving enough attention; they may actually be receiving so much that it creates a need for special service—all of the time!

How can we give children the attention and feeling of belonging they need without giving in to an endless stream of small annoyances? Understanding the message or belief that prompts the mistaken goal of undue attention will help us decide how to respond in ways that will encourage children instead of reinforcing the mistaken belief. The following sections describe things you can do.

Use Active Listening to Deal with the Belief Instead of the Behavior

Let's go back to the doctor's office. How else might Mom have responded to Ann? When Mom realizes that Ann is feeling neglected because Catherine is receiving so much of her attention, she can deal with Ann's belief rather than her behavior. This could be done through active listening. Active listening means getting into the child's world and making guesses about what she might be feeling. It is important to check out your guesses. Mom could say, "It must be hard for you to see me giving so much attention to Catherine. When I'm so worried about her, you might feel that I don't have any love left for you." If Mom has guessed correctly, Ann will feel validated for her feelings. This could bring so much relief that she may cry as she acknowledges the truth of her mother's guess. She might be able to give up her belief that she doesn't have belonging and significance—and her need to misbehave.

Notice and Compromise

Mom might tell Ann that she will read her one book if Ann will agree to look at another book quietly afterward and let her mother look at a magazine. By asking Ann to honor her need for some quiet time, mother has not just "given in" to Ann's demands for attention but has understood Ann's needs and respectfully stated her own needs.

Involve the Child to Gain Useful Attention Through Cooperation

Mom could ask for Ann's assistance in caring for her sick sister. (Do you remember the sign on the hat that said "Involve Me"?) She might ask Ann how they might help Catherine feel more comfortable. By involving Ann in the process of caring for Catherine, Mother will be giving Ann a meaningful role and directly meeting Ann's need to feel necessary and valued.

ENCOURAGEMENT FOR UNDUE ATTENTION SEEKERS

- Use active listening to deal with the belief instead of the behavior.
- Notice and compromise.
- Involve the child to gain useful attention through cooperation.
- Give a reassuring hug.
- Encourage the child's ability to entertain and soothe himself.

Mother then might ask for Ann's support by explaining how tired she is. Ann might offer to give her mother a neck rub. When adults ask children for their help and cooperation, children can be remarkably thoughtful. Ann might even suggest that she read her mother a story! This could become a much more peaceful and satisfying time for all.

Give a Reassuring Hug

Another choice might be to hug Ann and tell her that Mother loves her very much. It can be very powerful to forget about the behavior and give a reassuring hug that says, "You belong and you are significant in my life." This is often enough to stop the misbehavior. And it feels much, much better for everyone than nagging and lecturing.

Encourage the Child's Ability to Entertain and Soothe Himself

None of us is born knowing how to amuse ourselves; it takes time and encouragement from parents and caregivers for children to learn this skill. Children quickly become accustomed to looking to adults for entertainment and diversion and may never learn how to occupy quiet moments, cure boredom, or discover the endlessly interesting occupations of childhood for themselves.

Encourage your child to learn to entertain himself—and recognize that this is a process that will take time and patience. Provide story tapes and teach your child to operate the tape player himself; explore the world of puzzles, art projects, and quiet games. Then, when your child seeks undue attention say, "I love you—and I have faith in your ability to take care of yourself for a little while." It does take time, but a child who has discovered ways to fill empty moments is less likely to demand that adults do so, and the ability to entertain himself is one your child will use for a lifetime.

Misguided Power, or "You're Not the Boss of Me!"

Four-year-old Beverly is standing beside the computer, gazing curiously at the key-board. Interesting pictures and patterns move across the colored screen; Beverly has watched Mom and Dad do this and is determined to try. She looks carefully around her (she's been warned not to touch the computer) and, when she sees no Mom in sight, gives the keyboard several taps.

Mom turns the corner just in time to see Beverly's action. She flies across the room, grabbing Beverly firmly by the elbow, totally hooked by her small daughter's misbehavior. "I've told you not to touch the computer! Now you've messed up my work," she says angrily, and proceeds to slap Beverly's hand. Beverly responds by twisting free of her mother's grip and smashing her small fist down on the keyboard.

This scene continues for the next several minutes until Mom, exasperated beyond belief, picks Beverly up and puts her into her room for a "time-out." Beverly is outraged and launches into a major tantrum; Mom storms out to repair her damaged files. Right now, not only is Mom feeling angry and provoked, but she is also feeling defeated. And by a four-year-old!

What is the message behind Beverly's behavior? Beverly is saying, "I don't believe I am important unless I have power or at least don't let you boss me."

Identifying the Goal of Misguided Power

WHEN BEVERLY AND her mom were struggling over the computer, her mom first felt provoked and, finally, defeated. Beverly's mother reacted with some powerful statements: "I've told you . . ." and "You've messed up my work!" Beverly's response to her mother's ineffective interventions was to intensify her own behavior. And so the battle rages on.

An important aspect of the mistaken goal of power is that both participants—and note that it takes two—are very determined to "win." Neither is willing to give an inch. When parent and child are locked in combat this way, the result is a power struggle. The problem with power struggles is that "winning" always takes place at someone else's expense. When that someone is a child you love, the victory may not be worth the price.

"Let Me Help; Give Me Choices!"

IF YOU HAVE heard an impassioned "You're not the boss of me!" shouted by a child, you might well suspect that the goal involved is power. The child whose goal is power can be imagined wearing a bright red or orange hard hat. Printed in bold letters on this hat is the command "Let me help; give me choices."

When four-year-old Beverly and her mom fought over the computer, they began a pattern of determined power struggles that might have set the tone of their relationship for many years. Fortunately, Beverly's mom learned about her own responsibility in maintaining their power struggle. She then changed her behavior and thus opened the way for Beverly to change her belief system and her behavior.

Offer Limited Choices

Beverly's mom sought out a parenting class, and she eventually learned how to empower Beverly by giving her power in appropriate ways. She gave Beverly limited choices instead of demands. "Would you like to walk with me into the other room, or shall I carry you?" "Mommy's work is for Mommy to do. Would you like to read a book or go and play with your Legos?"

Turn Misguided Power to Useful Power by Asking for Help

A power struggle is often defused by asking a child for her help. Mom let Beverly know how much she needed her. "Honey, we are a family, and you are so important to me. I don't know what I would do without you. What do you think we could do about the computer?" Asking for help often redirects the child and the parent away from power struggles and toward the power of cooperation.

Shut Your Mouth and Act—Kindly and Firmly

Another way to disengage from a power struggle is to be firm but kind. When Beverly continued to hit the computer keyboard, she was "throwing down the gauntlet," challenging her mom to fight. Instead of picking up the gauntlet, Mom can stop talking and act. She can kindly but firmly pick Beverly up and take her into another room. There need be no further mention of the computer until after a cooling-off period, which is often necessary before a child will listen to a limited choice or an appeal for help.

By not lecturing or shaming her daughter, Mom does not invite further resistance. Even if Beverly chooses to have a tantrum, Mom has defused the power struggle by refusing to become engaged.

ENCOURAGEMENT FOR SEEKERS OF MISGUIDED POWER

- Offer limited choices.
- Turn misguided power to useful power by asking for help.
- Shut your mouth and act—kindly and firmly.
- Ask if a positive time-out would be helpful.
- Make a date for problem solving.

Tantrums are less likely when children feel the energy of kindness along with firmness. This does not mean that tantrums can be entirely avoided, but avoiding a tantrum is not the goal. The goal is to kindly and firmly act upon what you have said.

Ask If a Positive Time-Out Would Be Helpful

When adults and children engage in power struggles, both have stopped thinking rationally and are reacting irrationally. It is usually impossible to solve a problem at the time of conflict, because objectivity is lost. Positive time-out may be required before win/win solutions can be found. After involving your child in creating a positive time-out area (see chapter 13), a power struggle might be interrupted by asking, "Would you like to go to time-out until you calm down?"

If your child really understands that time-out is not punitive and has helped create a place designed to help her feel better, she will often choose this option. If, however, your child says no, you might say, "Well, then I think I'll go until I feel better." What powerful role modeling that would be! It is appropriate to follow up a positive time-out by working on a solution together. Beverly and her mom might agree that Beverly can play her own computer games when Mom is there to help, that Mom gets to have some uninterrupted time to work, and that Beverly can ask Mom when she wants computer time.

Make a Date for Problem Solving

With preschoolers, problem solving might be accomplished by helping them explore what happened, what caused it to happen, and what ideas they have to solve the problem. Four- and five-year-olds are also very good at participating in family meetings (see chapter 15). After a cooling-off period (positive time-out) or even at the time of conflict, it might defuse the power struggle to ask, "Would you like to put this problem on our family meeting agenda, or would you like me to?" Actually, simply putting the problem on the family meeting agenda can serve as a cooling-off period during which everyone waits until the scheduled meeting to work together on solutions.

Revenge, or "I'll Make You Feel As Bad As I Do!"

It is bedtime. Dad is getting three-year-old Alice ready for bed. Dad says it is time to put on her jammies, but Alice is having great fun playing with bubbles in the sink and doesn't want to stop. Just as Dad is becoming impatient, Alice spills a cup of water on the floor. Dad immediately becomes angry, thinking Alice spilled the water on purpose. He picks Alice up and spanks her on the bottom. Alice begins to cry, and Dad has to wrestle her into the pajamas as she kicks and struggles.

When Alice is finally in her pajamas, Dad grumpily goes over to pick out a book for a bedtime story. Alice's lower lip puffs out. "I hate that book," she pouts, "and I don't want you to read to me! I want Mommy!" What a blow! Dad feels terrible: his own daughter doesn't love him. He is hurt and disbelieving.

Alice may be saying, "Daddy hurt me, so I'll hurt him back" in the only way she knows. The third of the four mistaken goals is revenge.

Identifying Revenge

DAD WAS SHOCKED that Alice would deliberately spill water all over the floor. He was trying his best to get Alice to bed while his wife was working late, and now, on top of everything else, his feelings are hurt. He feels bad that he spanked Alice. He didn't like doing it, but he didn't know how else to respond to her behavior.

First of all, did Alice deliberately spill the water? Young children spill a lot of things. Their muscle control is still developing. If Dad had understood the developmental nature of Alice's action, he might not have seen it as misbehavior. By getting into Alice's world, he would have understood that Alice simply had an accident or made a mistake, and he could have helped her get a sponge to clean up the puddles. Working together to mop up the spill might even have distracted Alice enough that the jammies would go on easily.

Even if Alice had deliberately spilled water, spanking is unlikely to help matters much. Spanking teaches children that "might makes right." It can invite many responses, and few of them are what parents intend. In this case, a spanking invited revenge. Both Alice and her dad wound up feeling hurt.

As we examine Dad's feelings and reactions and Alice's response, we see the clues that indicate the mistaken goal of revenge. Whenever an adult feels hurt by the behavior of a child, it is likely that the child is feeling hurt, too. This probably was not the first time Alice had received a spanking. She knows it isn't fair because she didn't mean to spill the water, but she doesn't have the skill to speak up for herself. She is telling her dad in the only way she knows (through the coded message of her behavior) that she feels hurt, both physically and emotionally. Others aren't fair to her, so she will get revenge.

"Help Me, I'm Hurting; Acknowledge My Feelings"

WHEN YOU PICTURE the child whose goal is revenge, imagine a black baseball cap turned backward. On the back is written the plea "Help me, I'm hurting; acknowledge my feelings."

When adults can begin to see a child who is hurtful as a "hurting" child, they feel motivated to respond to that child differently. Instead of giving in to the instinctive desire for retaliation and punishment, they can choose to offer care and support. If a child is feeling hurt, does it make sense to make that child feel worse?

Deal with the Hurt Feelings

First of all, Dad can move to the heart of the matter by dealing with Alice's hurt feelings. Dad could say, "Your behavior tells me that you might be feeling

ENCOURAGEMENT FOR REVENGE SEEKERS

- Deal with the hurt feelings.
- Apologize if you caused the pain.
- Listen to your child's feelings.
- Make sure the message of love gets through.
- Make amends, not excuses.

very hurt right now. I'll bet it hurt your feelings as well as your bottom when I spanked you." Getting into her world and acknowledging her hurt feelings is very validating for a child. She will feel understanding, belonging, and significance.

Apologize If You Caused the Pain

Alice's dad really does love his daughter, and he immediately regretted spanking her. His attitude can invite Alice to change her beliefs when he can take responsibility for his own behavior by apologizing. Dad can tell Alice that it was wrong of him to spank her. (It would be even better not to have spanked her, but he may still make mistakes as he learns new ways to respond.) Dad can reassure her that it is wrong for people to hurt each other, and no matter what she does, she does not deserve to be hit.

If you have never had the experience of apologizing to a child, swallow your pride, admit that adults aren't always right, and apologize the next time

"HELP ME PUT THINGS RIGHT"

Q. My four-year-old threw his cup of juice onto the floor when I told him it was time for his nap. The cup cracked and broke. I think his feelings were hurt because he didn't get to go to the park this morning. I want to respond to his hurt feelings but I don't think his behavior should go unpunished, do you?

A. Sometimes adults take the approach that if a child misbehaves "for a reason," he is no longer responsible for his actions. Ignoring misbehavior does not teach life skills. Nor does punishment, which translated usually means "you must suffer." What does help is to give children the opportunity to make amends.

If an item is damaged, it is appropriate to work out a way for the child to replace or repair it. That might mean doing a few helpful tasks to earn the money. It might mean helping come up with a plan to repair the damage, such as patching you make a mistake with your child. Children are delightfully quick to forgive, and you may discover that the hugs that follow apologies bring you even closer together.

Listen to Your Child's Feelings

Dad might take a moment to observe his small daughter closely. He can notice the jutting lip, trembling chin, and the tears beginning to fill Alice's eyes. And he can ask Alice—with genuine interest—how she is feeling. If she is too young to articulate her feelings, he can ask her if she thinks that Daddy doesn't love her. Alice will probably respond with a verbal (or nonverbal) signal that lets her dad know he has understood correctly. He can ask Alice why she threw water on the floor. She can explain that "it spilled" or was "on accident." When Dad and Alice have this kind of conversation, they are developing a new sense of trust.

When a child is feeling hurt, it is difficult for her to move beyond her emotions to solutions. Therefore, it is very important to address the feelings first.

a tear in a book. It might mean taking money out of his piggy bank. Even a young child can do some small task to contribute toward replacing the broken cup.

All of the solutions listed focus on teaching responsibility. Taking away television for a week does not achieve the same life lesson. Spanking, shaming, or yelling do not teach desirable life skills either. A child might learn fear of retaliation, escalate to more hurtful behavior himself, or decide that he is a "bad" person. None of these outcomes includes learning to take responsibility for his actions.

Children feel so much better about themselves when they are given a chance to make amends for misbehavior, to "put things right." If this is done in a spirit of love instead of anger, a child can regain a measure of self-esteem in the process. Few children feel pleased with themselves when they lose control of their behavior. They need encouragement to learn from their mistakes and tools to repair the damage, while parents need to change their attitude of shame and blame to one of support and true discipline.

Make Sure the Message of Love Gets Through

Dad now has a chance to tell Alice how much he does love her and how important she is to him. When a child is feeling hurt, this message can do so much to heal the pain. Dad also can share how he felt. When Dad can listen to and respect Alice's feelings and then explain his own, each will learn a great deal about the other. The love connection is rekindled.

If Dad tries these new ideas, he just might find himself snuggling close to his precious daughter as they read a bedtime story together. Even a painful and damaging experience can be healed when the message of love and caring gets through. Through her dad's example, Alice will be learning new tools herself, storing them up for the day she gets her own child ready for bed.

Make Amends, Not Excuses

Alice did not spill the water intentionally. If she had, once she and dad had dealt with her hurt feelings, it would have been necessary to address the mess. Dad might offer to help her wipe up the spill or supply her with a mop or sponge to enable her to do so herself. If Alice resorts to tears or retreats into hurt feelings again, her dad can make this encounter an opportunity to teach (rather than continuing the revenge cycle) by kindly and firmly continuing to "help" Alice clean up the puddles, and then wordlessly continuing with her regular bedtime routine.

Assumed Inadequacy: "I Give Up"

It is Jean's birthday; she is turning five years old today. Jean lives with her grandparents. When she enters the kitchen, her grandparents eagerly watch for her reaction to the brand-new birthday bike proudly displayed in the center of the room with a big red bow. Jean looks anxiously around and doesn't comment on the bike. Grandmother impatiently asks, "Well, what do you think? Do you like it?" Jean doesn't respond. Grandma then says in a coaxing voice, "Jean, look at your wonderful new bike."

Jean shakes her head and mumbles, "I can't ride a bike." Grandpa rushes over to reassure Jean. "That's no problem, sweetie, you'll learn in no time." Jean says nothing and does not go near the bike. Her grandparents look at one another in exasperation and shrug their shoulders. "What's the use?" they think to themselves, and Grandpa dejectedly begins to pour Jean's cereal and milk for her.

Jean's grandparents have been successfully convinced to "give up" on her. They feel hopeless both about themselves and about Jean. Somehow Jean has come to believe that she is not "good enough," that she is truly helpless. She acts upon this belief by convincing others of her inadequacy. Jean's grandparents love her, but they mistakenly believe that the best way to show that love is to do things for her, such as pouring her cereal and milk, which she could easily do for herself.

Of all the four goals or messages, children displaying assumed inadequacy are often the most overlooked. Because they are so busy shrinking back, they don't create the havoc that children acting upon the other three goals do. Children communicating this message often become nearly invisible.

This goal is rarely found in children younger than age five unless they are given little or no opportunity to develop a sense of autonomy. It can be especially baffling when highly productive and goal-oriented parents see this behavior in their child. What parents value as personal drive and determination may overwhelm these children and convince them that they are truly incapable. The fourth and final of the mistaken goals is assumed inadequacy, or giving up.

Identifying Assumed Inadequacy

JEAN'S GRANDPARENTS TRY not to feel hopeless, but Jean looks so tiny and helpless. They do their best to protect her and to make up for the fact that her parents aren't around. Grandma and Grandpa react to Jean's helpless behavior by doing things for her. Grandpa pours her milk, a task she might take pride in learning to do for herself. They are there to supply her every need. They endlessly buy her things and make plans and choices in which she has no participation. Jean's response is to retreat further, to act passively, and to refuse to try anything new. The feelings, reactions, and responses all give clues that the behavior is assumed inadequacy.

"Show Me Small Steps; Celebrate My Successes"

CHILDREN WHO DEVELOP a belief in their own inadequacy may have adopted the perfection myth. They believe that because they cannot do things perfectly, they might as well give up. When children understand that mistakes are part of how everyone learns, they can break the power of the perfection myth.

When a child is criticized for the mistakes she makes, it is easy to understand how she might develop the belief that she can't do anything right. Criticism is not always overt. As a toddler, Jean was always dressed in beautifully ironed, frilly dresses. She was admonished to "keep clean," and her grandmother would become very upset when Jean got paint or food on her clothing. Jean's perception was that messy was "bad." Because she was often messy, Jean eventually began to believe in her own inadequacy. It seemed that every time she tried to paint a picture or pour her own juice, she made a mess. Jean decided that she couldn't do anything well. Her action, based on this belief, has become inaction. The child who pursues this mistaken goal may be pictured wearing a drab-colored ski hat pulled far down over her face. What you will find stitched on the front (if you look closely enough) is "Show me small steps; celebrate my successes."

Feeling inadequate or giving up is a very lonely place to be. Since their goal is to be left alone, these children are rarely much trouble to others. There are many things parents can do to meet this child's needs.

Have Faith in Your Child and Let Her Do Things for Herself

Parents may not realize that doing too much for children (probably in the name of love) is very discouraging. It is very easy for children to adopt the belief that "I'm not capable." Another possible belief is "I am loved when others are doing things for me."

Stop doing things for your child that she can do for herself. When she says, "I can't," have patience; say, "I have faith that you can handle this task." Encouraging a child who believes that she is inadequate requires a great deal of patience, gentle perseverance, and faith in the child's abilities.

ENCOURAGEMENT FOR ASSUMED INADEQUACY

- Have faith in your child and let her do things for herself.

- Take time for training and encourage even the smallest steps.

- Teach that mistakes are wonderful opportunities to learn.

Take Time for Training and Encourage Even the Smallest Steps

It is not surprising that Jean does not know how to ride a bicycle; no one does without teaching and practice. Instead of feeling frustrated, Grandma might share a story about her own experiences learning to ride a bike. Perhaps she could tell about how foolish she felt the first time she fell and her brothers and sister laughed. When Grandma shares a story such as this, she is also telling Jean that feeling embarrassed is okay. Because Grandma felt that way, it is easier for Jean to express her own fears. Children don't know that it was ever hard for adults to learn new things unless they are told such stories. Staying on a pedestal may be good for your image, but it can cripple the growth of closeness and trust.

Children watch us as we struggle to learn new things. They may believe we always succeed easily (and feel inadequate because they do not), or they may watch us try something and meet with repeated failure. How we react—whether we can laugh at ourselves and keep on trying or whether we give up in discouragement—will be giving them clues about their own experiences. Never underestimate the power of role modeling.

Children who have already developed the belief "I'm inadequate" may resist attempts at training. This is why small steps are important. Grandpa might start by letting Jean sit on the bike inside the house. He might be sure the bike has training wheels and show Jean how they work. Before starting her down the block, he can reassure her that he will not let go until she is ready. Of course, he might start by ceasing to fix her cereal and teaching her how to pour her own milk (from a small pitcher). Remember that when teaching new skills, especially to discouraged youngsters, it helps to make every attempt to foresee problems—and to ensure a child's success.

Teach That Mistakes Are Wonderful Opportunities to Learn

What is our attitude toward our own mistakes? Remember, we learn much more from what we see than what we hear. Criticism is difficult for most of us to accept. For a child who believes she is inadequate, criticism only reinforces her belief in her inadequacy. One of the healthiest things we can learn to do for such a child is to stop all criticism.

If Jean messes her dress up with paint or mud, Grandma may consider dressing her in more durable clothes. What a great message it would send if Grandma could learn to say, "Wow, you are covered with paint! You must have had a great time painting today."

Be Aware of the Hidden Message

"WHEW," YOU MAY be saying, "I had no idea there was so much going on in my child's head when he acted that way." It is important to understand that children do not consciously decide to pursue one of the mistaken goals; they are only rarely aware of their own beliefs and are not out to baffle their parents with a game of "guess my goal." It also takes time to translate awareness of your child's mistaken goal into kind, firm, and encouraging action.

When parents can be aware of the message hidden in their child's behavior and when they can observe their own feelings and reactions, then they can take steps to encourage a discouraged child and to celebrate a child's willingness to take risks and make mistakes. In so doing, parents nurture children who believe they are capable, lovable, and worthwhile.

21

Mistaken Goals in the Preschool Setting

MISBEHAVIOR—the coded messages children send us about their beliefs—doesn't happen just at home with parents. Misbehavior happens everywhere young children go. And just like parents, teachers and caregivers can learn to decipher children's mistaken goals and respond in ways that teach and encourage.

Undue Attention in the Preschool

IT SHOULD COME as no surprise that where groups of children are gathered, the desire for undue attention appears.

At the Tiny Treasures Child Care Center this morning, there are twelve children in Marcia's classroom, all four- and five-year-olds. Johnny is five. At about 10:00, he finds Marcia; his shoe is untied and he asks her to tie it for him. Marcia does so, and Johnny goes off to play. Less than five minutes later, he needs help sharpening a pencil. Marcia helps him do that, too, but no more than two minutes pass before she notices that Johnny has begun to mess around with Ben's blocks. Marcia reminds him that these are Ben's blocks and Johnny needs to choose something else to do. By 10:15, Johnny's shoe is again untied. . . .

By now, Marcia is longing for recess time or her break. In addition to feeling annoyed by Johnny's constant demands, she is also feeling guilty that she doesn't enjoy being around this child very much.

These feelings are the first clue that Johnny's behavior is motivated by the mistaken goal of attention.

Marcia's reactions to Johnny's behavior are fairly typical. She does things for Johnny that he could reasonably be expected to do for himself—or be learning to do on his own. She also spends a good deal of her time reminding Johnny to stop certain behaviors. The second clue that the goal is undue attention is that Johnny stops his behavior for a short while when Marcia reprimands him, but he soon finds ways to seek more undue attention. Every teacher will recognize a child they have known in Johnny. These children successfully keep the adults in their lives busy with them most of the time. Isn't it remarkable that Johnny's shoes have an above-average capacity for coming untied?

The Belief Behind Undue Attention

WHAT ARE JOHNNY and other children like him really saying by their behavior? Remember that Johnny wears a large, colorful hat declaring, "Notice me. Involve me." When a child seeks undue attention, he is acting on a deeply held belief that he can belong or count only by being noticed or by keeping adults busy with him. It is important to understand that preschoolers often seek attention. In fact, they truly need a large amount of it, and chants of "Look at me! Watch what I'm doing!" are frequent as they seek validation in our eyes. This is developmentally appropriate, and is not the same as the kind of "undue" attention that is very irritating.

When we know how to decode their mistaken goal messages, we understand that what children who misbehave are really saying to us is "I'm a child and I just want to belong." But because we're human, too, it's hard to hear the plea for belonging when we survey the crayon damage on the classroom wall or feel exhausted after a morning of Johnny's demands!

Those of us who work in school settings are certainly familiar with children like Johnny. Even when his teacher is able to understand that Johnny's behavior is a cry for attention, it is not always possible to give one-on-one attention in group settings. Still, a number of things can be done routinely with all of the children that will greatly diminish constant bids for attention such as Johnny's.

ENCOURAGEMENT FOR UNDUE ATTENTION IN THE PRESCHOOL

- Teach nonverbal signals.

- Give special attention before the child seeks undue attention.

- Take time for training.

- Help children get attention in useful ways through meaningful involvement.

Teach Nonverbal Signals

Children can be taught signals to let the teacher know that they need her time or attention. Marcia might have taught the children in her class to gently place a hand on her arm to let her know that she is needed. Marcia's signal that she notices that child's request for assistance is to make eye contact with the child, wink, and say, "As soon as I'm free." This gives attention but in a reasonable way, while still allowing a child to feel acknowledged and important.

Give Special Attention Before the Child Seeks Undue Attention

Marcia could comment on something that makes each child feel special. She might greet Johnny and tell him she found a spider's egg sac and brought it in to the science table. She knows that Johnny is fascinated by spiders. Her special attention and recognition of his interests might make him feel included and cared about in just a brief conversation.

Another way to say "I notice you" is to greet children individually. Some teachers take the time to give every child special attention with a hug or a handshake as they enter the preschool or child care center. This provides a very real message that says "I care about you and am glad you are here." When children feel this kind of belonging and significance, they may not need to seek undue attention. Large centers may want to designate one teacher as the "morning greeter."

Take Time for Training

Now, about Johnny's shoes. Marcia could create a training plan to help Johnny learn to tie his own shoes. After an adequate amount of demonstration and practice, it would be reasonable for Marcia to tell Johnny that she would love to watch him tie his own shoes. Eventually Johnny would be encouraged to tie his shoes and come back to show Marcia when he has been successful. Johnny is being given attention but in ways that help him feel capable, not in ways that reinforce the constant flow of small annoyances or demands for inappropriate special service.

Help Children Get Attention in Useful Ways Through Meaningful Involvement

As discussed in chapter 20, the "hat" message for the mistaken goal of undue attention is "Notice me. Involve me!" It can be very effective to ignore a "misbehavior" while redirecting a child to get attention in a useful way.

Five-year-old Melanie complained to her teacher, "Brent stole the trike I was playing with." It just so happened that the teacher had watched Melanie abandon the trike while she went to get a drink of water. The teacher put her hand on Melanie's shoulder and said, "Honey, would you please blow the whistle to let everyone know it is time to come in for lunch." Melanie quickly forgot her bid for undue attention and ran to every part of the playground blowing the whistle and waving for the kids to come in.

Just as children often make the mistake of trying to get undue attention, adults often make the mistake of getting hooked instead of finding a way to redirect children into feeling a sense of belonging and significance in useful ways. It is important to remember that encouraged children do not need to find mistaken ways to find belonging and significance—at least, not as often!

Power Struggles in the Preschool

It is a lovely, sunny day at the Silverport Preschool. Over by the apple tree, three-year-old Sarah and her teacher, Julie, are glaring at each other. Julie says it's time to go inside. Sarah refuses to go. Julie emphasizes that playtime is over and everyone else has gone inside and Sarah must come in right now. Sarah latches onto the side of the climber. Julie's face is turning pink and she begins to threaten her small pupil, "If you don't come in this minute, you won't be allowed to come outside the rest of the day."

Sarah sticks out her tongue. "You can't make me!" she taunts. Julie heads over to pick her up and carry her inside, but first she has to chase Sarah down.

Julie is really angry (and a little embarrassed—after all, this is a three-year-old) and feels that her authority has been challenged. As Julie carries the writhing, kicking, screaming child inside, she says through clenched teeth, "When I say it's time to come inside, you will do what I say."

What do you think? Will Sarah meekly obey Julie next time? What is the message behind Sarah's behavior? She may be saying "I want to be the boss and have some power in my life!" Her invisible hard hat is saying, "Let me help. Give me choices." Sarah's way of achieving power is by proving that "you can't make me!"

Identifying Misguided Power

THIS TEACHER FELT angry; she also felt that her legitimate authority had been challenged. These are the typical feelings adults have when they are involved in a power struggle—and these feelings provide the first clue to identifying misguided power.

As we've mentioned before, a power struggle can't be staged alone. Sarah needed Julie's reactions to engage in the battle. Julie reacted to the situation by using her superior strength to overpower Sarah and carry her inside. She made Sarah do what she told her to do. But did Sarah ever give up her end of the fight?

Recall the way that Sarah grabbed onto the play equipment to fortify her position. An additional clue that the goal is power is that the behavior intensifies. Sarah's response is yet another intensification and is characteristic of the mistaken goal of misguided power.

The Belief Behind Misguided Power

THE CHILD WHO acts upon the mistaken goal of misguided power will spend a great deal of energy in finding ways not to cooperate. Sarah had to clutch the playground equipment fiercely to maintain a hold that her teacher couldn't loosen. In the heat of battle, this ferocity may be described as "stubbornness." When the same child is learning to do a complicated math problem or running those last few miles of the marathon, this same trait may be seen positively as "tenacity." The underlying belief of the mistaken goal of misguided power is "I belong only when I am in control. No one can make me do things."

How might Sarah's teacher give her power in appropriate ways? There are several possibilities.

Ask the Child to Help

If there is a pattern of power struggles between Julie and Sarah, Julie could work to break the cycle by asking for Sarah's help—which invites Sarah to use her power in productive ways. Julie might say, "Sarah, I need your help. Would you please tell the boys in the far corner that it is time to come in?" An opportunity to help seems to appeal to the child who is seeking misguided power. Helping provides her with an opportunity to have power—but in a useful way. Remember that few people—including little ones—enjoy feeling powerless or victimized. All of us need opportunities to experience self-control and to learn

---

ENCOURAGEMENT FOR MISGUIDED POWER SEEKERS IN THE PRESCHOOL

- Ask the child to help.

- Offer limited choices.

- Do the unexpected.

- Seek win/win solutions.

that personal power can be used in helpful ways. It is not the *need* for "power" that is mistaken; it is the misguided use of power that creates problems.

Offer Limited Choices

As we've mentioned, one of the best ways to empower a child is to give her limited choices in which all alternatives are acceptable. Asking a child if she is ready to come inside now implies the hidden option of not being ready to come inside. If that is not an acceptable alternative, do not include it in your choices, stated or implied.

Sarah's teacher could ask Sarah whether she would like to lead the class inside at the end of playtime or hold the teacher's hand and follow the others. These are limited choices, both of which are acceptable. Staying outside is not one of the choices. If a child answers by naming an alternative that was not a choice given, such as "stay outside," simply respond, "That is not one of the choices." Another option might be to let Sarah choose which equipment to play on before going inside and to say that the bell would ring in two more minutes. These approaches would give Sarah time to consider her behavior and the opportunity to feel empowered, which might encourage her cooperation.

Giving choices is a respectful way to treat children, not a "gimmick" designed to trick a child into compliance. Choices empower a child, meeting the need for power and belonging in acceptable ways. And meeting the underlying need will address the real cause of the misbehavior rather than the symptoms only.

Do the Unexpected

Adults and preschoolers sometimes find that their behavior has become rather predictable. Julie and Sarah probably have enacted this little scene (or a variation of it) many times before. Instead of responding to Sarah's challenge in her usual way, Julie could do the unexpected. When Sarah refused to come inside, Julie could have said, "I'll bet you can't catch me." Julie could then run away from Sarah. What a surprise that would be for someone who is clinging fiercely to the railing! What is the point of hanging on to the railing now? Sarah just might let go to chase her teacher, and when she caught her, Julie could give her a big hug and walk peacefully inside with her. The standoff evaporates; both are winners.

Seek Win/Win Solutions

Another secret to dealing with power struggles is to seek win/win solutions. It is when both people involved remain committed to being the only winner that the power struggle escalates. Why assert our own power when it inevitably means a child must be the loser?

Five-year-old Chad refused to share the blocks with anyone. He said he needed all of them. As soon as the teacher recognized that she was about to engage in a power struggle, she instead said to Chad, "I need your help. You are so good at problem-solving—I'll bet you can think of a way to solve the problem we are having now. What ideas do you have for a solution that works for everyone?"

Chad wasn't quite ready to give up his misguided power and said stubbornly, "I need all of the blocks!" The teacher didn't take the bait. Instead she said, "I'll be back in a few minutes so you can have a chance to think about it. I know you can think of some good ideas. In fact, I'll bet you can think of at least two possibilities." She then walked away.

The wind had been taken from Chad's sail. He had nothing to fight against. It wasn't much fun to have all the blocks to himself with no one to challenge his power. Instead, he was intrigued by the challenge to come up with a good solution.

When the teacher returned in a few minutes to ask Chad about his ideas, Chad said, "We could set the timer for how long one person could have the blocks before giving someone else a turn." The teacher said, "That sounds like a good one. What else did you think of?" Chad beamed as he said, "I could go find something else to do!" The teacher said, "You thought of two good ideas. You decide which one works best for you." Chad happily turned over the blocks to another child and ran off to the housekeeping area. In that area, Chad wanted to play in the sink, but another child was using it. Chad said, "I'll bet we can think of a solution!"

Revenge in the Preschool

It is a Tuesday morning, and four-year-old Eric has been throwing the toy dinosaurs across the room. His teacher, John, comes over and removes the toy dinosaurs, telling Eric he cannot have them for the rest of the day. Eric is furious. Eric remembers that when Zachary threw the blocks into the corner yesterday, nothing happened to him. This isn't fair! Eric stomps off.

A little while later, John makes the charming discovery that Eric has stuffed the toilet full of toilet paper and has clogged it up. John shows Eric the mess he has made and asks, "How could you do such a thing to our school?" Eric doesn't hesitate. "I hate this place," he says, "and I'm glad the toilet is broken."

John tells the little boy that he will have to write a note to Eric's parents about this and that Eric will also have to stay in at recess. Before the day is over, Eric has also managed to cut Sally's hair.

Right at this moment, John is deciding to call in sick tomorrow. He just can't take another day of this child. Eric's message is "I've been hurt, so I'm going to hurt others back. Life is unfair!"

John is undoubtedly feeling pretty discouraged and hurt himself. He has devoted so much time and energy to becoming a teacher, and what's the use? John also feels disgusted and disbelieving, and he is baffled by Eric's disdain for the school's property.

Identifying Revenge

ADULTS (AND CHILDREN) often cover their hurt feelings with anger. John's reaction to Eric's behavior was to hurt back through reprimands and punishment. This created a revenge cycle.

Eric's response was to escalate his behavior by stomping off to stuff the toilet full of paper, proclaiming his hatred of this place, and to cut Sally's hair. Children are very good at revenge cycles. They have many weapons to hurt adults who can't see the message behind the behavior and don't know how to get out of the revenge cycle.

Eric's backward-facing cap declares, "Help me, I'm hurting; acknowledge my feelings."

The Belief Behind Revenge

A CHILD WHO has chosen the mistaken goal of revenge believes that if he can't belong (which must hurt a lot), at least he can get even. Unfortunately, it is difficult for most adults to love and enjoy a child who is hurting others and destroying property. By acting upon his belief that he doesn't belong, this child behaves in ways that prove his point.

It can be difficult to deal with a child like Eric. Once his teacher realizes that Eric feels he has been treated unfairly and is hurt, he can respond to Eric's real need. Eric wants to feel belonging, to be a real part of the group. How can that be achieved?

Deal with the Hurt Feelings Through Validation and Expression

Before Eric's behavior can change, he must feel understood. He needs to have his feelings validated, and he needs to express them in acceptable ways. John can spend time with Eric and help him find acceptable ways to express his feelings of hurt.

Young children aren't consciously aware that their misbehavior is motivated by hurt feelings. However, when an adult correctly guesses what they are feeling, children feel understood and validated. The best way to start the learning process is through modeling. John could say, "Eric, when you behave that way, I feel hurt. My guess is that you might be feeling hurt too. Can you let me know when you are ready to talk about our hurt feelings?"

If Eric does not want to say anything, the teacher might tell about a time that he felt really hurt. John could tell about feeling hurt when he wasn't chosen for the baseball team and that he took the ball after recess and hid it so that the other children could not find it. Eric will probably feel more willing to talk with John about his own hurt feelings after hearing John's story. When those hurt feelings have been acknowledged and admitted, Eric can begin to feel better.

By spending this kind of time with Eric, his teacher can gain Eric's trust by showing that he accepts Eric, even when Eric is not feeling likable. Remember, a child must deal with the hurt feelings before he can move forward to find solutions to the problems his behavior may have caused. Eric may well need a little time to cool off before he is ready to discuss his feelings.

Teach the Difference Between Feeling and Doing

Learning to name the feelings inside of himself gives a child a new tool. By learning to stop, acknowledge, and name his feelings, Eric can slow down and

ENCOURAGEMENT FOR REVENGE SEEKERS IN THE PRESCHOOL

- Deal with the hurt feelings through validation and expression.
- Teach the difference between feeling and doing.
- Ask if positive time-out would be helpful.
- Allow the child to share his perspective.
- Schedule a time (after the conflict) to work on solutions.
- Repair the damage; put things right.
- Work to help the child feel a sense of belonging.

take time to think before he acts. Eric needs to learn that there is a difference between feeling hurt and acting on those hurt feelings.

John decided to tell Eric, "What you feel is always okay, but what you do is not always okay. Later let's brainstorm some things we can do when we feel hurt that doesn't hurt others or damage our school." John was wise enough to postpone the brainstorming session, because Eric needs some time to recover.

Ask If Positive Time-Out Would Be Helpful

After John has taught his children about positive time-out, he can suggest that Eric go to time-out until he feels better. John could even ask Eric whether he would like company in time-out or if he would like to go alone. If Eric wants company and John has a few minutes, he could offer, "Would you like me to go with you or would you like a buddy to go with you?" Children who feel they don't belong usually jump at the chance to have someone go with them— they can cool off and feel belonging at the same time.

Allow the Child to Share His Perspective

After Eric has cooled off and feels better, John and Eric can talk about why Eric is feeling hurt and look for ways to help him feel better again. Eric could tell John how he felt about John's reaction to the block throwing incident. Perhaps John could remind him that the consequence for throwing blocks was decided at the morning's class meeting. That would explain why another child had been treated differently the day before. Or John could ask Eric to suggest a solution that would feel more fair to him. By dealing with the hurt feelings, John and Eric can move on to problem solving together.

Schedule a Time (After the Conflict) to Work on Solutions

Eric can be taught different ways to act when difficult feelings arise. Later that morning, John asked Eric to join him for a brainstorming session. John started by offering the suggestion that the next time Eric is feeling hurt, he can come

WHEN A "HURTING" CHILD HURTS ANOTHER CHILD

Understanding that a child's mistaken goal might be revenge does not make hurtful actions acceptable. Making amends for physical aggression involves three steps.

1. *Provide damage control.* Separate involved children or place one child out of reach of the offending child. Often this means placing both children in a cool-off area until they are calm enough to make better choices.

2. *Address hurt feelings.* Take the time to find out what might be causing a child to feel hurt. Allow the hurt feelings to surface. Sometimes, we can do nothing to erase the cause of a child's pain. Parents fighting with each other, illness in a family, or other life events are usually beyond our control. Simply allowing a child a safe place to express his feelings and to feel supported and listened to might be the full extent of our reach as caregivers. But it is an important and healing role.

to John and practice naming the feeling. John told Eric kindly that he will always try to be a good listener. John then asked Eric what ideas he had. Eric had been learning about "using his words" and said, "I could tell someone I don't like it when they hurt my feelings." John said, "That sounds good. Anything else?" Eric couldn't think of anything, so John prompted, "How about putting the problem on the class meeting agenda?" Eric said, "I could do that." John ended their discussion by saying, "You have three good ideas. I have faith in you that you will choose the one that works best for you the next time you feel hurt."

It is important to remember that this process may need to be repeated many times before Eric will learn to name his feelings, accept them as okay, and find acceptable ways to handle his feelings. After all, many adults have not learned this because many of us did not receive this kind of training.

When we demonstrate acceptance of a child's feelings, we encourage his sense of belonging by sending the message that it is safe for him to have all kinds of feelings. This is a form of unconditional caring.

3. *Make amends.* If one child hurts another child, what can the first child do to help the child he harmed feel better? He might suggest offering to provide a service such as clearing the other child's place at the table for him, reading a story to a younger child, or drawing a picture for the offended child.

Children may also choose to offer an apology, but forcing him to say "I'm sorry" teaches a child to "mouth" words without meaning them. If an apology is initiated by a child it will have more impact.

Adults may suggest any of these or other options after asking a child if he needs suggestions for ways he might help the injured child feel better again (an apology may be one of the suggestions given and a child may indeed choose it if it isn't forced on him). Making amends is part of learning to take responsibility for one's actions—an ability all of us need to cultivate and practice.

Repair the Damage; Put Things Right

What about Eric's destructive actions? Remember, making a child feel worse is unlikely to encourage that child to act better. Retaliation and punishment are typical adult reactions to destructive behavior, but they often provoke a child to respond with more revenge.

When a child destroys something, it is reasonable to expect him to take responsibility for replacing the damaged item or addressing the damage he's done. When Eric stuffs the toilet with paper and causes it to overflow, he can be expected to help clean up the mess. (Of course, Eric will be more likely to cooperate in the clean-up efforts when his feelings and the belief behind his behavior have been dealt with, as we have already discussed.)

Now Eric and John can discuss how Eric could help clean up the mess in the bathroom. Notice that the focus is on the mess in the bathroom, rather than the mess Eric made. This is not the time for blaming but for working together to find a solution to the problem. It takes time, but this kind of respectful and caring approach is much more likely to lead to improvements in Eric's behavior.

Eric hasn't "gotten away with" anything; he will agree to a plan for repairing the damage he has done, and John will follow through and see that the plan is implemented. When the focus is on solutions, the result just may be a change in the behavior. Then the revenge cycle can be broken.

> Retaliation and punishment are typical adult reactions to destructive behavior, but they often provoke a child to respond with more revenge.

Work to Help the Child Feel a Sense of Belonging

We have explored a number of ways that John can help Eric deal with one day's behavior, but to make a lasting change in the way Eric sees himself, John must focus on ways to give Eric a sense of belonging in the classroom. It is important that John help Eric see the ways in which he is liked by others to help him feel a sense of belonging. During a class meeting or circle time, John could begin a discussion of how good we feel when others want to do things with us. John could then say that he has chosen Eric to pass out the morning snack. He could ask who would like to share this task with Eric. Several hands would go up and a helper would be chosen. By focusing on "sharing the task with Eric," John has sent a different message than if he'd simply asked, "Who else wants to serve the snack?"

Afterward, John could spend a moment with Eric and comment on how many children raised their hands to do something with him. Did Eric feel good when so many children raised their hands to pass the snack with him? In this way, John would be helping Eric to be an important and contributing member of his class, as well as helping Eric perceive himself as a likable person with whom others want to share tasks. This sort of processing is a crucial piece in helping Eric to form different beliefs about his experiences.

Assumed Inadequacy in the Preschool

For Paul, it is just another day at swim class. Paul is five years old, but he is still in the group with the three-year-olds. The instructor, Tom, is trying to get everyone to blow bubbles in the water. Paul hates to get his face wet and blows little puffs well above the surface. Tom comes over and suggests that Paul pretend to "blow out the birthday candle." Paul only folds his arms around himself, puts his chin into his chest, and gives a tiny shake of his head. After a minute or two, Tom gives up and goes on to the next child.

A little while later, the other children are holding onto the edge of the pool and practicing kicking in the water. Paul sits on the side, refusing to get into the pool. Tom offers to hold Paul while he kicks, but Paul refuses and turns his body away from the pool. Eventually Tom gives up and leaves Paul alone.

Paul has successfully convinced his swimming instructor to leave him alone. Paul believes that because he is not "perfect," he must be hopeless. He acts upon this belief by convincing others to give up on him, demonstrating to perfection the mistaken goal of assumed inadequacy, or giving up. Paul's imaginary ski hat, pulled low over his face, reads, "Show me small steps; celebrate my successes."

Identifying Assumed Inadequacy in the Preschool

TOM MUST STAY alert to the needs of all of the children in his swim class— he can't spend all of his time with Paul. Tom feels hopeless when he can't convince Paul even to try the various activities. Tom cannot force Paul into the water or make him blow bubbles. His only choice seems to be to leave Paul alone, to give up on him. What else can he do?

Paul's response is to retreat further. He isn't fighting or being aggressive. In fact, he makes it pretty easy to ignore him and leave him alone.

The Belief Behind Assumed Inadequacy

IF PAUL ONLY tried, he might prove to be a terrific swimmer. Where did he acquire his belief in his own inadequacy? As it happens, Paul has very athletic parents who excel in most sports. They run, they rollerblade, and they bike. When Paul attempts to join them, it's difficult for his parents to hide their impatience at how much he slows them down. They love Paul very much; they just don't know how to adjust their activities to Paul's level.

Paul believes that because he is not as good at sports as his parents are, he might as well not try at all. He can't seem to do anything well enough. They are "perfect" and Paul, obviously, is not. It is safer to be helpless. If Paul can convince others that they can't expect much from him, they will leave him alone.

Encourage Even the Smallest Steps

How might Tom encourage Paul when he is backing away from the pool? Tom might say, "Paul, I know it took a lot of courage for you to join in the bubble blowing. I want you to know I really appreciate that kind of effort." A simple message, but what a powerful one! Tom did not assume that learning to swim was easy; in fact, he acknowledged how hard it is for Paul. Tom took time to notice the small step that Paul had been willing to take. Over time, this kind of gentle encouragement may help Paul take additional risks.

Focus On What a Child Can Do

Adults can learn to focus on what a child can do, to help him to see his own abilities first through others' eyes and eventually, through his own. All too often, teachers are occupied by the attention-seekers or are busy waging power

ENCOURAGEMENT FOR ASSUMED INADEQUACY IN THE PRESCHOOL

- Encourage even the smallest steps.

- Focus on what a child can do.

- Break up the tasks into small steps and celebrate success.

struggles with defiant children. Yet the child whose mistaken goal is assumed inadequacy or giving up is the one who can least afford to be ignored.

Break Up the Tasks into Small Steps and Celebrate Success

Adults who live and work with small children can learn to recognize and encourage small steps towards success and to have realistic expectations. Rudolf Dreikurs said, "Work for improvement, not perfection." When Paul's parents learn to enjoy just being with their son, sharing their pleasure in the activity, and encouraging his enjoyment rather than achievement, Paul will feel much more capable and encouraged.

An important part of encouraging small steps is to break a task down into small pieces that don't seem so intimidating to a discouraged child.

Four-year-old Steven was feeling very discouraged about his assigned task of picking up the blocks after his tower had fallen. His preschool teacher helped him break up the task into "doable" steps by saying, "There are three colors of blocks: blue, red, and yellow. How would you like to find two friends, and each of you could pick up a different color block?"

Steven was delighted with this idea. The teacher was helping him learn that it is okay to ask for help but that he can still do his part. Steven found two friends (his teacher gave him the hint that his friends might be more willing to help if they could choose the color of blocks they wanted to pick up), and the task was accomplished very quickly. However, the accomplished task was secondary to the encouragement Steven felt through his experience of success.

Paul's teachers, too, can be instrumental in helping him believe in himself. The key words for a child with this mistaken goal are "Believe in me!" and "Encourage, encourage, encourage!" As difficult as it may seem sometimes, try to have faith in the discouraged child. He sees himself mirrored in your eyes, and the energy of your belief in him is contagious.

Will It Make a Difference?

TEACHERS AND CAREGIVERS sometimes feel frustrated by the enormity of the task they face each day. It is no easy matter to teach and manage dozens of small, active people—especially when so much of what they believe about themselves and their world is shaped at home, out of the teacher's control.

Still, each of us can only do his or her best. The hours that children spend with their caregivers each day may be the closest many will come to feeling belonging and significance—and every hour is worth the work it takes to create. Better still, when parents and teachers can work together to truly understand children's behavior and deal with it effectively, the results for children can be nothing short of miraculous!

PART SIX

Child Care and Special Needs

If you are the parent of a preschooler, you have undoubtedly heard the debate raging around the subject of child care. There are those who claim that children should *always* be at home with parents during their early years and others who claim (just as loudly) that children *always* benefit from child care or preschool programs.

We believe that decisions about whether or not to work (or stay at home), whether or not to place children in child care, and whether or not to enroll children in preschool programs are decisions that can best be made by a child's parents. For many families these days, child care is a simple fact of life; it is not possible, whether parents wish it or not, to be at home with their children all of the time. It is also a fact of life that the quality of care a young child receives is vitally important, second only, perhaps, to the quality of parenting. Yet choosing child care that is both affordable and beneficial is difficult; there are so many options and it is sometimes hard to know how children will respond.

In chapters 22 and 23 we will take a look at the issue of child care. We will explore how to choose a quality child care setting and how to help both adults and children thrive. In chapter 24 we will explore the world of children with special needs and what parents and teachers can do to understand their sometimes challenging behavior and help them to reach their full potential.

Parenting is a challenging job, one that becomes immeasurably more difficult when done in isolation. Building a community of support and resources may be one of the wisest things that you will ever do as you raise your young child.

22

Your Child and Child Care

*C*ara's husband has two more years of graduate school to finish. She has just discovered that an unexpected baby is on the way. Her family depends on her income.

Jim has two children. The oldest is four and the youngest is eighteen months old. His marriage has just ended in divorce, he has sole custody, and is unwilling to give up a career that provides him with a way to support his family.

Bethany is director of research, midway through a ten-year project. If her research produces the results she expects, it may mean a cure for a type of cancer that has been considered hopeless. Bethany just turned thirty-four; she and her husband have decided that they can wait no longer to begin their own family.

Elena's neighborhood has no children. Her daughter is three now; Mitra is lonely and wants playmates. Elena does not want her to watch television all day. A preschool has opened on the next block, but she's not sure if it's the best thing for Mitra.

Keiko was such a devoted parent that she didn't leave her first baby until he was six months old. Then she left him with a sitter for only two hours and called at least once an hour to make sure everything was all right. The baby slept soundly the entire time, but she was still not comfortable leaving him.

Child Care: A Modern Necessity

THESE STORIES AND their variations are endless. Whatever the underlying issues, the reality is that many parents work and many children are in child care or preschool. And leaving a young child in someone else's care can be agonizing for parents. Most wrestle at least occasionally with guilt and doubts: "Am I being a neglectful parent if I don't stay home with my child?" "I don't have a choice—I have to work—but will my child be scarred for life? Or will it be good for my child to experience a good preschool or child care center?" And perhaps the most important question of all is "How do I find quality child care?"

> It may help to know that reputable university studies have demonstrated (even though many political groups do not like the results) that children do very well in a "quality" child care situation.

For most parents of young children, finding (and feeling comfortable with) a baby-sitter, nanny, or caregiver presents a major concern. Perhaps the idea of a night out together does sound wonderful—but how do you find a responsible, trustworthy caregiver for your young child?

It may help to know that reputable university studies have demonstrated (even though many political groups do not like the results) that children do very well in a "quality" child care situation. (NICHD Early Child Care Research Network. "Characteristics of Infant Child Care: Factors Contributing to Positive Caregiving." *Early Childhood Research Quarterly,* 11, 1996, 267–306.) These studies found that "family factors" (primarily maternal sensitivity and responsiveness) appeared to be more powerful predictors than child care regarding child outcomes—except for "poor-quality" child care.

This knowledge may help you feel confident about your decision to find quality child care whether you need it for a night out, a special event, or for full-time work. Children absorb the energy of your attitudes and react to them. If you feel fearful, so will your child. If you feel guilty, your child may "feel" an opportunity to use manipulation. It is ironic, but both working parents and stay-at-home parents seem to feel some degree of guilt and regret about their choice—whatever it is. Guilt rarely does anyone any good. The key is to make the best decision you can in your own special situation—and then to relax. You will find this easier to do when you know how to find quality child care. (For a more detailed discussion on the issues of child care versus stay-at-home parenting, please see *Positive Discipline: The First Three Years,* Prima Publishing, 1998.)

Living with Your Child Care Decision

ONCE YOU HAVE made your decision, you still may have feelings of sadness and anxiety about leaving your child in any kind of child care arrangement. Several things may help. The first step is to recognize that this is a necessary choice for you and your child. When a parent can accept the need for (or see the value of) child care in the life of the family, other concerns begin to fall into place.

The next step is to deal with the many questions you may have about handling the details of daily life when child care is part of your family's routine. "How can I handle leaving my child in the morning?" "What about pickup time in the evening? How do our home routines change or alter when we are away from our child all day?" "What about my child's friends?" "Will my child be safe?" "Will my child be loved and feel loved?" "What can we do to make it all work?" Many of these questions will be resolved once you feel confident that you have selected a quality child care situation. In this chapter (and chapter 23) we will discuss criteria you can use to evaluate the child care you are considering or have selected.

One of the most important criteria is to find a center or home that welcomes parents anytime. These centers have nothing to hide and will treat you as a respected partner in your child's care. If you feel like an intruder when you visit your child's preschool, child care center, or licensed home, find another where you feel welcome.

The New Extended Family

CHILD CARE TODAY often takes the place of the extended family of aunts, uncles, grandparents, and cousins that past generations grew up with. These days, there may be no sister or cousin to compare notes with when Belinda pulls a neighbor's hair or Jeff wakes up with a fever in the middle of the night.

Parents need other adults as their own support system when raising a child. Today's child care center can be such a resource. It is a place to meet other parents, share concerns, and learn from one another.

Your child's caregivers should be knowledgeable and ready to answer your questions. In truth, a quality child care center needs to be a place for families, not just for young children.

Parents can work with centers to sponsor parenting classes, speakers, and parenting groups. Most parents have similar concerns and are reassured to learn that other children behave in some of the same ways.

Today Steve felt at his wit's end. He had been working overtime, his wife was out of town with their older son at her sister's wedding, and it was all he could do to get three-year-old Rebecca up and ready for child care. And when he rushed in the door at the center, he realized that he had forgotten to pack Rebecca a lunch.

Mrs. Ball, the caregiver, came over to greet Rebecca. She noticed Steve's harried look and gave him her full attention as he told her how overwhelming the week had been. "And," he added sheepishly, "I forgot Rebecca's lunch today."

Mrs. Ball reassured him that what he was doing was very stressful and his feelings were understandable; she also offered to give Rebecca some crackers and peanut butter, milk, and fruit for lunch.

A child care center or preschool should be part of a family's support system. Sometimes having another adult there to listen means everything to a frazzled parent. Maybe things aren't like the "old days," but there are lots of ways that today's realities can be turned into opportunities. A good preschool can actually enhance life for you and your children.

There is a saying that "it takes a village to raise a child." Make your child care part of that village. Empower yourself to find quality care, or make it happen through your efforts to improve and enhance what is available.

Separation

PARENTS OFTEN FEEL not only sad but guilty when they leave their children in child care. (Working parents, please do not claim all the guilt for yourselves. The opportunities to feel inadequate and torn by separation from children are many and varied. Every parent experiences some degree of pain.)

Although a child might be doing the crying in the morning at child care or on an evening when a parent goes out with friends, the most important aspect of dealing with those tears is how parents handle the separation. The parent who, though sad, believes that her child will be well cared for and secure while she is absent communicates that confidence to her child. It is well worth the investment of time to get to know the adults who will be caring for your child.

The Child Care Day

YOUR DAILY ROUTINES will be influenced and altered by the schedule, commute, and details of your child's care. Some families will have to include food preparation time if they must bring in all or part of their child's food. Getting dressed and out of the house, coping with nap time, establishing departure routines, and keeping up with your child's budding and shifting friendships are common issues that may overtake the whole family.

Even the most effective and smoothly functioning lifestyle can be derailed by a two-week bout with the chicken pox! Remember that everyone has a bad day now and then, and how smoothly your day goes depends on many different elements. These include the mood and condition of parents, children, caregivers, traffic, and maybe even whether anyone remembered to put the milk back in the fridge the night before. With so many opportunities for disaster, make it a daily habit to celebrate what goes right.

It can be difficult to remember in the midst of rushing out the door, but even though two-year-old Nick insisted on wearing one purple sock and one orange sock and five-year-old Susan dropped the jar of honey on the kitchen floor, do take a moment to rejoice in the fact that Nick dressed himself at all and that Susan was helping set out breakfast things without being asked. There will always be imperfections: use your energy to focus on the daily victories.

Morning Hassles

ROUTINES ARE CRITICAL for getting out of the house in the morning. We've discussed children's differing perceptions about time and the "process versus product" thinking that prevails in early childhood (see chapter 6). These traits sometimes work against a smoothly flowing morning. What will work in your favor with young children is their attachment to routines. They thrive when the events in their lives are predictable. Establishing clear routines for getting the little ones to child care can prove to be the difference between a calm or hectic morning.

The Jasper family has four members. Dad has to be at work by 8:30 A.M., Mom begins work at 9:00 A.M., and their twin daughters, who are three years old, must be taken to child care. Since they have only one car, the family commutes together and both parents deliver the girls to child care each morn-ing. They have found several things that work well for them.

Each evening the twins help pick out the clothes they will wear the next day. The family discovered that this wasn't quite enough for Amy, because she hated to take off her warm nightgown in the chilly mornings. After a number of frustrating mornings, Amy and her mom agreed that Amy could sleep in the shirt she would wear the next morning. This satisfied Amy; she was willing to get up and dress since she already had on a warm T-shirt.

> Establishing clear routines for getting the little ones to child care can prove to be the difference between a calm or hectic morning.

The next part of the routine involved lunches. Since their caregiver did not provide lunches, either Mom or Dad would pack them the night before, with occasional "help" from the twins. (At a family meeting they had agreed that Mom and Dad would alternate weekly the jobs of packing lunches and helping the twins lay out their clothes and take baths.) Whoever packed the lunches also made sure that all coats and shoes had been located and were laid out near the door so there would be no last-minute panic over missing items.

Advanced planning and preparation the night before eliminated a lot of decisions (and opportunities to get into struggles) in the morning; the established routines kept things running smoothly. Some mornings Dad would begin breakfast and give everyone wake-up calls while Mom showered, then he would shower while she finished preparing breakfast. They would trade duties on alternate weeks.

The twins knew that they had to be dressed before they could have breakfast. Mom or Dad was available to help with difficult buttons or shoe tying, but the girls usually did a good job of getting their clothes on each morning. Both Mom and Dad had begun training and encouraging their daughters' efforts at dressing themselves when the twins were two years old.

Amy liked to pour the milk each morning. Her parents kept a small pitcher in the refrigerator that she could manage. (There was a sponge by the sink that the girls had been trained to use when the occasional spill occurred.) Both Angie and Amy were given things to do each morning to help with breakfast. Setting out napkins, putting salt and pepper on the table, and mixing the juice were among the jobs they could do. Angie and Amy felt good about the contributions they made each day. While the twins helped one parent clear up the breakfast things, the other parent got the car out and everyone's gear loaded up. Then, relaxed and smiling, out the door they went.

Does this sound like a fairy tale? Yes and no. It is possible to set up careful routines and achieve this kind of morning harmony. It did not happen overnight. First Mom and Dad hassled with each other over who should be doing what each morning. When they finally worked things out, they clearly understood each other's expectations and weren't spending lots of energy bickering.

Then Amy and Angie had to conduct a few tests to see if their parents really meant that they had to be dressed before they could come to breakfast. This meant that once or twice Amy and Angie did not have time to eat before leaving in the morning. Their parents knew that they could survive an hour or two until morning snack.

It also meant that on at least one occasion, one or both of the twins arrived at their child care in pajamas with Mom or Dad carrying a paper bag of clothing. Amy and Angie's parents did not mistreat their daughters; they gave them the opportunity to become responsible in ways that were respectful by learning from the results of their own choices. It also meant that Angie and Amy soon believed that their parents meant what they said, and both girls peacefully participated in the morning routines.

Usually the result was a hassle-free morning routine. Notice the word "usually." There was not always a smooth beginning to the day. Sometimes Mom or Dad overslept and got a late start or was just plain grouchy in the morning. Other times, no amount of routine would get Amy into her clothes. They learned to celebrate improvement instead of looking for perfection.

Another family, Susan and her son Jeffrey, also devised a smooth morning routine. Susan and Jeffrey had the additional stress of a bus to catch. Susan was enrolled in the community college, so missing a bus could mean missing a class, which would hurt her final grade. Jeffrey was four years old and attended a child care center about three blocks from his mother's college.

Susan and Jeffrey also began their routine the night before. Jeffrey was in charge of picking out his clothes. Because her child care provided meals, Susan had only her own lunch to pack. She took the extra precaution of stacking the things she needed the next morning in a box by the back door; she also checked to be sure she had change for the bus and a change of clothes for Jeffrey so there would be no last-minute panic looking for missing items in the morning.

After tucking Jeffrey in at night, Susan still had studying to do. Jeffrey had had to learn that there were limits to their bedtime preparations. In the summer, when school was out, Susan worked on establishing a clear and consistent bedtime routine. Jeffrey then knew what to expect at bedtime and everything went smoothly.

In the morning Jeffrey also had to get dressed before breakfast and do the job of setting out bowls for cereal as his mother finished dressing. They had to be at the bus stop by 8:05, so at 7:30 Susan set the stove timer to buzz in twenty minutes. When it went off, Jeffrey and Susan knew it was time to gather their things and head to the bus stop. This left only about five minutes for last-minute emergencies such as an urgent trip to the toilet or changing the shirt that got milk spilled on it.

No morning routine works perfectly all the time. With training, thoughtful planning, and respect—both for one another and for agreed-upon rules—mornings can proceed much more smoothly, at least most of the time!

Although their morning is hectic, Jeffrey is learning that he is an important part of a team. Because he and Mom have worked out these details at their family meetings, he feels involved and willing to help in the morning. When problems arise, the two work out new solutions. Once, when Jeffrey complained that he was sick of cereal, they agreed to make time for scrambled eggs once each week, but that would mean getting up ten minutes earlier and Jeffrey would help scramble the eggs. Instead of feeling deprived or burdened, Susan communicates to Jeffrey how much she loves him and finds ways to help him feel valuable and capable.

No morning routine works perfectly all the time. With training, thoughtful planning, and respect—both for one another and for agreed-upon rules—mornings can proceed much more smoothly, at least most of the time!

Arrival

NO MATTER WHAT happened before you got there, the moment arrives when you and your child are at the child care center. Some things will help both of you to feel better about the day ahead. Arrive early enough to create a smooth transition. Take a moment to look around the center with your child. Find out what the teacher is planning for the day. Prepare your child if you find out there is a substitute; meet the substitute and make sure you introduce your child to any new person she will be with that day.

Notice any changes in the environment. If a new toy or climber is out, explore it with your child. Sometimes you may have time to read a story or do a puzzle with your child before you leave. If time does not allow that, ask him what he will play with when you leave. This will allow you to feel more connected, and you and your child can visualize what he will be doing after you have gone.

When it is time to leave, go (dragging out the farewell leaves you, your child, and the caregiver emotionally drained), but never just disappear. Tell your child that you are leaving. Tears may follow your announcement, but if you are respectful and honest, your child will learn that she can trust you. If your child clings to you, gently hand her into the caregiver's arms so that she can be held and comforted as you leave. It helps to have a special place for children to stand or be held to wave to parents as they leave.

Even when parents leave in a respectful and loving way, children still may cry. The important thing to remember is that your child will learn that she can trust the adults in her life—and that she can trust herself. This is reaffirmed every day by the fact that you do, in fact, return (and that she does survive these separations). Eventually the tears will disappear and the routine of morning departure for parents and children will be smooth and happy. (If you feel the need, call the center midmorning to reassure yourself that the tears were brief and all is going smoothly. Your peace of mind will be worth it.)

Departure/Evening Pickup Time

WHEN YOU ARRIVE to take your child home, allow time for a friendly greeting and a bit of reentry. You are both about to begin a new segment of your day.

When Madelyn White arrives at closing to take her three-year-old daughter, Anna, home, she finds her playing with some dress-up clothes. Madelyn gives Anna a hug and comments solemnly on the orange wig and flowered purse that Anna has chosen. Madelyn then tells Anna that she may play for five more minutes.

During that time Madelyn gathers the notes about Anna's day that have been left by the morning teacher. She also signs up to bring a casserole to next week's potluck. When she returns to the dress-up area, Anna is still wearing the orange wig. Madelyn comments on how much Anna must enjoy that wig; perhaps she will be able to wear it again tomorrow. She then tells Anna that it is time to leave. Anna reluctantly leaves her toys and takes her mother's hand. Anna gets her coat and together they hunt down her missing shoe. Madelyn signs Anna out for the day and mother and daughter leave the center together. Madelyn feels comforted that her daughter is so happy at her preschool that she doesn't want to leave.

By taking time to reconnect with her daughter and giving Anna time to conclude her play, Madelyn has set the stage for a calm departure. Anna may fuss anyway—after all, she was having a lot of fun—but she is likely to fuss less than a child who is dragged away from her play.

The school staff has contributed to a smooth departure by taking time half an hour before departure to have the children find everything they need to go home—coats, lunch boxes, art projects, notices for parents about the upcoming potluck. In spite of all this preparation, some children may not be as cheerful as Anna when their parents arrive to pick them up.

There is a good reason for children to be fussy at the end of their day. An important element of child care is that young children must cope with a highly social environment all day. That means that a certain amount of tension and stress may have built up in your child. When a child falls apart at her parent's arrival, it may be her way of saying that you are the person she can trust to love and accept her, no matter what side of herself she shows to you. Social expectations can be relaxed in the warmth of a parent's arrival.

A major transition in a child's day takes place when he is about to leave the child care setting, and young children need some gentleness to get them through this transition. Devoting time to him and his needs at this moment will ultimately benefit you both.

Family Support

WHATEVER A FAMILY'S configuration, resources, or location, all need support from time to time. Parents of young children need other parents with whom to share concerns, ideas, and stories. Children need both other children and adults in their lives to learn about the variety of people that populate their world.

Parenting classes, books such as this one, and other resources provide valuable tools for parents today. Many communities boast "moms" groups where parents can gather to share ideas and allow their children to play. In addition, the Internet has opened a vast world of information: sites such as that of *Moms Online* (*www.Momsonline.com*) provide forums for conversation, advice, and even opportunities to ask questions of recognized experts in a variety of fields. Caregivers also have access to an array of resources. Raising children involves the whole of society. What happens to children on every level matters to all people, young and old alike.

> Raising children involves the whole of society. What happens to children on every level matters to all people, young and old alike.

Whether your child stays at home with you or a nanny, goes to a relative's or friend's home for care, or attends a child care program, the type of care that is available will affect you both. In truth, child care affects everyone, either directly or indirectly. The environment and the teachers who work with your children help to shape their future—and the future of our society. Quality care is a must. Child care centers should be safe, pleasant, nurturing places for children to be.

Choosing a Child Care Center

THE IDEAS WE have explored here will work much more smoothly when you and your child feel comfortable with the child care choice you have made. How should you choose a child care facility? It is extremely important not to "bargain hunt" for child care. Although cost must be considered, it should not be the most important factor in your decision. Many extremely important hours of your child's life will be spent in the child care that you choose.

Simply put, find the best care possible. If quality care is unavailable, make what you find into quality care by providing the caregivers with information, such as this book. Actively work to bring training to your area if it is lacking. First, though, it may help to know what a good child care facility is. Let's take a closer look in the next chapter.

23

Identifying Quality Child Care

IF YOU ARE one of the many parents who need to find regular care for your child, there are a number of factors to consider. Don't be in a rush to choose: be sure to visit several different child care programs. Take notes on what you see. Are the children happy? Do they move around the center confidently? Do the teachers get down on the children's eye level to talk with them? Is the art work displayed low enough for children to see it, or is it only at adult eye level? Is the building clean? Are there visible safety hazards? Do the teachers look cheerful or frazzled? (Do remember that even the best teachers can have tough days!) Does the equipment provided allow children to play freely, to dress up, to learn, and to be active? Or are children expected to be quiet, sit still, and "be good"?

Good Child Care: "How Can I Tell?"

PARENTS SOMETIMES LOOK at lists of qualities and requirements for good child care and feel overwhelmed. You may be wondering how you will ever know if the facility you are considering meets these standards. There is a relatively simple solution: ask. Child care is an important decision, and your confidence as a parent will influence your child's comfort with and response to her new setting. Don't hesitate to ask for all of the information you need to make an educated decision. If a center or provider seems reluctant to answer your questions or to allow you to observe them in action, it's probably wise to look elsewhere.

You might want to copy the checklist below and take it with you when you visit prospective child care facilities. Let's take a look at what all of these indicators really mean.

The Child Care Center or Home

Most states or cities require centers and homes to meet a variety of licensing requirements. Seeing licenses posted tells you the requirements were met. Be sure to check dates to be sure that licenses are current (although many states are so backlogged that long intervals between licensing are common).

Centers with low staff turnover indicate that the staff are well treated, receive fair compensation, enjoy their work, and feel supported by the center's administration. When staff do not receive decent wages, they go elsewhere, often leaving the child care field.

SELECTING CHILD CARE

Identify quality child care using the following indicators on this checklist.

1. The center or home has:

    • Licenses displayed and current

    • Low rate of staff turnover

    • Local, state, and/or national accreditation

    • Loving, child-centered environment

2. The staff is:

    • Well trained in early childhood development and care

    • Working as a team

    • Staying up-to-date through training programs

    • Adequately paid

Look for special licensing. The best known is the NAEYC (National Association for the Education of Young Children), which takes a multifaceted approach. Centers spend several months doing self-assessments and correcting any weak areas; they then are visited by independent accreditors, usually on several occasions. This accreditation is only valid for two years, then must be repeated. Programs displaying this type of accreditation truly have earned it.

Next, evaluate the physical aspects of the center. Is this a loving, child-centered environment? Is the space where your child will be spending her time clean and well-maintained? Look for toys and equipment placed at the child's eye level, easily accessible. There should be places to climb safely and that encourage movement. A room designed for infants should have child-safe, unbreakable mirrors at the floor level, as well as rails or small, sturdy furniture that a child can use to pull herself up as she learns to walk. Balls and rolling toys on the floor will help your child with eye-hand coordination and encourage him to move and crawl.

3. Discipline is:
   - Positive rather than punitive
   - Kind and firm at the same time
   - Designed to help children learn important life skills

4. Consistency shows:
   - In the curriculum
   - In the way problems are handled
   - In day-to-day center management

5. Safety is demonstrated by the:
   - Physical setting
   - Program health policies
   - Preparedness for emergencies

Whenever possible, there should be child-sized equipment. Small pitchers, drinking cups, and child-size tables and chairs are very helpful for young children. If child-size items aren't available, then some adaptation of adult-size equipment will help. An example would be to make sinks or toilets more accessible by providing sturdy step stools.

The Staff

Training and experience make it more likely that caregivers will truly understand the needs of young children, provide activities that meet those needs, and have developmentally appropriate expectations. Studies report that when child care providers complete training, they give more sensitive and appropriate care. Education added to low turnover indicates experienced caregivers, a winning situation for everyone involved.

Look for the types of training staff receive. Are there special training requirements? Montessori and Waldorf programs have specialized training curriculum for their teachers. Community college, undergraduate, and master's-level degree programs in early childhood studies exist in every state.

> Training and experience make it more likely that caregivers will truly understand the needs of young children, provide activities that meet those needs, and have developmentally appropriate expectations.

Look for harmony. When there is discord at a center, the children feel it. Remember, young children can "read" the energy of the adults around them, and they respond to what they sense. Centers that encourage cooperation—among children and staff members—model the value of teamwork. Look for regularly scheduled staff meetings, in-house communication tools, and an atmosphere of camaraderie.

Doctors, stock market analysts, child care teachers—all must stay knowledgeable about current information in their fields. Child care workers are professionals too. Do staff at the center you're considering attend workshops? Are there in-house training programs, or are employees encouraged to take part in additional educational programs? Do staff stay current by taking part in seminars, workshops, and special topic trainings such as Positive Discipline? Teachers learn about new research, get inspired by and reminded of basic concepts, or feel encouraged when they hear others share solutions to common dilemmas.

Discipline

Is there a written discipline policy? In what manner are problems handled? Are there texts on discipline recommended by the center? Ask what teachers do about a child who hits, bites, or grabs toys. Find out if teachers receive any training in how to deal with problems that arise. Does the center condone spanking? Is the attitude at the center positive or punitive? Are children being shown what to do more often than being reprimanded about what not to do?

Notice how teachers interact with children.

- Do teachers speak to children in a respectful way?

- Does the teacher get down to the child's eye level when talking to him or do teachers yell instructions across the room? One-to-one communication indicates more appropriate and effective caregiving.

- Are boundaries made clear or does a teacher giggle uncomfortably when children run up and slam into her?

- Is there follow-through? Do teachers do what they say? Does the teacher call out to a child to "Put down that stick!" and then proceed to chat with a coworker while the child brandishes the stick overhead? Or does the teacher walk over and calmly remove the stick after giving the child a moment or two to do so himself?

- Do staff members see themselves as teaching skills to children? Is the child who grabs a toy seen as one who needs to learn social skills or as a "bad" boy who won't share and must be punished?

- What lessons do children learn about their own abilities? Do the teachers put on everyone's coats, socks, and shoes or do they help children do so themselves? Who washes a child's hands before lunch? Look for programs where skills are being taught and children are not simply objects to be fed, dressed, and carted around without their involvement.

What type of atmosphere do you sense when you visit? Happy, peaceful children are a good sign. (Please note: this doesn't necessarily mean quiet children!) The level of activity should indicate that the children are involved in and enjoying whatever they are doing.

Consistency

Consistency in the curriculum means that certain activities are provided regularly. Show and tell, daily story time, or singing are examples. Children thrive on routine—at their care facility as well as at home. Consistency also means that learning objectives exist and are implemented. Contrast a well-defined program to a place where children are given some old egg cartons to cut up, plopped down in front of the same container of blocks every morning, or left to watch endless videos and television programs. In the context of a clear curriculum, some of these activities may be fine. Just be sure that your caregiver values hands-on learning, healthy activity, and developmental growth—not just silence and obedience.

Is there consistency from teacher to teacher or class to class in the way problems are handled? Does one teacher refuse to allow children to help prepare snacks while another turns snack time into a yogurt "finger paint" free-for-all?

Centers with consistent programs encourage children to develop trust, initiative, and a healthy sense of autonomy. These traits are important at home, and they are also important where your child will spend so much of his time.

Consistency begins with center management.

- Are expectations made clear?
- Are events well organized?
- Are finances handled in a businesslike manner?

Safety

Safety includes the physical setting, the program health policies, and the emergency preparedness of the center. A program with exposed electrical cords, unimpeded access to a laundry cupboard, or broken-down play equipment does not provide an environment that is safe for little ones.

Mr. and Mrs. Jamison visited their daughter's center and saw the staff and children participating in a fire drill. They were impressed with the level of compe-

tence shown at the center—and it even got them thinking about the need to develop their own evacuation plan at home.

Find out if staff have current CPR and first aid training and HIV/AIDS training. Under what conditions will sick children be sent home? Look for fire safety procedures and earthquake or other emergency preparedness. Ask how injuries are handled. Reassure yourself that the adults in this place know how to care for your child under a variety of circumstances.

Nannies and Sitters As Caregivers

Q. *I have a wonderful sitter who is great with my one- and two-year-old girl and boy. My only concern with her is that she does not discipline her own three-and-a-half-year-old; consequently, her child is a tyrant and my two-year-old is starting to behave like the sitter's daughter. This child screams, hits her mother, and tells her mother "no" or "shut up." My son is starting to act this way at home, and it takes at least an hour to settle him down to our rules. I don't want my children to become tyrants as well. In all other aspects this sitter is wonderful. What do I do?*

A. Your sitter's daughter did not develop such behavior in a vacuum. Although you feel satisfied with her treatment of your children, we suspect she is not very effective at setting limits. The behavior of her daughter is a big clue. Does her daughter act this way all of the time? It could also be true that her daughter is jealous of sharing her mom's attention and so devotes her energy to misbehaving in order to keep her mom busy with her. Talk over your concerns; ask the sitter how she feels about her daughter's behavior and see if the two of you can come up with a win/win solution. If this does not resolve the problem, you may face a decision about whether or not to change your child care arrangements.

Choosing a sitter or a nanny requires careful consideration. Always check references, interview candidates (without children present), and set up a trial visit where you, the caregiver, and your child can get acquainted. Conduct transactions in a business-like manner; provide sitters with emergency, medical, and health-related information, and honor agreements paying for a sitter's time in the event of a last-minute cancellation.

The advantages of employing a sitter or nanny include not having to take your child out of the home for care. Children sleep, eat, and play in a familiar and consistent environment. There is often more flexibility if parents must work varied schedules or if jobs include traveling.

On the other hand, a child at home with a nanny misses opportunities to develop social skills unless she plays regularly with nearby friends and relatives or attends a part-time preschool program. Most parents worry about the danger of abusive or neglectful care. Nannies and sitters are alone with children. The only protection available is caution, careful screening, and a thorough checking of credentials.

TIPS FOR FINDING A SITTER OR NANNY

- *Ask your friends.* If you have friends or coworkers with young children, ask them for a list of names and phone numbers. Knowing that people you trust recommend someone is probably the best way to feel comfortable when you leave your child with a sitter.
- *Ask your preschool.* If you have a child care center or preschool, the director may have a list of names. If you don't take your child to child care, a reputable preschool in your neighborhood may still be able to refer you to sitters.
- *Check with organizations you trust.* Your local church, high school, or youth organization may be able to provide you with the names of trustworthy caregivers. Churches, schools, and other organizations often have young people who are willing to baby-sit—and some have even been trained. A few phone calls may get you in touch with a reliable baby-sitter.
- *Form a baby-sitting co-op.* If you know other families with young children, agree to form a co-op where you trade child care duties one evening or

If a sitter brings along a child of her own, more variables get involved. Some things to consider in this instance include:

- How old is the additional child?

- Will the additional child detract from your child's care?

- Does the presence of another child provide a playmate and the opportunity to build important social skills?

No matter whom you select to watch your children while you're away, be sure you've talked with him or her enough to feel comfortable—and to be sure that person shares your philosophy of raising children. If your child is old enough to communicate easily with you, check her perceptions occasionally to

weekend day each week. If four families form a co-op, each couple might have three Friday nights or Saturday afternoons out each month, for example, and one evening or day as the "sitters." A co-op can provide you with reliable, free child care—and regular times to spend as a couple, with friends, or just taking time to care for yourself. Keeping track of the hours you watch children and making sure the balance sheet stays even will make things work for everyone.

- *Don't forget your relatives.* Grandparents, aunts, uncles, and cousins may be more willing than you think to provide child care in exchange for the opportunity to spend time with the youngest members of the family. As long as your relatives know they have the right to say no (and as long as you don't wear out your welcome), your extended family may provide you with a great deal of child care, and children can benefit in countless ways from relationships with other members of their family. (See also the next section.)

be sure everything is going well. And always listen to your heart; your instincts will help you know when changes are required.

Grandparents and Other Relatives

MANY CHILDREN SPEND their time with grandparents or other relatives while parents work. In fact, many grandparents today are actually raising their grandchildren because the children's parents are unable to do so. Being cared for by relatives gives children opportunities to forge strong family bonds, and many of us have fond memories of times spent with our extended families. There may also be problems, disagreements, and clashes between the generations.

Q. *How can I raise a well-mannered four-year-old if his grandmother lets him get away with murder and spoils him rotten? He stays with her while I work part-time, three days a week in a nearby office. I feel like I always have to be the bad guy since she won't discipline him. I'm even afraid that he loves her more than me. I need help.*

A. Parenting disagreements with grandparents are often more about the relationship between parents and their own parents or in-laws than about what goes on between young children and their grandparents. Such conflicts stem from the need to move to an adult-to-adult relationship with one's own parents, who sometimes continue to see us as that adorable chubby-cheeked darling they dandled on their knee only yesterday—or as the "problem child" who hasn't learned anything in the years since childhood.

Love is not a contest. It sounds a bit as though you and your child's grandmother are using your child as way to prove superiority over one another. Children love their parents. They also love their grandparents. It is possible to love both without diminishing the love for either.

> Children love their parents. They also love their grandparents. It is possible to love both without diminishing the love for either.

Children are remarkably bright. They know quickly what behavior is acceptable in different circumstances. If Grandma lets young Andy decorate her kitchen table with marshmallows, Andy will still be able to remember that marshmallows have a different function at home. He may of course try to talk you into this modification while whining about how "Grandma lets me do it." Just smile and remind him that the rules at home are different.

(For an expanded look at grandparent/parent issues, refer to *Child Care Information Exchange* magazine's January 1998 article by Roslyn Duffy, entitled "From a Parent's Perspective." To contact the magazine and request a reprint of the article, call 800-221-2864 or e-mail *ccie@wolfenet.com*.)

Unfortunately, when child-rearing philosophies, expectations, and rules clash, tolerance may not be enough. If parents make a sincere attempt to achieve a healthy relationship with parents, in-laws, or other family members, and differences cannot be resolved, further action may be necessary.

"What If I Have Doubts?"

WHENEVER A PARENT feels truly uncomfortable with a caregiver, related or not, the situation must be addressed. Suspicions of abusive treatment, exposure to harmful conditions, widely differing philosophies regarding discipline, or concerns about children falling behind developmentally merit immediate attention. If you believe your child is at risk, do not hesitate: Remove him from the environment and find a caregiver you can trust and feel comfortable with.

If the concerns are not threatening to your child's safety or health, work toward solutions. Communicate your concerns and voice ideas, wishes, and requests in a respectful fashion. Listen nonjudgmentally to your caregiver's ideas. Work on solving problems together. As with any care setting, when adults work together, children benefit.

Your child will, in all likelihood, spend at least part of these important preschool years in the care of someone other than his or her parents. The time and energy you invest now in making child care arrangements that work for all of you will be repaid many times over in peace of mind, enjoyment, and learning.

24

When Your Child
Needs Special Help

WHY DO SOME children need special help? Countless parents spend sleepless nights wrestling with that question. "Why did this happen to my child?" "If only I was a better parent. What have I done wrong?" "Why does my child act this way?" It seems as though everyone has suggestions, offers unsolicited advice, or knows what you "should" be doing. Even though you try many different ways of guiding, encouraging, and training your children, sometimes nothing seems to work.

Most parents look for ways to do a better job; in fact, the Positive Discipline series of books exist for exactly that reason. Yet despite all of the information and advice available, there are still children for whom life just seems harder. They struggle in school; they have trouble making friends; they can't seem to manage basic skills. Some bounce off the walls; others don't seem interested in much of anything; and still others can't stop talking long enough to get anything done. These children (and families) may need more than improved parenting skills. Attention deficit disorder (ADD), fetal alcohol syndrome (FAS), autism, sensory integration disorder, dyspraxia, and other developmental delays are among the conditions preschoolers, their families, and their caregivers may encounter. How can you tell when your child needs special help?

Taking a Closer Look

FOR MANY FAMILIES, a child's preschool years are burdened by stress and anxiety.

Katrina will never forget those panicked midnight trips to the hospital as baby Sandy's small face took on a bluish tint. Asthma threatened to steal Sandy from Katrina throughout her infancy and toddlerhood. Now, as she watches her four-year-old daughter race across the playground and take a tumble in the dust, Katrina must learn to give her daughter room to explore and grow while continuing to care for her health.

Carol and Brad Ford have their own worries; they agonize over their son's stuttering. No matter how many people advise them to ignore Jacob's tortured language, both parents feel fiercely protective when other adults and children hear him struggling to speak. Their pain only makes Jacob more anxious. Is his problem somehow their fault?

Most parents are quick to blame themselves when their children encounter repeated problems. Special needs that involve behavior or development create anxiety, guilt, and confusion for families. Guilt will not help you or your child. Accurate information and support will help you let go of guilt and replace it with beneficial action. The first step, of course, should be a physical or neurological evaluation from a doctor who specializes in the area of your concern.

If it is your child's behavior that troubles you, it's usually best to start at the beginning. Take a moment to think about the information already presented in this book. Consider your child's age and developmental level. Evaluate your own parenting style, lifestyle priority, and expectations.

> Special needs that involve behavior or development create anxiety, guilt, and confusion for families. Guilt will not help you or your child.

Consider your child's temperament and his individual needs and abilities. And consider the possibility of coded messages in his behavior. It may be wise to write down your observations to share with a professional. Most parents will find the answers to understanding their child's behavior somewhere in this information. But if you've carefully considered these things and you still find that you don't know where to begin to help your child, it may be time to look deeper.

The Reality of Special Needs

CARL WAS A difficult baby from the start. He never stopped moving, overreacted to every noise, and had difficulty nursing because everything distracted him. Richard, four years old, darts all over his preschool classroom and always seems startled by the sound of the gerbil moving in its cage, even when he's sitting across the room coloring. Kim just can't sit still or pay attention for more than five minutes, no matter how hard she tries. These children may not be misbehaving; they may be struggling with things that are genuinely difficult for them.

The disorder known as ADD or ADHD (attention deficit disorder without or with hyperactivity) is a chronic lifelong cluster of behaviors. It does not appear overnight. According to some estimates, 5 to 10 percent of all people experience symptoms such as difficulty sitting still and paying attention or act-

WHEN ALL ELSE FAILS

Q. My daughter, now four years old, has had an ongoing problem with getting dressed. She complains that her clothes "hurt." She takes about fifteen minutes to put on socks, pulling them on and off, often dissolving into a tantrum because they hurt. The same goes for underwear. I have tried buying all different types of underwear and socks, as well as allowing her to pick them out in the store and make her own choices in the morning. She asks me to cut all the tags out of her clothes because the tags hurt. And forget about wearing tights! She has always seemed sensitive to sounds, smells, and tastes. I have tried helping her get dressed; I have tried ignoring her as she throws a fit over her socks, but what else can I do?

ing impulsively. Attention deficit disorder (or the fear of it) brings many desperate parents to counselor's offices, parenting classes, and into the arms of would-be miracle fix-it claimants.

Whatever special needs a child has, knowing that those needs are real and not the result of poor parenting, inadequate teaching, or a child's "deliberate" misbehavior brings a great deal of relief. Parents of children with virtually any chronic condition experience a sense of frustration, sadness, and grief, as well as anxiety. They also need to develop specialized skills. Knowing that you're not alone works wonders; so does information about finding help and support.

It is important to remember that especially before the age of five or six, temperament and normal development account for many "problem behaviors"; in fact, many medical professionals will not diagnose a condition such as attention deficit disorder until a child is older. Such conditions are, however, very real. Parents need to know that it is wise both to ask for help and to trust their own wisdom regarding their children. (After all, who knows a child better than his or her parents?)

All children, whether or not they have special needs, need to feel belonging and unconditional acceptance and will benefit from teaching, encouragement,

A. Many people struggle with the way their bodies process sensory information. While your daughter's complaints may seem trivial or imagined to you, they may be quite real. Your daughter really may feel that the socks are hurting her. There is a condition known as "sensory integration disorder" that might affect your child. Although there is no consensus as to this diagnosis, there are treatment options that might help. Consult an occupational therapist or a pediatric neurologist for further information. You may also find useful support on the Internet.

Most important, accept that your child really does feel pain and resist the temptation to engage in power struggles with her. Treating her behavior as a parenting problem will not be helpful; accepting the validity of her complaints and finding help and support will.

and understanding. All can be helped to reach their fullest potential as capable, happy human beings.

Labels: Self-Fulfilling Prophecies?

NO ONE WANTS his child to be labeled. Labels such as "clever," "clumsy," "shy," or "cute" all define who a child is in others' eyes, creating an image that may prevent that child from being appreciated and experienced for who she really is. On the other hand, some labels simply describe what is obvious. Labeling a child who wears glasses as "the little girl with glasses" doesn't necessarily cause people to prejudge her behavior.

Sometimes a child's cluster or pattern of behaviors is equally obvious. Diagnosing such a child as having attention deficit disorder or fetal alcohol syndrome can be helpful. Most parents and teachers find it easier to encourage and support a child who has ADHD than one who has been labeled "disruptive," "squirmy," or "a troublemaker."

Adults often must struggle with their own attitudes and expectations about children who are different or special.

When Veronica Corelli was told that her four-year-old daughter was going to need glasses, she went home and cried, grieving that her "poor" little girl was going to be "disfigured" with glasses. Abruptly, she stopped and listened to what she had just told herself. She had described her daughter as "poor" and the glasses as "disfiguring." Veronica asked herself whose problem this was. Her four-year-old would want and need her mother's support and acceptance. In fact, the glasses would help her to see better and would enable her to grow and develop normally.

Veronica realized that the real problem was her own attitude. If she wanted to provide her daughter with the help she needed, Veronica had to recognize the value of that help. From that moment on, she chose to support her daughter and obtain whatever care she might need, including glasses. Her daughter's "disability" had existed only in her mother's own mind.

In the same way, identifying a problem by way of a diagnosis does not define who the child is. It is simply a convenient word for a child's uniqueness and special abilities. Because most diagnoses result in a certain amount of distress, we usually hear a great deal about the many associated problems. But it is equally important (if not more so) to look at the assets and attributes a child possesses. Children who have attention deficit disorder, for example, are often highly intelligent and creative: their brains simply process information differently. Understanding those differences can be helpful rather than hurtful.

When a child lacks one ability, growth is likely to occur in other areas. A person who cannot see often develops acute hearing. Everyone has both strengths and weaknesses. What are your child's special gifts? A gentle spirit, a lively sense of humor, or a tender heart often will outweigh the liabilities that accompany "differentness"—if we choose to let them.

Denial

A FEAR OF "labels" or denying a child's special needs does not help anyone. Sometimes we feel more concerned about our own ego (or what people will think) than about what is best for our child. It requires a brave heart to accept and parent your children as they really are, to give them what they really need.

Lauren Avery taught parenting classes in churches and schools and was well respected as an educator in her community. She was also a skillful and effective parent who had raised three children. Imagine how embarrassed and despairing she felt when her fourth child came along and reacted differently to everything her mom did. By the time Grace was five, things were getting out of control. Three out of five days each week, Lauren would carry a screaming child who was throwing a wild tantrum out of the preschool, trying to ignore the knowing glances and stares of the other parents. She tried everything she knew, but nothing seemed to work with Grace.

> Sometimes we feel more concerned about our own ego (or what people will think) than about what is best for our child. It requires a brave heart to accept and parent your children as they really are, to give them what they really need.

Finally she decided that she simply had to accept Grace for the child she was. When Grace threw a tantrum at the preschool, her mother took her to the car and read a book until the tantrum was over. Then she drove home without lecturing. Grace still wasn't able to control her behavior, but Lauren quit worrying about what others were thinking and put her child's needs first.

Learning to Accept

IT IS OFTEN easier for adults to respond to children who have a highly visible disorder or who behave in extreme ways rather than children whose disorder may be less obvious. If Sally, whose limbs are contorted with cerebral palsy, accidentally bumps into a classmate while struggling to maneuver the stairs, a teacher probably will not tell Sally that she must stay in from recess for pushing her classmate.

Nor will Sally's mother be called in for a conference and told that if she would just improve her parenting skills and be more firm, Sally would not have to struggle so to feed herself or learn to walk. Unfair as it seems, parents of children with ADHD, FAS, and dyspraxia often receive such criticisms and advice because these conditions are not as obvious, clearly defined, or well understood as physical disabilities.

> Adults and other children need to learn and practice the art of offering respect, rather than blame, to those who are different.

While learning Positive Discipline parenting skills will help both you and your child, parenting is not the *cause* of your child's behavior or condition. Parents and caregivers are, however, all too human, and it is sometimes easy to "scapegoat" a child whose behavior or appearance is different. Adults and other children need to learn and practice the art of offering respect, rather than blame, to those who are different. Tolerance, patience, and encouragement will go a long way towards helping all people (including children) live together peacefully.

Invisible Differences

LET'S LOOK A bit more at the case of children with ADD. Because children with ADD are often impulsive and find it difficult to sit quietly, their behavior is typically labeled "misbehavior" and others are quick to suggest remedies. Parents find themselves accused of ineffective parenting; they also feel considerable guilt and may believe they have failed as parents. Perhaps most difficult of all, they are living with a child whom they love dearly but with whom they struggle a great deal of the time.

When accurate, a diagnosis of ADD can be an enormously healing step for both parents and child. It establishes that this child is not merely disruptive, fidgety, or defiant. Difficult behavior can be understood as a symptom to be overcome rather than a series of intentional misdeeds. An ADD child is not a troublemaker, even when her behavior gets her into trouble.

Imagine that you are a small child and sometimes, for reasons you don't comprehend, you become terribly upset and begin to scream and kick. Wouldn't your loss of control be frightening? Your parents might decide your tantrum occurred because you couldn't have a toy when you wanted it, or you didn't want to turn off the TV when you were told to, or you thought the teacher had scolded you unfairly. They might also imply that you are somehow at fault or "bad." It's not hard to understand why a child may begin to see herself as "bad." The reality—that she has little ability to control her behavior regardless of the circumstances—is scary.

Learning to understand the difficulties a child may face does not mean we condone inappropriate behavior. In fact, having clear, reasonable expectations and following through with kindness and firmness is essential. Parents and teachers can learn to respond in ways that are productive and do not reinforce a child's image of himself as a "bad kid." Again, all children need love and encouragement, regardless of their special needs or circumstances.

"Getting Away" with Misbehavior

Dee Harris has two daughters. The younger daughter, Megan, is five years old and has been identified as having ADHD. Sheila, her older sister, is seven and does not have ADHD. Before they go shopping, Dee takes the time to discuss her expectations with her two daughters. She has found this especially helpful for Megan, who has difficulty with transitions (a common characteristic of children with attention deficit disorder). They discuss the behavior that is expected as well as what is on the shopping agenda.

Late one Friday afternoon, Dee follows the usual preshopping routine with her daughters. Megan remembers their agreement that this is not the day they will get ice cream cones, and she proudly reminds her mother of this fact.

At the store, however, Megan sees a child happily licking an ice cream cone. In Megan's mind, seeing another child with an ice cream cone means she wants one herself; Megan immediately believes that she must have an ice cream cone. Soon a tantrum is under way. What happened to Megan's agreement that there would be no ice cream today?

The characteristic impulsiveness of attention deficit disorder translates "wants" almost immediately into "needs." All children behave impulsively at times, and most show other traits symptomatic to ADHD on occasion. But ADHD is suspected when the traits show up consistently, the child can't control them, and there is no psychological cause for them. (Taylor, John F. *Helping Your Hyperactive Child;* Prima Publishing, 1994.)

Dee stops shopping and asks Megan if she can regain control by herself or whether they should leave the store. The tantrum continues, so mother and daughters leave the store, with Megan hitting and screaming. The tantrum rages on in the car; when they arrive home, Megan runs into her room and slams the door. By now

KEEPING THE BALANCE

Q. I have twin boys. One of them was born profoundly deaf. Because of the special classes, doctor's appointments, and treatments this child needs, the one with hearing must put up with lots of waiting. He has always been very helpful, patient, and "easy."

Since their third birthday, though, things have changed. In the last month the unaffected child has become defiant, whines all the time when he doesn't get his way, and has become somewhat withdrawn. This is the opposite of his personality just a few months ago. I have wracked my brain trying to find out what is different now in our lives, daily routines, or family situation. Do you have any suggestions, or is this just a phase and it too shall pass?

A. It takes a great deal of patience and sensitivity to raise children with special needs. We often say that children are wonderful perceivers but not very good interpreters, and children often believe that the special therapies, doctor's appointments, and treatment that their special needs sibling receives indicate more

Dee is struggling to maintain her own control. She is angry, discouraged, and exhausted. Sheila, hurt and disappointed, is thinking, "I didn't do anything to spoil the shopping trip. Why did I have to miss out on the fun?" It's hard not to resent a little sister who behaves this way.

It's important to note that Dee does not spoil either of her daughters. She does not respond to unreasonable or demanding behavior by abandoning agreements she has made. There was nothing wrong with her parenting.

"Well," some parents might say, "if my child acted that way in a public place, I'd sure let her know how I felt about it. That mother should have spanked her daughter, or refused to let her have ice cream for a month!" But think for a moment. Has Megan "gotten away with" misbehavior? Will punishment or humiliation help her to change her behavior in the future? And did Megan want to lose control? Did she intend to misbehave? It may be hard

parental love and attention. Attention isn't just a matter of quantity—it's a matter of the beliefs and feelings that children form about how much they (and their siblings) receive and what that tells them about their special place in the family.

It's also wise to remember that while children develop at different paces emotionally as well as physically, three-year-olds are often experimenting with what we call "initiative"—forming their own plans, wanting to do things their own way, and (occasionally) practicing that by becoming defiant, whining, and generally less compliant.

You're probably right that some of this will pass, but be sure to include regular "special time" with each of your children. This doesn't mean spending money or huge chunks of time: fifteen minutes to go for a walk, throw the ball, or read a story are usually all it takes. As your boys grow, they will learn to speak to each other (and you) in sign language—and this can become your shared "secret" language. During your special time, ask your sons to share their happiest and saddest times of the day; be prepared to listen well and to share your own. The key to each child's behavior lies in what he believes about himself and his place in his family.

for her mother, who is experiencing a seething (and very human) mixture of anger, guilt, and blame to remember, but Megan may not have consciously chosen to defy her mother. She was proud of remembering her agreement with her mother and she knows that her mother follows through on those agreements. Dealing effectively with Megan's behavior means recognizing her special needs.

What can Dee do? When she and Megan have calmed down, they can discuss what happened in the store. They might also discuss ways Megan could help her sister feel better. Maybe Megan could offer to do one of Sheila's chores or play a game with her. Sheila, too, has needs that should not be ignored.

Megan almost always feels terrible when she loses control of her behavior; she can feel her mother's exasperation and disappointment, and it's hard for her to bear. Perhaps the most important thing Dee and Megan can do now is to work on ways Megan can cope with those out-of-control feelings. ADHD is something they can acknowledge and face together; they can choose to be a family, loving and supporting one another.

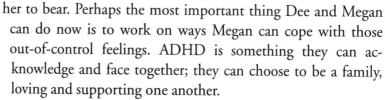

It would be easy to allow Megan to feel that she is "bad" or "difficult," and because her mother is human, she will sometimes make mistakes and say or do things she later regrets. But as we've seen before, mistakes aren't fatal. And Megan's behavior may not change anytime soon. Facing reality, learning coping skills, and getting support will help both mother and daughter survive the difficult times.

Despair or Pride

FINDING OUT THAT your child does not fit your "ideal" comes as an emotional blow. But once adults move beyond their fear of labels and their own denial, they can stretch their horizons wider to see the wonderful gifts their child has, not in spite of learning or behavioral differences but sometimes because of them.

It undoubtedly takes time and determination, but you can learn to celebrate the very things that make your child require special help. People with asthma have competed in the Olympics; Temple Grandin, autistic herself, shed new light on autism and became famous for designing new systems of animal management; and Thomas Edison (along with scores of other famous people) is believed to have had ADD. What would the world be like without the invention of electricity?

What About Treatments?

Robert Adams had struggled with his son, Charles, to the point of desperation. When Charles was five years old, his teacher suspected Charles might have some "borderline" ADHD characteristics. Robert was horrified, and not a little offended by this suggestion. He signed up for parenting classes, bought piles of books, and did his best to be a better father.

But Charles' problems continued. By the age of seven, he was having trouble with schoolwork and friendships, and his difficulties were affecting the entire family. Everyone seemed tense and touchy; arguments were frequent. Finally his dad decided it was time to look for help.

This time, Charles' doctor made a clear diagnosis of ADHD. After months of counseling and trying various approaches, Robert agreed to try medication. Within a week, Charles' behavior was much improved. It was difficult for Robert to believe that those tiny pills could have such an influence on behavior—and equally difficult to admit that his son might need this kind of help. But whenever Charles missed his medication over the next few months, his behavior deteriorated dramatically. Robert began to see his son in a different light and began to enjoy the calm, interesting child he was becoming. Charles, too, was changing; finally he could be himself, rather than a desperate little person always struggling with the effects ADHD had on his daily life.

Medication can be part of a comprehensive and loving approach to helping a child with ADHD. However, even we three authors have differing opinions regarding medication. This only emphasizes the importance of doing your own research and deciding for yourself what works best for you and your child.

Again, listen to your inner wisdom; trust your knowledge of and love for your child. Be sure he understands what ADD is (one youngster informed his counselor that he was a "psycho" because he had something called ADD) and that it does not mean he is sick or "bad." Be willing to change what doesn't work for your family. Build a supportive team of family, friends, and helping professionals who can give you and your child the encouragement you need.

The Importance of Self-Care

EVENTUALLY, MOST CHILDREN with the sorts of conditions we have discussed will leave home and embark on life as independent adults. Just as you teach your child to set the table and do other age-appropriate tasks, you can allow him to understand and learn to maintain his own body.

Sandy, the child with asthma, learned to carry her nebulizer in a backpack that she kept with her at all times. Sandy attended public school, participated in sports, and promptly began medication at the onset of any symptoms. Sandy had learned to recognize her needs, monitor her body's warning signals, and live a full life; asthma was just one factor in it, not the controlling factor. Her mother encouraged Sandy to see herself as being in control of her own health, capable of meeting her own needs, and not as a helpless victim in need of coddling. What a brave, difficult, and necessary task for any parent of a special needs child.

Preschoolers should never be left to handle or take medications without supervision. But they can learn to recognize the signals their bodies and emotions send them. Even young children with metabolic disorders or other conditions requiring a special diet can be aware of their body's needs, accept the special foods they require, and help measure and prepare those foods. When parents allow children to become involved and responsible (in age-appropriate ways, of course), they not only help ensure their child's future health and well being but also build self-confidence and a sense of capability.

Look for the Positive

WHATEVER THE PHYSICAL, behavioral, or emotional challenges you and your child face, focusing on your inadequacies as parents or caregivers will not help. Find support for yourself, take care of your own needs, and accept and learn from your mistakes. Educate yourself, your child, and your caregivers about the condition affecting her, practice applying both humor and hope to each day's struggles, and get help for any child who needs it. Above all, make every effort to discover and celebrate the qualities that make each child special, unique, wonderful. Those qualities are there—we only have to look.

CONCLUSION

THE YEARS OF early childhood are often overwhelming for parents. Preschoolers have an amazing capacity to take center stage in a family's life, often leaving the adults around them breathless with laughter—or exhaustion. Each day seems to bring a new discovery and, sometimes, a new crisis. It may seem as though the kitchen counter will never be cleared, the laundry will never be done, these years will never end.

But they do. Our job as parents and teachers is to make ourselves unnecessary. From the first moments of our children's lives, we steadily guide them toward independence—loving and supporting them when they falter, keeping constant faith that they will grow and bloom. We hover nearby as inconspicuously as we can, holding our breath when they stumble, rejoicing when they continue on their way.

Yes, the preschool years are busy ones for parents and teachers. These years of testing and exploring can sorely try our patience, and we may catch ourselves longing for the day when our child is older and needs us less. But if we are wise, we will take time to enjoy and savor these years that pass so swiftly.

Far sooner than you think, you will look across the room and stare in amazement at the stranger you see. Gone is the preschooler with the chronically runny nose; in his place is a grown-up looking child, ready for school and new friendships, ready to move further and further from the circle of your arms.

Our children will face life equipped with whatever love, wisdom, and confidence we've had the courage to give them. There will surely be struggles, bumps and bruises, and tears; yet if we've done our job well, our children will know that mistakes are opportunities to learn and that life is an adventure to be enjoyed.

There is a beautiful fable about two little girls who discovered the value of struggle and perseverance. They found two cocoons hanging from a branch, and as they watched in awe, two tiny butterflies emerged. The little creatures were so damp and fragile that it seemed impossible they could survive, let alone fly.

343

The girls watched as the butterflies labored to open their wings. One girl, fearing that the butterflies would not survive, reached for one and gently spread its delicate wings. The second girl offered the other butterfly a twig to cling to; then she carried it to the window ledge, where the sun could warm it.

Both butterflies continued to toil valiantly, testing their new wings. The one on the ledge eventually opened its wings, paused for a moment in the sun's gentle warmth, then flew gracefully away. But the butterfly whose wings had been pried open never found the strength to fly and perished without ever taking wing.

It can be painful to watch your young ones struggle, to know that you cannot always save them from trouble and pain no matter how vigilant you are. But wise parents know that, like the butterfly, children gather strength and wisdom from their struggles. It takes a great deal of courage—and a great deal of love—to refrain from lecturing and rescuing and to allow our children, with our encouragement, teaching, and love, to taste life for themselves and learn its lessons.

We can't fight our children's battles. And even the most loving parent cannot guarantee that his children will never know pain. But there is a great deal we can do.

We can offer our children trust, dignity, and respect. We can have faith in them, and in their ability to learn and grow. We can take the time to teach them: about ideas, about people, about the skills they will need to thrive in a challenging world. We can nurture their talents and interests, and encourage each small step they take. We can give them the gifts of competence and responsibility.

Best of all, we can love and enjoy them, laugh and play with them. We can create memories they—and we—will cherish all our lives. We can steal into their rooms at night and feel again and again that overwhelming tenderness as we gaze on our children's sleeping faces. We can draw on that love and tenderness to give us the wisdom and courage it takes to do what we must as parents and caregivers.

This book is all about learning from our mistakes and celebrating our successes. As authors and as parents, we hope you have found it useful. But the ultimate answers will always be found in your own heart and spirit; you will parent (and teach) best when you do so from your heart.

Take a moment now and then to savor this special time of childhood despite the inevitable hassles and frustrations; enjoy your children as much as you possibly can. These are precious, important years, and we can only live them once.

REFERENCES

Adler, Alfred. *Understanding Human Nature.* Translated by W. Beran Wolfe. Greenwich, CT: Fawcett Publications Inc., 1954.

Chess, Stella, M.D., and Alexander Thomas, M.D. *Know Your Child.* New York: Basic Books, 1987.

Dreikurs, Rudolf. *Fundamentals of Adlerian Psychology.* Chicago: Alfred Adler Institute, 1953.

Erikson, Erik H. *Childhood and Society.* New York: Norton, 1963.

Ferber, Richard. *Solve Your Child's Sleep Problems.* New York: Fireside Books, 1985.

Glenn, H. Stephen, and Jane Nelsen. *Raising Self-Reliant Children in a Self-Indulgent World.* Rocklin, CA: Prima Publishing, 1989.

Harlow, Harry F. *Learning to Love.* New York: Ballantine, 1971.

Healy, Jane M. *Endangered Minds: Why Children Don't Think and What We Can Do About It.* New York: Simon & Schuster, 1990.

Munsch, Robert, and Sheila McGraw. *Love You Forever.* Willowdale, Ontario, Canada: Firefly Books Ltd., 1986.

Nelsen, Jane; Cheryl Erwin; and Carol Delzer. *Positive Discipline for Single Parents.* Rocklin, CA: Prima Publishing, 1994.

Nelsen, Jane; Cheryl Erwin; and Roslyn Duffy. *Positive Discipline: The First Three Years.* Rocklin, CA: Prima Publishing, 1998.

Nelsen, Jane; Lynn Lott; H. Stephen Glenn. *Positive Discipline A–Z.* Rocklin, CA: Prima Publishing, 1993

Nelsen, Jane; Riki Intner; and Lynn Lott. *Positive Discipline for Parenting in Recovery.* Rocklin, CA: Prima Publishing, 1996.

Piaget, Jean. *The Origins of Intelligence in Children.* New York: International Universities Press, 1952.

Sammons, William. *The Self-Calmed Baby.* New York: Little, Brown, 1989.

Shore, Rima. *Rethinking the Brain: Research and Implications of Brain Development in Young Children.* New York: Families and Work Institute, 1997.

INDEX

FOR MORE INFORMATION

Workshops, seminars, and facilitator trainings are scheduled throughout the United States each year. Workshops include:

Teaching Parenting the Positive Discipline Way
(a two-day workshop for parent educators)

Positive Discipline for Parents
(a one-day workshop)

Positive Discipline in the Classroom
(a one-day workshop for teachers and school personnel)

Dates and locations are available by contacting:

Positive Discipline Associates
P.O. Box 788
Fair Oaks, CA 95628
1-800-879-0812
E-mail: posdis@aol.com
Web Site: www.positivediscipline.com

The authors also provide dynamic lectures, seminars, and conference keynote presentations. For more information or to schedule a presentation, call 1-800-879-0812.

ORDER FORM

To: Empowering People, P.O. Box 1926, Orem, UT 84059
Phone: 1-800-456-7770 (credit card orders only) Fax: 801/762-0022
www.positivediscipline.com

BOOKS	Price	Quantity	Amount
Positive Discipline for Single Parents by Nelsen, Erwin & Delzer	$16.00	_____	_____
Positive Discipline: The First Three Years by Nelsen, Erwin & Duffy	$16.00	_____	_____
Positive Discipline by Nelsen	$11.00	_____	_____
Positive Discipline A-Z by Nelsen, Lott & Glenn	$16.00	_____	_____
Positive Discipline for Teenagers by Nelsen & Lott	$14.95	_____	_____
Positive Discipline for Preschoolers by Nelsen, Erwin & Duffy	$16.00	_____	_____
Positive Discipline for Blended Families by Nelsen, Erwin & Glenn	$15.00	_____	_____
Positive Discipline for Parenting in Recovery by Nelsen, Intner & Lott	$12.95	_____	_____
Positive Discipline in the Classroom by Nelsen, Lott & Glenn	$14.95	_____	_____
Positive Discipline: A Teacher's A-Z Guide by Nelsen, Duffy, Escobar, Ortolano & Owen-Sohocki	$14.95	_____	_____
Raising Self-Reliant Children in a Self-Reliant World by Glenn & Nelsen	$12.95	_____	_____
Understanding: Eliminating Stress and Finding Serenity in Life and Relationships by Nelsen	$12.00	_____	_____

TAPES AND VIDEOS

	Price	Quantity	Amount
Positive Discipline cassette tape	$10.00	_____	_____
Positive Discipline video	$49.95	_____	_____
Building Healthy Self-Esteem through Positive Discipline cassette tape	$10.00	_____	_____

SUBTOTAL _____

Sales tax: UT add 6.25%; CA add 7.25% _____

Shipping & Handling: $2.50 plus 50¢ each item _____

TOTAL _____

(Prices subject to change without notice)

METHOD OF PAYMENT (check one):

_____ Check made payable to Empowering People Books, Tapes & Videos
_____ Mastercard, Visa, Discover Card, American Express

Card # _____ Expiration _____/_____
Ship to _____
Address _____
City/State/Zip _____
Daytime Phone (_____)_____

ABOUT THE AUTHORS

Jane Nelsen is a popular lecturer and co-author of the entire POSITIVE DISCIPLINE series. She has appeared on *Oprah* and *Sally Jesse Raphael* and was the featured parent expert on the "National Parent Quiz" hosted by Ben Vereen. Jane is the mother of seven children and the grandmother of fifteen.

Cheryl Erwin is a marriage and family therapist in private practice. For the past nine years she has also been a consultant, writer, and speaker on parenting issues. Cheryl lives with her husband and fourteen-year-old son in Reno, Nevada.

Roslyn Duffy cofounded and directed the Learning Tree Montessori Child Care. She currently directs the Better Living Institute, maintains a private counseling practice, conducts parent and teacher training programs, and appears as a featured speaker in person, on local National Public Radio, and on *MomsOnline* Internet magazine. Her column, "From a Parent's Perspective," appears in *Child Care Information Exchange* magazine. Roslyn lives in Seattle, Washington, with her husband and four children.